Muslim, Christian, Jew

Muslim, Christian, Jew

The Oneness of God and the Unity of Our Faith . . .

A Personal Journey in the Three Abrahamic Religions

ARTHUR G. GISH

CASCADE *Books* · Eugene, Oregon

MUSLIM, CHRISTIAN, JEW
The Oneness of God and the Unity of Our Faith . . . A Personal Journey in the Three Abrahamic Religions

Cascade Books
An Imprint of Wipf and Stock Publishers
199 W. 8th Ave., Suite 3
Eugene, OR 97401

www.wipfandstock.com

ISBN 13: 978-1-61097-363-2

Biblical quotations are from the Revised Standard Version of the Holy Bible, copyright by the National Council of Churches of Christ in the United States of America.

Quotations from the Qur'an are from Abdullah Yusuf Ali, revised and published by The Presidency of Islamic Researches, IFTA.

Cataloging-in-Publication data:

Gish, Arthur G.

   Muslim, Christian, Jew : the oneness of God and the unity of our faith . . . a personal journey in the three Abrahamic religions.

   xxvi + 210 p. ; 23 cm. —Includes bibliographical references.

   ISBN 13: 978-1-61097-363-2

   1. Islam—Relations—Christianity. 2. Judaism—Relations—Christianity. I. Title.

BM535 G45 2012

Manufactured in the U.S.A.

This book is dedicated to the courageous Muslims, Christians, and Jews who live their faith on a daily basis working for justice, peace, and true reconciliation in the West Bank, Gaza, and Israel. It is upon this foundation of faith and action that we all should look to for inspiration and hope for our world.

Contents

Foreword

I FIRST ENCOUNTERED MEMBERS of the Christian Peacemaker Teams in Jerusalem in the early 1990s. It was the height of the first Palestinian Uprising and I was speaking in Jerusalem, at Sabeel, the Palestinian Christian liberation movement organization. Because of the urgency of situation on the ground, the venue was full. It was also tense. Could I bring an important word to the violent, yet hopeful, reality on the ground of Israel/Palestine?

I was known to some, having earlier written a book on a Jewish theology of liberation. My own position came from the context of Jewish history and the Jewish future. As a people just recently decimated by an endless assault on our people, known now as the Holocaust, were we now to embark on a state-sponsored project of permanently oppressing another people, the Palestinians? From the Jewish side, simply put, this was and is the question. It seemed to be the question of the people in the room as well, some of who were Palestinian Christians, but with most of the audience being expatriate NGO workers from Europe and America with little or no religious affiliation. Nonetheless, we were all together on the urgency of the situation. This was a Kairos moment. Would Israel and Jews around the world embrace this moment as a chance, perhaps the last chance, to change direction?

I remember the scene vividly. When I rose to speak, I felt a guiding hand, as if I was beginning to speak and, at the same time, when I spoke I heard a peculiar echo as if someone else was speaking and I was simply a vessel through which the words were conveyed. I felt strange, like having an out-of-body experience. At the same time, I felt deeply rooted, totally connected, at one with myself and my environment. Who was that me/ not me speaking? How can I define my out of body/totally connected experience?

I didn't know then and don't know now—I certainly don't claim that it was God placing the words I spoke in my mouth. How could I as a post-Holocaust Jew make such a claim? The question I had grown up with and studied was the question of questions: Where was God at Auschwitz? But as I spoke at Sabeel the question now seemed to have shifted: Where is the prophetic at this moment of crisis?

I have come to understand the prophetic in the following constellation: "The prophetic is the indigenous of the people Israel; It is the greatest gift to the world; Without the prophetic there is no meaning in the world; There may be no meaning in the world; The prophet is the one who embodies the possibility of meaning in the world."

Of course, we also know that the people Israel are the great strugglers against the prophetic. This is one way of looking at Jewish history, as the struggle within the people Israel over the prophetic itself. The contemporary manifestation of this struggle was right before our eyes. There were those Jews like myself in Israel and America—Jews of Conscience—who were supporting the Palestinian right to be free in their own homeland. There were other Jews in Israel and America who were crushing the Palestinian uprising.

So Palestinians were struggling against great odds and were waiting for our decision. On which side of the prophetic do we stand? Or more to the point, since Jews stand on both sides of the prophetic divide, which side would win out?

It is clear which side won—at least for now. The forces of repression and oppression are clear victors. Yet the question remains as to the ultimate cost to Palestinians and to Jews themselves. In the air is the profound uncertainty of how long this deepening injustice can survive. Walls fall in every period of history. The Iron Curtain walls fell in Berlin and beyond; Apartheid South Africa is no more.

The choice before us is transformation or catastrophe. Most often the transformation happens within catastrophe when the bodies are piled so high that we have to climb ladders to see beyond the carnage. Israel may or may not escape this catastrophe. As I spoke at Sabeel, the choice was ours. At some point, the choice denied may be imposed from without. The danger ahead is incalculable.

The Christian Peacemakers that Art Gish writes so movingly about already knew the cost of indecision. As Christians, they know all too well the ravages of empire when it invades and infects the deepest ground of religious belief. Jesus, the prophetic Jew, is in Christianity quickly caught up in a whirlwind of empire violence. His witness is consumed and revamped for the purposes of the state and power, so much so that those oppressed by the Empire Christian Jesus have no choice but to fight against his very presence and those who proclaim it. Christians of conscience, then, are fated to struggle against the very Christianity that claims Jesus, all the while attempting to disentangle a vision and a purpose that has been so conformed to power that Christian dissidents are seen by most Christians as deviants and heretics.

So when members of the Christian Peacemaker team approached me after my talk, I was interested, though a bit confused, with what they were saying. If I was hearing them right, they were totally opposed to the anti-Semitism that was central to Empire Christianity and they were totally opposed to the oppression of Palestinians by anyone, including Jewish Israelis. For them it followed logically that they would be present as human shields to protect Palestinians from the abuse of Jewish settlers and the Israeli military—while maintaining their stand against anti-Semitism.

It was a mouthful for me to digest, especially since I had been involved in the interfaith ecumenical dialogue that had become the interfaith ecumenical deal. Stated succinctly, this means that the necessary and creative dialogue of Jews and Christians after the Holocaust has morphed into a deal where Christians repent for the sins of anti-Semitism and remain silent about Israeli abuses of Palestinians. If Christians speak critically about Israeli policies against Palestinians, the Jewish establishments in Israel and America, as well as the local rabbis and university Jewish Studies and Holocaust Studies academics, accuse them of reverting to anti-Semitism.

The Christian Peacemakers I met in Jerusalem were contravening the rules of the interfaith ecumenical dialogue. They were breaking the interfaith ecumenical deal. By doing so, they charted new ground in the history of Christianity, both within their own community and with Jews. Christian Peacemakers refuse to demonize Jews or romanticize them.

Jews are good and self-sufficient within their own covenant; Christians have been wrong in demeaning Jews. But Jews also can act unethically and regarding Palestinians are doing so; Jews are wrong in their policies toward Palestinians and need to be confronted.

Having absorbed this fascinating new configuration of Christian-Jewish relations, I visited the Christian Peacemaker apartment in Hebron, a city that is heavily Palestinian and Muslim but with Jewish settlements and the Israeli army calling the shots. Kathleen Kern was the leader of the group there, and in our first conversation, she told me that she had read three of my books. I was amazed at this and asked her why she was drawn to my writing. Her response: "Because you portray a different face of Jewishness than the one I experience here."

How beautiful and deep an expression of life that is, especially when that life is lived as a witness in a context of suffering and hope. I was stunned by Kathleen's comment. She was teaching me about my own writing, parsing the words for the message that I was communicating, a message that I didn't fully understand yet. For me, it was an epiphany. In the middle of Hebron, a Christian struggling with her faith was reflecting back my own faith. We were on the same side, wanting the face of Jewishness to be what it is called to be.

Christian Peacemakers were also spreading the prophetic they first encountered in the Hebrew Bible and reflecting it back on Jews—not for the sake of their conversion from an out-dated Jewish faith to the pristine triumphal real Christian faith, but for the sake of Jews and Christians—and Muslims—so we could join together in a faith pilgrimage that only makes sense as a community of believers confronting the obstacles of the world. The obstacles, often as not, are our fellow Christian, Jewish, and Muslim believers.

This is where I part company with Art Gish or at least want to add an additional note to his moving words that he draws from his diverse and difficult commitments in the world. While the Christian Peacemakers I met, and Art Gish in these pages, draw near to the origins of their Christian faith tradition—and also calls Jews and Muslims to draw near to the origins of our faith traditions—the challenge as I see it is to recognize that the Judaism and Jewish life as we have known and inherited it is over. This is true for the Christian and Muslim life explored in these pages. Of course, there are aspects of these three traditions that are worthy of contemplation and recovery. However, they are important only in a new configuration that allows for the particularities of the three to continue in a transformed context that will not be defined by their differences.

This transformed context is what I call the New Diaspora. This is the world of the exiles from all three religions and from geographic and cultural locations around the world. Though they hope one day to return to their original community, they are fated to live out their lives in exile. This is also where their children and grandchildren will be raised and will live. It is only by recognizing that the exiled Others that we live with are our new community that we can use the shattered fragments of our inheritances to nourish and support each other in future.

In the New Diaspora, truth claims are chastened by history. As with our journey, they are broken, in fragments. These fragments are closer to the truth of their own founding than they are as we received them through our various traditions. Whether it was Moses, Jesus, or Mohammad, what has become of them is known only through the traditions that claimed and lifted them out of their historical encounter. Instead of imitating their encounter, we are called to have our own encounter in our own time.

So do not harken back to the truth claims that follow inspired leaders in the traditions that have conformed to empire power! Rather look for the prophetic as it arises in our own lives. As well, band together against the forces of injustice and oppression wherever they might be and against whoever wields the unjust power, even if those wielding it have recently faced an annihilationist assault. Fragments of our own religious background may be helpful to us. They may be helpful to others from another background. Think of Kathleen Kern sharing with me what was helpful for her. Think of her witness—and her words—nourishing me.

The end is near, as it always is. Art Gish has seized his moment to be faithful in the world. It is up to us to seize our moment.

Dr. Marc H. Ellis
University Professor of Jewish Studies
Professor of History
Director, Center for Jewish Studies
Baylor University, Waco, Texas

Introduction

A RT GISH HAS WRITTEN an inspiring book for secular and spiritually motivated people who still question the possible constructive and powerful role that religion can play in building a culture of peace in the Middle East and around the world. This book is full of wisdom that is rooted in the reality of the Israeli-Palestinian conflict, and it is rich with practical experiences of how religious leaders can act for solidarity and justice. The prime assumption of the three Abrahamic religions "being different branches of the same tree" is a powerful vision and a metaphor that captures the need of Arabs and Jews in Israel-Palestine and elsewhere to overcome their narrow exclusionist tendencies and to see the commonalities in their faiths as a source of compassion and a call to act for justice. Unlike some other interfaith publications, this book recognizes the destructive and dark interpretations in the three Abrahamic traditions that led to violence and hatred of the other. Yet, the author manages to systematically provide counter arguments and issue a loud cry for nonviolence based on the three faith traditions.

The author has chosen to begin the plea for genuine interfaith dialogue by introducing his personal journey with Christian Peacemaker Teams in Hebron, which is full of inspiring and real stories. Their work in Palestine and Israel since 1995 is a living testimony for the type of interfaith activities one can engage in order to promote justice and compassionate understanding of other faith traditions.

Inter-religious advocacy and nonviolent resistance efforts involve danger and require deep faith. The author shares some of the pain, danger, and sacrifice that have been endured while working for peace in Hebron. However as a committed peacemaker, operating out of humility, he does not delve enough into such examples and stories, leaving the reader wanting to know more and more. Despite the suffering associated with these confrontations of prejudice and violence, the author maintains the capacity to appreciate and understand the other.

"I have been cursed, spit upon, stoned, kicked, and beaten by Jews in Hebron, in addition to receiving numerous death threats from them. On the other hand, I have been humbled by the deep commitment of Israeli activists who are working side by side with Palestinians for a peaceful future."

Interfaith dialogue is about the capacity to see the other and maintain your own faith. Art Gish amazingly captures this with all his stories and experiences, especially when he prays in a synagogue and manages to find peace and connectedness. However, he does not stop there. He proceeds with his symmetrical interfaith peace-building strategy and enters mosques and prays with Muslims, too.

When dealing with interfaith dialogue many are afraid of the contradictions and inconsistencies that emerge within them as a result of the interaction. In his book Art Gish takes them on. "How do I resolve the seeming contradictions between the Torah, the Qur'an, and the gospel? Maybe the contradictions are not as deep as most of us think they are." This interfaith manuscript is truly a guide for those of us who wish to delve into deeper layers of inter-religious understanding and learn how to internalize what we preach for in these dialogue groups. "When I enter the synagogue or mosque, I am declaring to the powers that be that I will not submit to their culture of fear, that I will not cut myself off from any of God's children. My allegiance is to God."

Many practical implications can be derived from this book, especially from the stories and personal examples that Art Gish shares when he encountered the exclusivist sentiments among religious Muslims and Jews. He has identified such tendencies as most destructive and obstructive of genuine interfaith dialogue. One can take these examples and stories and construct a practical guide for interfaith dialoguers on how to become more aware of their exclusivist consciousness and stand firmly against injustice.

Another courageous and unique segment in this book is the chapter on Abrahamic sources of violence. Art Gish masterfully handles the sensitive subject of Abrahamic religions and violence. The various faith groups in an interfaith setting rarely deal with this topic. Indeed, recognizing that the three faith groups have engaged in violence is a crucial step in gaining trust and building confidence in interfaith dialogue groups.

Art Gish does not offer a concrete future direction in his conclusion. However, he invites readers to join him in recognizing the core and true calling of each of the Abrahamic faiths and to rise above their empty weekly or daily preaching, "I have become weary with listening to empty preaching," and go beyond the "glitters and lies of Western society." The spiritual transformation of Art and of Palestinians and Israelis is offered as an illustration for the possibilities to be changed by the experience of the other and as a way forward in affirming the humanity in each person in the world regardless of their faith or nationality.

Mohammed Abu-Nimer, PhD
International Peace Building and Conflict Resolution
School of International Service
American University, Washington, D.C.

Preface

Arthur G. Gish

ONE OF THE BEST ways to communicate big ideas is through stories. It is stories, not doctrines or ideologies that can touch us deeply and transform our lives as well as our understanding of the world. The Jewish, Muslim, and Christian scriptures are built on narratives. Much of this book is a collection of stories of many incredible experiences I have had over the years with people of other religions.

I have included some theoretical and historical material, based on the best of modern scholarship, concerning some of the more important issues between Judaism, Islam, and Christianity, and some introduction to the three religions to give readers background and insight into some of the issues raised in interfaith relationships. This book is not a scholarly treatise, however.

I see this work partly building on the work of John Howard Yoder, and especially his important book, *The Jewish-Christian Schism Revisited*, by extending his vision of Jewish/Christian reconciliation to include Islam.[1]

This book is written primarily for Jews, Muslims, and Christians who seek a better understanding of the other two faiths, but also for anyone who is a spiritual seeker, who is open to the possibility that maybe there is something in the Judeo/Christian/Islamic tradition that could speak to the longing in their hearts. I have found exciting depth and meaning in the

1. Yoder, *The Jewish-Christian Schism Revisited*.

Hebrew, Christian, and Muslim scriptures. This book is rooted in those scriptures. I hope Jews, Muslims, and Christians will find their deepest beliefs embedded in these pages.

This book is written for people who see the spiritual emptiness of Western technological society. Worship of self, power, money, and technology has led us to disaster. Although its positive contributions are enormous, Western civilization has also brought us to the point of physical and spiritual destruction. The denial of God has not led to liberation. The achievements of science have not satisfied human spiritual needs. Western values of materialism and individualism are not sustainable.

Is there a road out of the present confusion? Could commitment to the God of Abraham, Sarah, and Hagar, the forerunners of all three religions, point to a way out? Do the three Abrahamic religions have an answer? Do God's revelations to humanity contain wisdom for us? Is there one God who is the Creator and Sustainer of all that is?

I have chosen to limit the scope of this book to the three Abrahamic religions, partly because that is my own experience, and partly because members of the three religions comprise over half of the world's population. Just to deal with these three religions is already a huge task. This is not to deny the biblical and Qur'anic affirmation that God has spoken through prophets in every age to every people. There are universal truths at the core of all the great world religions. Those truths are true because those truths came from God.

The three religions are bound together by scripture, history, and their daily interaction throughout the world. They cannot naturally be separated, except by force. There cannot be real peace in the world without peace and just relationships between Jews, Christians, and Muslims. Participants in most of the violent conflicts in the world today use at least one of these three religions to fan the flames of hostility, suspicion, and violence. The daily interactions between these people throughout the world, combined with the large amount of weaponry owned by all three groups, make dialogue and just relationships between us extremely important.

Partisans of each of the three religions, people who have deep biases against one or both of the other two religions, have written much of the literature about the three religions. In addition, another genre of literature, written by secular scholars, has a bias against religion in general. This book expresses deep respect for all three Abrahamic religions.

People who hate any or all of the three Abrahamic religions may be critical and accuse me of white-washing the cruelties committed by those of the religions they hate. I could have mentioned more atrocities than I have from all three religions, but chose instead to focus on ways in which all three religions have risen above the worst in their histories. We do not need to prove that people do bad things. We need to see that possibilities for respect, cooperation, and peace not only exist, but that there is a rich history in all three religions for this hope.

This book certainly does not claim to speak for all Jews, Christians, or Muslims. People within each religion have mutually contradictory beliefs. This book is one particular understanding of the three religions. There will be people in each religion that will disagree with my understanding of their religion. Those disagreements, I pray, will be the basis for continuing dialogue.

I am aware that the perspective of this book comes out of privilege, out of my special status in the world as a white, educated, male U.S. citizen who has had the opportunity for travel and exposure to other cultures, personal and economic security, and the freedom to explore new ideas. My privilege colors my perspective. I am deeply grateful for the freedom I have. Partly due to my privilege, but also because I refuse to give in to my fears, I have the freedom to go anywhere, to do anything I believe God wants me to do. I have had many experiences in the Middle East of riding buses, visiting villages, sleeping in Jewish and Muslim homes, while experiencing the barriers of race, nationality, language, culture, and religion evaporating between us, so that we could simply enjoy and appreciate each other.

I am also aware that in many times and places the ideas expressed in this book would have led to my imprisonment and possible execution. Therefore, I am grateful to the many people in all three religions who have rejected exclusive ideas and are open not only to friendship, but also fellowship with people of other religions.

The idea of interfaith dialogue may sound threatening to some groups of people, particularly minority groups whose existence may be threatened, groups who have used their religion as a cohesive force to survive over the centuries by resisting oppression and pressures to assimilate into the dominant cultures around them. I think of, for example, Jews or the Amish who survived centuries of oppression by being exclusive.

Each community has established its own boundaries. There may be good reasons for those boundaries, and they need to be respected. In some cases, religious and cultural isolation may be a legitimate survival mechanism. We need to remember, however, that those boundaries are artificial barriers. It is essential that those boundaries not be elevated above God, above the call to love our neighbor. Often boundaries had legitimate reasons when they were created, reasons that may no longer exist. Boundaries without a legitimate basis exist in opposition to God.

Although I would personally make more narrow definitions of faith, in this book I use the words, Jewish, Muslim, and Christian loosely, referring to anyone who even vaguely identifies with one of these religions. All three religions are diverse and none would fit any narrow definition. References to Christians, Jews, or Muslims committing atrocities do not mean that those people are true, practicing Christians, Jews, or Muslims. This is not the place to employ more narrow definitions.

Sadly, there are people in all three religions who will feel threatened by some of the ideas in this book. It need not be so. I would hope that people in all three religions would see their faith affirmed in this book.

In no way has my involvement in Judaism and Islam compromised my Christian faith or made me less Christian. I hope Christian readers of this book will be able to discern my continuing Christian faith. I believe what I am doing is wholly consistent with following Jesus. I hope that my love for all three religions will not be a stumbling block for my Muslim, Jewish, or Christian friends. I really do affirm and accept your faith. I am your brother.

The vision in this book of the three religions being different branches of the same tree should not be seen as support for a sanitized, weakened religion which could form the basis for a new world order of capitalist and corporate control of the planet. I completely reject a pluralism in which one can worship any god as long as one pledges allegiance to the empire, a pluralism that weakens the faith and identity of religious communities. The Judeo/Christian/Islamic vision in this book will be seen as subversive by anyone seeking worldly power to control and oppress other people. People who worship the true God regularly make trouble for their rulers. My goal is not to reduce our heritage to some weak mush, but to recover the radical vitality of God's revelations.

I beg God's forgiveness for any false or harmful views expressed in this book. I tried to be honest in what I have written, but I know I can be sincerely wrong. I hope nothing in this book is disrespectful to God or God's revelations, or brings discouragement to any people of good will. I ask God's forgiveness for everything I write that is wrong.

I pray that through this book some people will deepen their faith and resolve to serve God.

Acknowledgments

I WANT TO THANK those who read and criticized earlier drafts of this book. Their comments were very helpful. A big thank you to Dale and Debbie Gish, Joel Gish, Jonathan Maffay, Robby Labovitz, Niel Bernstein, Elijah Ray, Liam Joshua Cohen, Mary Ann Garber, Steve Heinrichs, Nancy Beres, Bill Baldwin, Heather Irwin, Spruce Houser, Martha and Bill Faw, Bob and Trisha Lachman, Fatih Yildirim, Douglas Caffyn, and Dennis Bricker. Also thanks to Tim Kraus for editing and formatting the final manuscript for publication.

I am especially grateful to my Jewish and Muslim friends for the many ways they have been supportive and helpful, sharing insights, helping me overcome some of my ignorance and pointing out some of my mistakes. I have much to learn from people whose experience is different from my own.

And finally, a big thank you to my wife, Peggy Gish, a woman of great faith, who has opened her heart to people of other religions.

⇒ ONE ⇐

A Personal Journey

MAYBE MY FIRST EXPERIENCE of interfaith thinking came to me as a boy hearing prayers in languages other than my own. Occasionally missionaries or people from other cultures would speak to my church and give us a flavor of another culture by praying in the language of that culture. Although the prayers were in another language, somehow I knew those prayers were directed toward the same God I worshiped. They were just using different words. I was amazed that God could understand more than one language. My understanding of God was expanding, a process that has never stopped.

As a boy, both through church activities and personal reading, I became deeply immersed not only in the Christian Scriptures, but in the Hebrew Scriptures as well. I have always understood Judaism as the foundation for Christianity.

I began my faith journey in the Church of the Brethren, part of the Anabaptist, Free Church tradition. I grew up as part of a small minority tradition, part of a tradition that had experienced persecution for its cultural nonconformity, and for rejecting worship of the state and militarism. We rejected many of the moral values of the larger society, but did not seek to impose our values on the greater society. Growing up in a tradition not linked to the power structures of the dominant society made me more open to other groups who also have been persecuted minorities. I easily identify with groups who have moral commitments rooted in Scripture, and based in distinctive communities of faith, communities that would rather endure suffering than inflict suffering.

1

An important step in my relationship with Islam and Judaism has been my work with Christian Peacemaker Teams (CPT) in Israel/Palestine starting in 1995. Each winter since then, I have gone to Hebron in the West Bank for two or three months to be part of the CPT team there.[1] I was challenged with the idea that those who desire peace should be willing to take the same risks that soldiers take in their pursuit of war. That was a challenge to my faith, and caused me to turn more deeply to God. I could never be able to take those risks on my own strength.

The work of our Hebron team was centered in an apartment in the Muslim Old City, between the small Jewish settlements in the city. There were around 1200 Israeli soldiers in Hebron to protect the one or two hundred settlers who lived in the middle of 140,000 Palestinian Muslims. There often were clashes in front of our door. We were there to be a non-violent presence in the middle of the conflict, to listen, to observe, and to engage in nonviolent direct action, an ideal context for an experiment in nonviolent action and interfaith dialogue.

Those experiences in Hebron involved intense relationships between the three Abrahamic religions as they interacted in that tense city. We were immersed in the life and culture of Jews and Muslims in Hebron. We moved beyond polite dialogue to bringing Muslims, Jews, and Christians together in a common struggle for peace and just relationships between people of the three religions. We dared to face some of the difficult issues that are so often ignored in polite dialogue.

Judaism, Islam, and Christianity are each threatened by narrow-minded, violent extremists who put the narrow interests of their own people above our common interests. It has been a privilege to stand side by side with open-minded Muslims, Jews, and Christians in that struggle. I will not soon forget the many experiences of Jews, Muslims, and Christians working side by side in Hebron.

It is actually something of a miracle that a group of Christians can make a clear Christian witness in Muslim Hebron. For several years we had our daily morning team worship in the park across the street from the Ibrahimi Mosque and the synagogue at the Tomb of the Patriarchs and Matriarchs. We have had repeated acts of public witness for peace and justice in Hebron, with a clear Christian message, including Christian worship.

---

1. See Gish, Arthur, *Hebron Journal*, and Gish, Arthur, *At-Tuwani Journal*.

Muslims have many misconceptions of Christians that are not helped by the many Christians in America who uncritically support policies of the state of Israel that put Palestinian Christians, Muslims, and Jews, in jeopardy. Hopefully, American Christians living and working with Muslims will affect Palestinian Muslim perceptions of Christians.

My experiences of sleeping in Muslim homes, being invited to pray with Muslims, and sharing their lives made a deep impression on me. I was deeply impressed with the spirituality of Palestinian Muslim culture. As we worked side by side and took risks together, we came to trust each other. Religion seemed to be the number one topic many Hebronites wanted to discuss. Almost every day in Hebron I became engaged in intense religious discussions. The Muslims were not shy about sharing their faith with me and inviting me to become a Muslim. My times spent in Iraq with CPT have also been formative for me.[2]

Because of the importance of Hebron for Jewish faith and history, Jews from all over the world make pilgrimages to Hebron. Hebron, the burial place of Abraham and Sarah, Isaac and Rebekah, Jacob and Leah, and the capital during the first seven years of David's kingdom, has deep significance for Jews. My relationships with Jews in Hebron have been intense and have involved serious interaction with many segments of the worldwide Jewish community. This has included serious confrontations with Israeli settlers, daily interaction with Israeli soldiers who represent the whole spectrum of Israeli society, and working side by side with Israeli peace activists.

This interaction moved far beyond polite, sterile, empty, condescending dialogue to serious struggles with Jews that often went to the heart of both Jewish and Christian identity. I have been cursed, spit upon, stoned, kicked, and beaten by Jews in Hebron, in addition to receiving numerous death threats from them. On the other hand, I have been humbled by the deep commitment of Israeli activists who are working side by side with Palestinians for a peaceful future. I have the deepest respect for Israeli Jews who risk their lives and reputations to confront oppressive actions of their government and maintain relationships with Palestinians.

On January 30, 2003, I witnessed Israeli tanks and bulldozers demolishing the main Palestinian produce market in Hebron. It was a horrendous scene. Before standing in front of and stopping an Israeli tank, I

2. See Gish, Peggy, *Iraq: A Journey of Hope and Peace.*

confronted an Israeli soldier with the horror of destroying the food supply of hungry Hebron. "What you are doing is a serious violation of the Torah and Judaism," I told him. He responded, asking me in an angry, cynical tone of voice, "Are you a Jew?" Without thinking, I responded, "Yes, I am a Jew."

That was some kind of breakthrough for me. All my life, in some way or other, I have been wrestling with the Hebrew Scriptures and how to incorporate them into my Christian faith. I had always accepted the validity of God's revelations to the Jews. That morning, I realized I was in fact a Jew in my faith. That realization has changed my life.

I have also been wrestling with my relationship with Islam, and how to deal with the message of the Qur'an. I have been fasting during Ramadan since 1997. I have been deeply moved and challenged by the beauty, depth, and clarity of Muslim spirituality.

My relationship with Islam intensified one evening during the fasting month of Ramadan in Hebron on February 3, 1997. A man invited me to break the fast with his family. His goal was to get me to convert to Islam. My goal was to develop relationships with Palestinians. When it was time for the sunset prayer, my host invited me to join in the Muslim prayers. I told them that I couldn't do that, since I was a Christian, not a Muslim. They insisted that I pray with them, telling me there is only one God and that they wanted me to pray with them. "Why not," I thought. They showed me how to wash my hands, face, and feet in preparation for prayer. I then joined them, kneeling with my face on the floor. After eating, they took me to a mosque for about two hours of evening prayers. It was an amazing experience for me. A door opened for me that night to a whole new world.

On February 21, 1997, the same man and his friend, in a further attempt to get me to become a Muslim, took me to the Al Aqsa Mosque in Jerusalem for Friday Prayers. I was deeply moved by the experience. There was a spirit of universal love in the mosque. People from all over the world, from every race and social class, together prostrated themselves before the Lord of the universe. My friends introduced me to one of the imams who, arm in arm, led me out of the mosque, across the large courtyard where the Jewish Temple once stood, down into the Old City, up the Via Dolorosa, past the Church of the Holy Sepulture, into another mosque. They took me into a room, which soon filled with about 20 men, important Muslim leaders in Jerusalem. Apparently, my friends had asked the imam for help in getting me converted. Soon the whole group of men started working on me. I told them I was ashamed of how Christians have treated Muslims over the centuries, and apologized to them. I shared with them my faith and desire to submit myself totally to God's will. What followed was an intense time of honest dialogue, including some time talking about the meaning of the cross and nonviolent suffering love. At the end of our time, every one of those men hugged and kissed me. I felt blessed. I felt loved and respected. Since then, I have regularly prayed with Muslims in their homes and in mosques, and have included the Muslim way of praying in my own prayer life.

I later started regular participation in worship in the synagogue in Athens, Ohio. On October 13, 2005, I participated for the first time in Yom Kippur services, a total of seven hours of liturgy in a 24-hour period. Yom Kippur (The Day of Atonement) is the most sacred day of the Jewish year, a day of fasting, self-examination, and repentance. The day began at sunset on Wednesday evening. For the next 24 hours, there was a complete fast, no food or drink, with nothing to pass one's lips. People are to abstain from sex during this time.

Yom Kippur that year was during the holy month of Ramadan, the Muslim month of fasting, during which Muslims abstain from all food, drink, and sexual activity every day from dawn until sunset. Since I already was fasting for Ramadan, combining both the Jewish and Muslim fast was extra special for me by bringing together the two religions in a very personal and physical way.

I entered the synagogue Wednesday evening with eager anticipation. I knew this would be a formal, two-hour service. I put on a kippah (skullcap), as did all the men. The synagogue soon was packed with people, many whom I have known over the years. A woman played a flute as we gathered for worship. The rabbi began by declaring that we had God's permission to be gathered there, even though we were all sinners, even though we may not all agree, even though we may be on the opposite sides of issues. "By the authority of the heavenly court, with the permission of God, The Ever-Present, and with the permission of this congregation, we who have ourselves transgressed, declare it lawful to pray with others who have wronged either God or human beings."

That really struck me. I thought about the Israeli settlers in Hebron, Jews who have been so nasty to me, from whom I have received so much abuse. I have been given permission by God to worship with them. That jolted me. Was I ready to worship with them? I immediately recognized that I had to be ready to worship with them, even though I found that difficult, and yes, repulsive. How can I worship God who loves those nasty settlers and not be willing to worship with them, to be open to them?

I was given a copy of a call for repentance as I entered the synagogue, a reprint from *Tikkun* magazine, with two columns, one for people on the political left and one for people on the political right, calling each group to repentance. The focus was the Israeli/Palestinian conflict, calling both left and right to examine their self-righteous and judgmental attitudes. That challenged me to examine my views toward Israelis and Palestinians, to ask if my attitudes represent the Spirit of God who loves both Palestinians and Israelis.

I was deeply moved by the liturgy: the praise of God, the Hebrew prayers, and the deep expressions of faith. There was nothing in the liturgy or the sermon that I could disagree with. It was thoroughly biblical, to use a phrase from my childhood. It was the same faith I learned as a boy in my home and in my church. I had heard many of the same words used in Christian and Muslim liturgy. As I sat in the Yom Kippur service, I wondered, as a Christian, how could I not be Jewish? Judaism is at the root of my faith.

My belief that there is one faith at the core of Islam, Judaism, and Christianity was reconfirmed. I sensed the same Spirit of God in that synagogue as I sense in churches and mosques. I sensed the same longings in those Jews as I sense in Muslims and Christians. All of us want a relationship with God, to be accepted by God. There is one God who sends his/her Spirit to us all.

I was impressed by the lists of specific sins we were to repent from, and the biblical promises of God's forgiveness. As we went through lists of sins, over and over we repeated the words, "For the wrong we did before You," followed by a specific sin. Examples of the sins mentioned were malicious thoughts, oppressing others, contempt for others, hardening our hearts, betraying a trust, polluting God's creation. The people who compiled the prayer book took old texts and traditions and made them inclusive and contemporary, without, I think, compromising traditional Jewish faith.

The reading of the message of judgment and hope for Israel and for all humanity, embodied in Isaiah 57:14—58:14, summed up for me the meaning of Yom Kippur. Repentance must be personal, and it must include the dimension of social justice. I deeply appreciated the prayers for peace, including peace between Israelis and Arabs.

I was reminded of my daily need for repentance, my need for humility, my need for grace. My aching, hungry stomach reminded me not only of the suffering of the poor, but also of my selfishness, my wanting to satisfy all my desires, my need for more self discipline. My own frailty became more real to me.

We filed out of the synagogue in silence. I immediately headed for the mosque for evening Ramadan prayers. I sensed the same Spirit of God as I entered the mosque. I felt overwhelmed by feelings of gratitude that I have been given these wonderful, marvelous opportunities to worship God. I found myself silently repeating the few Hebrew prayers I knew as I bowed, kneeled, and prostrated myself with my Muslim brothers and sisters. I had also silently repeated Muslim and Christian prayers during the Yom Kippur liturgy.

The next morning we gathered at the synagogue for three hours of liturgy. We gathered again at 5:00 for another two hours of liturgy, after which we broke the fast by eating a delicious meal together. I then went back to the mosque for another round of Muslim prayers.

In addition to my participation in Jewish and Muslim worship those two days, both days began with a time of Christian worship around our communal breakfast table. I am a Christian.

As I thought about redemption during the Yom Kippur services, I remembered the kippah the Jaber family near Hebron had given to me about five years earlier. The Jabers had found the Jewish skullcap in their field the day after a group of Jewish settlers had come on their land during the night of January 2, 2001, and destroyed some of their property. Apparently one settler lost his kippah after a lot of exertion during the rampage at the Jaber home. I wondered if he also lost his religion in the process. When the Jabers offered me the kippah, I accepted it and had a feeling I might someday find it useful. It had lain on my desk since then; representing for me the oppression my Palestinian friends have been experiencing from their Jewish neighbors.

As I thought about atonement and redemption during the Yom Kippur services, it came to me that I should start wearing that kippah in the synagogue as a symbol of my faith that redemption and reconciliation are possible. I am sure the settler who lost that kippah would be horrified to know that I, a Christian and his perceived enemy, am now wearing his kippah. I wear that kippah not as any sign of disrespect, but as a sign of love and hope. Yes, even the Hebron settlers can be transformed by God's love. Maybe some day in heaven he and I can talk about this, after both of us have been transformed. Hopefully we will both get a big laugh out of this.

The next week after Yom Kippur, I again attended Shabbat services at the synagogue and wore my kippah. That beautiful, woven, many-colored kippah is now a symbol of my love for Judaism, and my hope that peace and reconciliation are possible. That kippah embodies why I worship in synagogues and mosques and churches. The dividing wall of hostility has been breeched again.

My experiences of worship with Jews have been very healing for me, something I deeply need. I was raised in an American culture that includes a deep strain of anti-Jewish bigotry. Of course, I was influenced by that bigotry. Add to that all the horrible experiences I have had with Jews in Hebron, and I am a person in need of healing and redemption. I need to hear Hebrew spoken by Jews in a loving context, Hebrew used to praise God instead of to curse. Yet seeing the prayer shawls, the kippahs, and hearing the spoken Hebrew prayers, raises deep feelings of anxiety in me, reminding me of my need for much more healing.

I continue to worship in the synagogue in Athens. I go to worship God, as a statement of peace and my love for Jews, but I also go because I find a source of healing there. I need to sing and pray with Jews. I need to hear the words of faith in God and longings for peace from Jews in Hebrew. I have heard too many curses in Hebrew.

Good Friday, April 14, 2006, was an ecumenical day for me, beginning with personal Muslim prayers before sunrise. Next came our daily time of Christian worship around the breakfast table. We read the story of government conniving, intrigue, and torture that resulted in crucifying Jesus, an innocent man. The biblical story sounded like the day's news. Before participating in the ecumenical Good Friday service in the Presbyterian Church building in Athens, I went to the basement and did Muslim ablutions in the sink. As the story of Jesus' arrest, rigged trial, and execution was read, I thought of all the undeserved suffering in our world, people continuing to die for the sins of others.

Immediately after the Good Friday service, I walked to the mosque for Friday prayers. I entered a different world in the mosque with Muslims from around the world, yet it was the same God I had been praying to all day. I heard in the Muslim sermon a message of redemption offered to all by the one God.

To round out the day, to make the circle of faith complete, that evening at 6:00, I went to the synagogue in Athens for the weekly Shabbat service. Since this was Passover, the theme was redemption, remembering how God liberated the slaves in Egypt.

The evening was not finished when I walked out of the synagogue. The local homeless shelter was holding a "Fast from Shelter" at the County Court House where evangelical Christians were spending the night on the street to remember homeless people. I joined the time of worship they had at the beginning of each hour. The theme at 8:00 was God's requirement that we do justice, love mercy, and walk humbly with our God.

Now it has almost become a tradition for me on Good Friday to attend the ecumenical Good Friday service, go to the mosque for Friday Prayers, and to the synagogue for Shabbat services.

As I worshiped in the synagogue five months later, on September 15, 2006, I was filled with a deep peace. I felt bathed in God's love. I felt accepted by the Jews there. I soaked in that peace and love. As we stood and chatted after the time of worship, I was stunned when I saw a young man wearing a green tee shirt of the Israeli Defense Forces. I recoiled in horror as I do in churches and mosques when I see someone in military uniform. Military uniforms symbolize for me the opposite of the Judeo/Christian/ Islamic vision. Images of Israeli military atrocities raced through my mind. I wanted to confront the young man as I have confronted many Israeli soldiers. I knew my angry urge was coming from my pain, not from any leading of God's Spirit. I kept quiet, greeted him in a welcoming spirit, and wrestled with my feelings of anger and sorrow. I thought of the stark contradiction between what those Israeli Defense Forces do and the beautiful vision of peace and trust in God I had just experienced in that synagogue. I thought of the long Jewish history of rejecting trust in military might. I left the synagogue full of joy for the peace and love I had experienced that evening, and full of pain and sadness for the foolishness of trusting in violence and the horrible suffering that misplaced faith causes. I left realizing again my own need for healing.

For some years I have been saying that Christians need to take both Judaism and Islam more seriously, for we are all part of the Abrahamic tradition. Now I am in the middle of a deep, creative struggle, trying to put together the Jewish, Islamic, and Christian influences in my life. How do I resolve the seeming contradictions between the Torah, the Qur'an, and the gospel? Maybe the contradictions are not as deep as most of us think they are. Maybe we need to look deeper. All three traditions call me to love God with my whole being, to submit my life to God, and to follow the path God has created for us.

This is more than a personal pilgrimage for me. A major challenge for people of faith is to resist the growing demonization of Islam, Christianity, and Judaism. I am deeply troubled by the great divide, the fear, the hostility, and bigotry in all three religions toward the other two. This demonization is a major threat not only to all three religions, but also to the lives of literally millions of people around the earth. Not only are people in all three religions calling for war against the other religions. Governments are taking up and encouraging these calls. Actually, much of the impetus for this demonization comes from governments and business interests to further their geo-political objectives. I want to do something to build bridges between the three religions. I feel called to embody in my own life the healing, the reconciliation, the unity I long for between people of different religions. I want to live what I believe.

Every time I enter the synagogue in Athens I am aware that people may hate me for associating with Jews. Each time I enter the mosque in Athens I assume that someone may be taking note of my associating myself with Muslims. When I enter the synagogue or mosque, I am declaring to the powers that be that I will not submit to their culture of fear, that I will not cut myself off from any of God's children. My allegiance is to God.

Can one be a Muslim, a Christian, and a Jew? Is that possible? Often the questions concern social identity rather than theological concerns. People in all three religions at first often react with surprise, considering the idea to be preposterous. But after understanding my journey, most, but not all, have been supportive. A Muslim questioned me about my faith and asked who was my prophet. I replied, "Moses, Jesus, and Mohammad." He was perplexed. On the other hand, one Muslim said to me, "In order to be a Muslim, one must be a Jew and a Christian, one must accept the Jewish and Christian faiths because Moses and Jesus were also sent by God."

After informing the Jewish congregation in Athens, Ohio, I met with the rabbi to discuss the possibility of my officially being recognized as a Jew. Sadly, the rabbi informed me that a key question I would be asked would be, "Are you disassociating yourself from all other religions?" Obviously my answer to that question had to be negative. I have received the same answer from various other rabbis, but many Jews have encouraged me to continue my participation in the Jewish community. I feel very welcome among them. I have no desire to push the issue. Rather, for the time being, it has seemed best to me to explore ways I can become more Jewish in my life. My first steps in this direction have been to regularly attend Shabbat services, participate in Jewish celebrations, learn Hebrew prayers, and avoid certain foods. I have been encouraged by the words I heard in the synagogue in Athens: "There is more than one way to be Jewish."

As I began relating to Muslims and Jews, it was clear to me that my first task was to listen and learn. I soon became aware of my ignorance. My task was not to challenge, but to open my heart to the people I knew so little about. First, I needed to get beyond all my misconceptions. Who was I, a Christian, to say anything to Jews and Muslims who have suffered so much from Christians? I had a great need to first learn humility.

My relationship with Islam and Judaism is primarily trying to learn and understand. This involves more than rational learning. I want to allow the spirit of Islam and Judaism to penetrate to the depths of my soul. Upon hearing the call to prayer from the minaret, I try to open my heart to hear and absorb that call to turn to God. In the same way, I try to allow the Hebrew prayers to soak into my soul.

I have had an advantage coming from my Anabaptist background, with the commitment to actually live out the vision presented in the Bible, and the belief that the Lordship of Jesus must relate to every area of life. A common Muslim critique of Christianity is the view that the church has spiritualized the message of the prophets with the result that the Scriptures apply only to one's inner spiritual life, with our socio/economic/political lives lived outside the parameters of God's revelations. I was raised to believe that I must follow Jesus in every aspect of my life. Discipleship has been seen as essential, with the result that I have to live my life in nonconformity to mainstream American views on issues such as violence, sexuality, and possessions. This is strikingly similar to the Muslim understanding of *tauhid*, the belief that every area of life must be submitted to the one will of God. It also seems similar to the Jewish idea of all of life being informed by Torah.

Because of my association with Judaism and Islam I will never be the same. I have been so changed by my experiences with Islam and Judaism that I can never go back to where I was before going on this journey. I have found values and practices in all three religions that I cannot abandon.

Participating in Muslim prayers, including prostrating before God, makes some Christian prayer seem casual and shallow. When Muslims join in formal prayer, first they wash (ablution), and then together prostrate themselves before God. One's whole body is used in Muslim prayer. That experience is awesome. I asked a Muslim friend why he did not pray the five daily Muslim prayers. He replied, "I am not worthy to bow down before the Lord of the universe." Although I do not agree with him, his words continue to haunt me. How seriously do I take prayer? Am I careless and casual about my relationship with God?

I repeatedly think about my friend when I participate in Christian worship, much of which focuses on me and what God will do for me. On the other hand, I deeply appreciate the informality, spontaneity, and freedom found in Christian worship. Although the Muslim liturgy is deeply meaningful for me, I also need the congregational singing and music that is often vital in Jewish and Christian worship.

It has been a long, exciting journey. I remember very well the fear I felt when I first visited the mosque in Athens. I didn't know what to expect. Would I be rejected because I was a Christian? I felt I was taking a big step into the unknown. I had been influenced by all the negative stereotypes of Muslims as violent people. I even had fears for my safety, but quickly realized how silly my fears had been. I was welcomed with open arms. They told me they had deep respect for Jesus and for Christians. There was nothing to fear.

I experienced similar fears when I first went to the synagogue in Athens. How would the Jews react to me, a Christian? Some of them had been upset because of criticisms I have voiced about Israel and the Occupation. As in the mosque, I was warmly welcomed in the synagogue. The Jewish people of Athens have been very gracious to me.

I learned from these experiences that I do not need to live in fear. I can take steps into the unknown. I can take risks. I can reach out to anyone, even to those whom I am told to fear.

I remember seeing a cartoon showing a box in the middle of a beautiful meadow. Inside the box was a fearful person, too afraid to break out of the small box. It felt safe only inside the box. Recently our cat gave birth to two kittens. Soon they were crawling around the boxes in the shed where they were born, but for several weeks they were afraid to come out of the shed and hid when they saw me. Gradually they overcame their fears and enjoyed the big beautiful world they had feared. There really isn't anything to fear in breaking out of our little boxes and experiencing the larger beautiful world God has created.

≈ TWO ≈

The Oneness of God

INCLUSIVE OR EXCLUSIVE?

OVER THE YEARS I have had many conversations with people who can see no validity or virtue outside their own religion, who believe their religion is the only true religion, that God accepts the prayers only of people of their religion, and only people of their religion will go to heaven. God will send all other people to hell. Often this includes denying the full humanity of those outside their religion, normally called racism.

Some Christians claim that their denomination is the one true church; that people in other Christian churches are going to hell. Large numbers of Muslims have told me that unless I am a Muslim, I will burn in hell. Some Shia and Sunni Muslims think only their Muslim group is acceptable to God. Judaism has its own history of belief that Jews are the only people of God. I have met Jews who claim that God loves only Jews, that only Jews have souls, and that Arabs are nothing more than animals. These people have their Scriptures and dogmatic arguments to bolster their bigotry, but I believe they miss the truth of their own religions.

I have met many bigots in all three religions, people who can only badmouth and belittle other religions. Some of this is based on misunderstandings and age-old lies. Some is based on modern forms of oppression and racism fostered by religious, political, and economic institutions. People have historical excuses to hate members of other groups. Christians have done horrible things in the name of Jesus. Muslims have oppressed others in the name of Allah. Jews have become oppressors when they have had political power.

Some Christians say that the Christian god is different from the Muslim god, that Christians and Jews must unite to fight the Muslim god. This bigotry is expressed every day in the Western media and in personal conversations. It results in wars and interpersonal violence. People in each religion suffer deeply from this bigotry, both in direct attacks and in the ways bigotry saps vitality from each religion. Abraham's family has become dysfunctional. How sad it is that people in all three religions have squandered the profound message they could be sharing with the world. The Star of David, the cross, the crescent, have been used to justify oppression.

People in each religion need to give up their horror stories about the other religions, be willing to take actions that can build trust, and work for new beginnings. Our horror stories enslave us and keep us from being open to God who wants to give us something new. We can lay aside our fear, mistrust, and feelings of being victims, and see God as the connection between us all. Religion can bring us together, instead of separating us. The closer we are to God, the closer we will be to each other.

There are various versions of a story of new arrivals getting a tour of heaven. When they approach a walled-in corner of the celestial city the angel tells everyone to be very quiet in order not to disturb the people there, because, as the angel explains, "The people in that section of heaven believe they are the only people here."

The biblical story of Ruth was written as a rebuke to exclusivist thinking, and stands in sharp contrast to the books of Ezra and Nehemiah. The point of the beautiful love story is that King David, the embodiment of true Jewishness, was not a pure Jew, that his grandmother was a Moabite, a non-Jew. David was a mongrel, a half-breed, not a pure Jew. In the eyes of the Israelites, Moabites were people to be despised. Yet the story of Ruth affirms that Moabites also are part of God's plan. Ruth, who was not brought up as an Israelite, is portrayed as the embodiment of the fulfillment of the law. Non-Jews are also God's people according to the book of Ruth.

Some people not only reject all other religions, but also believe their interpretation of their own religion is the only valid understanding of the truth. I recently heard a sermon that could have been preached in any of the Abrahamic religions. The preacher decried the lack of unity in his religion. So far, so good, but his answer to that disunity was to demand that everyone accept his narrow point of view. I recoiled in dismay. He was contributing to the disunity in his own religion. He had become part of the problem.

Many people in all three religions believe the troubles of the present time are God's judgment for not following their religion strictly enough. For example, lack of rain or too much rain is seen as a consequence of human sin. There is a grain of truth in this. Nature is in rebellion against human oppression. But there also is great danger in this belief, because it can form the basis for scapegoating. We can blame current troubles on any group we hate or fear, and play God by acting out our wrath upon that group. The answer, we are told, is to repent, to turn back to God, and follow some strict interpretation of pure Jewish, Muslim, or Christian faith. Only then will things change for the better. There is little concrete agreement on what this would mean.

Since people believe that their Scriptures are true, they conclude that since their beliefs are rooted in Scripture, their beliefs are true. This arrogance makes dialogue difficult. I have heard Christians say, "God said it, I believe it, and that settles it." Even if my Scriptures are inerrant, my interpretations of those Scriptures are certainly not inerrant. Much hostility could be avoided if we could remember that any reading of any text is an interpretation of that text. Recognizing that we see the Truth only partially can give us the humility to be open to seeking common ground with people of different perspectives.

I am uncomfortable with rigid dogmatism and narrow-mindedness, no matter how they are manifested. Fundamentalism is found not only in religious groups. It can be secular, political, or scientific. In every group there are those who believe they have the truth, and anyone who disagrees is wrong, if not damned.

Dogmatism cuts us off from God's grace, and from our neighbor. "We few are right, and everyone else is going to hell." In other words, God loves only me, and those who agree with me. Will theological and spiritual correctness justify me before God? Am I not in need of God's grace even if I am right? On the great judgment day all of us will realize how wrong we have been on so many levels. For me, faith means being open to God, and not needing to be in control. We can only trust in God's grace and mercy.

The important thing is not whether our intellectual doctrines are correct, even though I have spent a lot of time studying and thinking through doctrinal issues, but whether or not we have a living relationship with God, whether we love mercy and walk humbly on the earth. Who are we to tell God who God may or may not accept?

Our beliefs are important. They affect how we live. But much more important is whether I hold my beliefs with compassion and a yearning for justice. Even if I am totally correct in all my beliefs, if I do not hold them in love, I am totally wrong. The main question is not what doctrines we believe, but whether we are guided by God's Spirit, whether we are filled with love, and whether we are working for justice.

If my heart is not filled with love, the next logical step is for me to hate those who are not correct like I am. If I hate them, obviously God must also hate them. Therefore, I can ostracize them, marginalize them, dehumanize them, oppress them, and yes, kill them.

Faith in God is not a set of abstract beliefs separate from earnestly seeking to do God's will in our daily lives. Beliefs, doctrines, and theology are true to the extent they are lived. Jesus told the story of a father who had two sons. When he asked one son to go work in the vineyard, the son agreed, but didn't work in the vineyard. When he asked the other son to work in the vineyard, the son argued with his father and refused. But then the son reconsidered and did go work in the vineyard. "Which son," Jesus asked, "did the will of his father?"[1]

GOD IS ONE

At the heart of all three Abrahamic faiths is the affirmation that God is one. "Hear O Israel, the Lord your God is one (*Shema Yisrael, Adonai Elohenu, Adonai echad*)." Muslims make the same affirmation each day when they confess, "There is no deity except God (*la illaha illala*)."

When I was a student at Bethany Theological Seminary, Samuel Sandmel, a noted Jewish biblical scholar, gave a series of lectures on the development of monotheism in ancient Israel. At the end of his last lecture, I asked a very stupid question. I asked when the issue of monotheism was finally settled in ancient Israel. I have never forgotten his answer. He said, "The issue of monotheism has never been settled."

Indeed, it has not been settled. Still today, the radical concept of monotheism is too much for many people to handle. That is confirmed not only by the recent resurgence of polytheism in Western countries, but

1. Matt 21:28–31.

also by the confusion among adherents of the three Abrahamic religions. Repeatedly I hear Christians say that Allah is a different god than the Christian god. I often respond by asking them how many gods they think there are. Some Christians believe there are two gods, a good god and a bad god (Satan).

In 2003, a Jewish settler in Hebron approached a teammate and in a very angry way yelled at my friend, saying, "My god will kill your god," a bratty response, on the same level as "My daddy can beat up your daddy." As much as by the fear, hate, and bigotry expressed in his proclamation, equally troubling was his rejection of the Jewish belief in the oneness of God.

On January 31, 2008, I awoke in the morning to see six inches of snow on the ground, the first snow to accumulate in ten years in the South Hebron Hills in occupied Palestine. That day was special. People of all ages were throwing snowballs, a joyous time. I asked my Palestinian Muslim friends if snow had also fallen in the nearby Israeli settlements. They all said yes. There is one God who makes it snow on everyone, not just His favorite people, be they Muslim, Jewish, Christian, or anyone else. We deny the oneness of God when we make exclusive claims on God.

There was the concept in ancient tribalism that each tribe, each locality, had its own deity. Henotheism is the belief that there are other gods, but we worship only one god, our god. This is illustrated in the biblical and Quar'anic stories of Jonah, who thought that by getting on a ship and sailing away from the land of Israel, he could escape the god who was asking him to do something he didn't want to do, namely, to share God's salvation with Iraqis in Nineveh, a people other than Israelites. To his horror, he discovered that God was also present out in the middle of the sea. In both the Bible and the Qur'an, the prophet Jonah comes to realize that there is one God; that no one can escape from God; that God is everywhere, and cares for all people. To believe in the oneness of God is to view the world through something other than tribal lenses. Do we worship the Lord and Creator of the Universe, or a tribal deity we created? The gods we create reflect our own brokenness. They are petty, vicious, and act like spoiled brats.

Originally the proclamation that there is one God was an exclusivist claim that "My god is the true God and your god is a lesser god or no god." A deeper understanding of monotheism is an inclusive claim that all who truly seek God are seeking the same One Reality, that since we were all created by the same Creator, we all have a deep yearning for relationship with our Creator. Rather than ask if we worship the same god, a more productive approach is to ask how our understandings of God are similar and different.

The human longing for God, to connect to our Source, is universal. God does not belong to any group. God's grace is not limited to people of my religion. God's mercy is universal and eternal. "The steadfast love of the Lord never ceases."[2] Only the God who transcends the gods we create is worthy of worship. God is not ours, because God's love and mercy always includes the other, the stranger, and our enemy. The concept of monotheism is subversive to the notion of provincialism, because those other cultures and peoples also were created by God. The Western world-view is provincial because it excludes much of the rest of the world from its perspective. If there is but one God, the Creator of all that is, then that God somehow must also be involved in the lives and societies of peoples other than our own. Provincialism, ethnocentrism, and racism are antithetical to monotheism.

There is one God. All peoples are special to God, but no person or group of people is exclusively special to God. God is Lord of all nations, all cultures, and all peoples. We do not possess God. Any denial of this basic tenet of monotheism leads to racism. Divisions, oppressions, and wars are the result of denying that all of us are from God. Domination and oppression of others is a usurpation of the sovereignty of God.

The Hebrew Scriptures begin not with the beginning of one people, but with the origin of all people, and contain the vision of the day when we will all be one. God's covenant with Noah was for not only all people, but for all creatures.[3] Through Abraham, all the nations were to be blessed. According to Genesis 14:18–20, Abraham received a blessing from Melchizedek, a priest in Jerusalem, whose monotheism predated Abraham.

In Exodus 18:1–27, we find the amazing story of Jethro, a priest of Midian (an Arabic descendent of Abraham?), and Moses' father in law, coming to the mountain where God covenants with Israel. Jethro gives

2. Lam 3:22.

3. Gen 9:8–17.

Moses spiritual advice, proclaims that Yahweh is greater than all gods (*Allahu akbar?*), offers a sacrifice, and gives Israel his blessing. Jethro, however, leaves and does not become part of the Jewish covenant. This is not a story of conversion. Today, as we encounter Muslim Arabs, we encounter the descendents, either physical or spiritual, of this Arabic priest who had blessed Israel.

God is the God of all nations.[4] There is one God.[5] Malachi says God's name is great and worshiped among the Gentiles.[6] There is the hope in the Hebrew scriptures that one day all people will be included in God's rule, that all the nations of the earth will come to worship God in Jerusalem.[7]

Classical Jews have not seen it necessary for people to become Jews in order to be saved, because, as spelled out in the Talmud, there was a similar revelation for Gentiles in the covenant with Noah, by which Gentiles are to be judged. Jews have traditionally believed that if non-Jews abide by the seven commandments given to Noah, God will accept them. Pre-Christian Judaism recognized a class of non-Jews as people who "feared God."[8]

According to the Hebrew Scriptures, it was a mixed group of people who left Egypt in the Exodus.[9] Before the blessing of the first cup in a Passover seder at the synagogue in Athens, these words were read: "Israel left Egypt with 'a mixed multitude'; the Jewish people began as a multi-cultural *mélange* of people attracted to a vision of social transformation. What makes us Jews is not some biological fact, but our willingness to proclaim the message of those ancient slaves: The world can be changed, we can be healed."

Repeatedly, when I confront Israeli soldiers or settlers with their racist actions toward Palestinians, I recite the *Shema* ("Hear O Israel, the Lord your God is one") to them in Hebrew and remind them that there is one God who created us all. At the top of the hill going up to Tel Rumeida in Hebron there has been a barrier separating Palestinians and Israelis. The Palestinians have a very narrow space in which to walk,

4. Amos 9:7.

5. Isa 45:6.

6. Mal 1:11.

7. Isa 66:23.

8. For more discussion of the classic debate in Judaism on whether non-Jews are accepted by God and how to relate to non-Jews, see Novak, *Jewish-Christian Dialogue*.

9. Exod 12:38; Num 11:4.

while the Israelis have almost the whole street for walking and driving cars. No Palestinian cars are allowed there. I have often pointed out to Israeli soldiers enforcing the separation, that they are enforcing a system of Apartheid.

On February 22, 2009, an older Palestinian man started walking down the hill on the Jewish side of the barrier. A soldier stopped him, made him go back before he could then walk down on the Palestinian side. I told the soldier, "This is Apartheid." I said, "This is disgusting. One side for Jews and a narrow side for Palestinians." I repeated the Shema to him and said there is one God. "What you are doing is a denial of the oneness of God. There is one God. This is despicable." Often the soldiers defend their actions, but sometimes they recognize that what they are doing is racist. They stand there, looking helpless. Sometimes this results in extended conversations.

The Hebrew Scriptures go beyond calling us to love our neighbor. "The stranger who sojourns with you shall be to you as the native among you, and you shall love him as yourself, for you were strangers in the land of Egypt."[10]

The Christian Scriptures end with the vision of people "from every nation, from all tribes and peoples and tongues, standing before the throne and before the Lamb, robed in white, with palm branches in their hands.[11] The vision continues with God's angels and people from diverse cultures in profound worship of God. In Revelation 22 there is an image of the river of life flowing from the throne of God. The leaves of the trees growing beside the river are for the healing of the nations.

The Early Church accepted the Greek concept of *Logos* (Word), a concept of universal rationality in the universe. John argued that the Logos enlightens all people.[12] Paul believed that all people have some knowledge of God based in creation.[13] This became the basis for early Christian dialogue with Greek philosophy.

10. Lev 19:34.
11. Rev 7:9.
12. John 1:4.
13. Romans 1–2.

The New Testament makes various positive comments about non-Christians, including the affirmation that God has revealed him/herself to the whole world. Both the Jewish and Christian scriptures affirm that non-Christians and non-Jews can know God. Non-Jewish wise men from Persia (Iranians?) came to Bethlehem to honor the birth of Jesus.

A Roman military officer approached Jesus and asked Jesus to heal his servant. The officer went so far as to tell Jesus that it was not necessary for Jesus to come to his home. "Just say the word and my servant will be healed," he said. Jesus affirmed the faith of this pagan and said that he had not seen as deep faith in all of Israel as in this pagan. Jesus then went on to say that many would come from the east and the west into his kingdom, but people with "proper" faith would be rejected.[14] Jesus also was impressed with the faith of a Syrophoenician woman, a Greek pagan, and healed her daughter.[15] When Jesus encountered the Samaritan woman, he affirmed the validity of the Samaritan religion.[16] In the story of the Good Samaritan, it is an outsider of another religion who does God's will. In the Parable of the Last Judgment, Jesus says that many will be saved who did not know Jesus.[17] Jesus said that the pagan cities of Tyre and Sidon will fare better on the Day of Judgment than the Jewish towns that refused to repent.[18] Jesus prayed that we all be one.[19]

At Pentecost, Christians affirmed that God's Spirit has been poured out on all flesh, looking back to the vision of Joel.[20] Acts 2:9–11 records some fifteen of the many ethnic groups living in Jerusalem being present at Pentecost, including Arabs from Arabia. Paul also spent time in Arabia. The book of Acts and the Pauline letters tell the amazing story of early Christianity transcending ethnic barriers and including people from all these ethnic groups, in marked contrast to the racism and nationalism that took over much of later Christian history. Paul saw the covenant with Israel being extended to all peoples.

14. Matt 8:5–13.
15. Mark 7:24–30.
16. John 4:1–42.
17. Matt 25:40.
18. Matt 11:20–24.
19. John 17:20–26.
20. Joel 2:28–29.

Peter resisted reaching out to non-Jews before seeing a life-changing vision. However, Peter's first statement to the Gentile Cornelius was to affirm the legitimacy of the Gentile's faith: "Truly I perceive that God shows no partiality, but in every nation anyone who fears Him and does what is right is acceptable to Him."[21] Peter here was expressing his acceptance of the covenant with Noah.

When the Apostle Paul and his companions met Lydia, a Greek pagan, they recognized her as "a worshiper of God."[22] Titius Justice, also a pagan, is recognized as "a worshiper of God."[23] The first two chapters of Romans say rather clearly that God has spoken in some way to all people. Paul claimed, "For there is no distinction between Jew and Greek (and Muslim?); the same Lord is Lord of all and bestows his riches upon all who call upon him. For every one who calls upon the name of the Lord will be saved."[24] We are no longer foreigners and aliens, but fellow citizens. The dividing wall of hostility has been broken down.[25] We are now one. Although history has eclipsed this verse in that new walls of hostility have been erected between worshipers of the One God, those walls can again be broken down.

The vision of the Qur'an also is a universal vision. The knowledge of God has been given to all peoples.[26] Acts 14:17 says exactly the same thing. The Qur'an accepts the legitimacy of all the prophets that came before Mohammad. The Qu'ran makes clear that the Prophet Mohammad brought nothing new, but what had already been given to the messengers before Mohammad.[27] About one fourth of the Qur'an is devoted to stories of former prophets.

God has sent prophets to all peoples of the earth and their messages have consistently been the same: that we are to worship and serve God

21. Acts 10:34–35.
22. Acts 16:11–15.
23. Acts 18:7.
24. Rom 10:12–13.
25. Eph 2:14–22.
26. Qur'an 4:122ff.
27. Ibid., 41:43.

alone, avoid evil, and pursue the good. Since all people are created by God and have a desire to know God, and since God sent prophets to all peoples, we can discern God's work in every culture. The Qur'an bases religious pluralism both in God's creation and God's revelations. The people of all religions are to be respected.

> If it had been thy Lord's Will,
> They would all have believed,
> All who are on earth!
> Wilt thou then compel mankind,
> Against their will, to believe![28]

Some Muslims have interpreted this verse as God admonishing Mohammad for being too enthusiastic in trying to convince others of the truth of Islam. Consider these verses:

> And dispute ye not with the People of the Book, except in the best way, unless it be with those of them who do wrong. But say, "We believe in the Revelation which has come down to us and in that which came down to you; Our God and your God is One; and it is to Him we submit.[29]

Sura 57:27 states that God gave Jesus the Gospel, and put kindness and mercy in the hearts of his followers.

> To each among you have We prescribed a law and an open way. If Allah had so willed He would have made you a single people, but [His plan is] to test you in that he has given you, so strive as in a race in all virtues. The goal of you all is to Allah; it is He that will show you the truth of the matters in which you dispute.[30]

If God had wanted there to be only one religion, there would be only one religion. Acceptance of the legitimacy of other religions is a doctrinal principle in the Qur'an, based both in God's revelations to the other religions, and that those religions exist by God's will. All humanity has been given divine guidance. God gave a different law and way of life to each religion.[31] The Qur'an forbids anyone to call some paths superior.[32]

---

28. Ibid., 10:99.
29. Ibid., 29:45–46
30. Ibid., 5:48; Also see Qur'an 22:34, 67.
31. Ibid., 5:48.
32. Ibid., 2:136; 3:84; 4:152.

Diversity is a gift from God. The diversity that exists in the human family, as in the rest of creation, is part of God's creative intention. Differences of gender, age, race, religion (different prophets for every nation) are part of the creative structure of creation, differences that are to be accepted and celebrated. Islam accepts cultural and racial diversity. "O mankind! We created you from a single (pair) of a male and a female, and made you into nations and tribes, that you many know each other."[33]

In spite of criticism of Judaism and Christianity in the Qur'an, a sense of kinship with both religions is both assumed and expressed. Both are based on authentic revelations from God, both affirm the Oneness of God. The Qur'an says, "To you your religion, to me my religion."[34] The Qur'an goes beyond toleration to accepting that Jews and Christians also can be saved.[35] "Those who believe [i.e., the Muslims], and those who profess Judaism, and the Christians and Sabians, those who believe in God and the Last Day and act righteously, shall have their reward with their Lord; there shall be no fear in them, neither shall they grieve."[36]

The Qur'anic basis for an inclusive approach to other religions is the concept of *ahl al-ktab* (People of the Book), which at first referred to Jews and Christians. As Islam moved east into India, Muslims extended this concept to include other religions that have received a Scripture, including Zoroastrans, Buddhists, Sikhs, and Hindus. The Qur'an guarantees freedom of religion to these groups. The Qur'anic acceptance of the People of the Book is an acceptance of religious pluralism, wherein minority groups are free to express their religion and culture, and freely participate in the larger Muslim society.

If this is true, then other religions have a right to exist and must be respected by Muslims. The Qur'an repeatedly calls for respect for the People of the Book. Mohammad said, "On the Day of Judgment I myself will act as the accuser of any person who oppresses a (non-Muslim), and lays excessive burdens on him."[37] The Qur'an calls on people of all religions to live peacefully with each other. Christians and Jews were considered fellow believers. Only later in Muslim history were Christians and

33. Ibid, 49:13.
34. Ibid., 99:6.
35. Ibid., 3:113–15
36. Ibid., 2:62.
37. Abu-Nimer, *Nonviolence and Peace Building in Islam*, 76.

Jews considered unbelievers. The constitution Mohammad prepared for the city of Medina included Jews as part of the community (*ummah*). All believers in God are part of the community God is creating.[38]

The Qur'anic command not to make alliances with unbelievers,[39] often translated to mean Muslims should not make friends with Jews and Christians, actually says the same thing as the Christian Scripture, "Do not be unequally yoked with unbelievers."[40] These Scriptures do not prohibit having friends from other religions. Farid Esack interprets this to refer to becoming collaborators with those who oppress others.[41] The Qur'an allows Muslim men to marry Jews and Christians, a rather intimate relationship.

The attitude in the Qur'an toward non-Muslims is determined by their responses to the message of Islam. Warfare against non-Muslims is permitted only when non-Muslims threaten Muslims. The warfare must stop as soon as the non-Muslim hostilities cease. The shape of Muslim relations with other religious communities was shaped primarily by security concerns, not evaluations of the beliefs of those communities.

Many Muslims, and some Christians, argue that any revelation is valid only until a new revelation supercedes and abrogates the former revelation. The message of Moses was binding until the message of Jesus replaced the message of Moses. The message of the Qur'an now has replaced all former revelations. That is a later interpretation, not the teaching of the Qur'an. Ahmad Ibn Taymiyah, the great fourteenth-century Muslim intellectual from Damascus, argued that both the Torah and the gospel are still valid not only for Jews and Christians, but for Muslims as well.[42]

Criticism of Christians and Jews in the Qur'an is based on the hostile reactions of specific Jewish and Christian groups to Islam, and is not a rejection of the validity of Judaism and Christianity. All can find salvation if they believe in one God and do good deeds. It is interesting that the Qur'an

---

38. Qur'an 23:52.

39. Ibid., 5:31.

40. 2 Cor 6:14.

41. Esack, *Qur'an: Liberation and Pluralism*, 180–84.

42. Ahmad Ibn Taymiyah quoted in Madjid. *The True Face of Islam*, 96–97; for Madjid's vision of pluralism see pp. 93–107. How Muslim scholars have gotten around the explicit teaching of inclusiveness in the Qur'an is spelled out in detail in Esack, *Quran: Liberation and Pluralism*, 161–72.

repeatedly condemns Christians and Jews who saw God as accepting only their group. The Qur'an rejects the exclusiveness of Christians and Jews.

> And they say: "None shall enter paradise unless he be a Jew or a Christian."
>
> Those are their vain desires. Say, "Produce your proof if ye are truthful." Nay, whoever submits his whole self to Allah, and is a doer of good, he will get his reward with his Lord; On such shall be no fear, nor shall they grieve.[43]

Conservative Muslims refer to the clear statement in the Qur'an that Islam is the true religion.[44] There has been much discussion in Muslim history as to the meaning of both "Islam" and "religion." Does "Islam" refer only to those who adhere to Islam as a formal religion, or to people of faith who are living in submission to God? Is Islam only a formal social group, or a response and relationship to God? The word "Islam" means "submission to God," not a particular religious group. Many Muslim scholars have argued that interpreting this verse to refer to formal Islam is a later interpretation.[45]

Islam is not the first or only universal religion. The Torah is clear that God's revelation to Abraham and Moses was not just for the Hebrew people, but for all people. The intention was that Israel would be a light to the nations, that through Israel all the nations would come to know the one true God. Even though Jesus preached mainly to Jews as Mohammad spoke mainly to Arabs, Christianity also had a universal vision of proclaiming the good news to all peoples. Many ethnic groups were involved in the miracle of Pentecost and the church spread rapidly to various lands. Mohammad never saw Islam as a universal religion replacing other religions. At first, Islam was a religion for Arabs, and then later became universal.[46] The one religion of Abraham, Moses, Jesus, and Mohammad is not something that any group can own, but is meant for the whole world. That realization should lead us all to humility.

---

43. Qur'an 2:11–112.
44. Ibid., 3:19.
45. Esack, *Qur'an: Liberation and Pluralism*, 126–34.
46. Armstrong, *Muhammad*, 211–12.

TRUTH IS ONE

All truth comes from the same source. Since there is one God, it is not surprising that there is a consistency in expressions of God's Spirit wherever people around the world respond to that Spirit. We can expect to find the fruits of the Spirit (love, joy, etc.) wherever the Spirit is at work. A response to God's Spirit is a response to God's Spirit. Jesus is quoted in John 16:12–15 as saying that the Holy Spirit will guide us into new truth. On this basis, Christians must be open to what God's Spirit may teach us through other religions.

In John 1:9 we read that the Word of God is the Light that enlightens every person. If we walk in the Light we have fellowship with all others who also walk in the Light.[47] Christians identify that Light with God's love expressed in Jesus. However we understand or name that Light, the Light is the Light, no matter what we call it. God has many names, but also is nameless. The important thing is that we walk in that Light. The meaning of life is found in worship and obedience to God. Just the longing for God, even though never satisfied, is more wonderful and fulfilling than any physical hunger that has been filled.

One evidence for the oneness of God is the amazing universality of people understanding what is sometimes called "the moral law." Although there has been disagreement over what is good, seldom have people advocated that we choose evil over good. From primitive cultures to ancient Babylon, to the Greek philosophers, to modern religious philosophy, there is general agreement on rejecting dishonesty, oppression, and murder, and an affirmation of integrity, freedom, and altruism. These values were not made up by people, but rather are rooted in God's creation and made clear in God's revelations to humanity. We find answers to the deepest longings of our hearts in the Jewish, Christian, and Muslim Scriptures, truths that come from the One who created us all. The Scriptures affirm our longing to love and be loved.

To affirm the truth and validity of one's faith does not need to mean that there is no truth in any other religion. If people of another religion affirm the oneness of God, I can rejoice and embrace them in their faith. Truth is truth, no matter who believes it. All Truth is God's Truth. Truth is one. How can I reject anything that is holy and true? This does not imply relativism, for all views are not equally true.

47. 1 John 1:17. Compare this with Sura 24:35 in the Qur'an.

No religion contains all Truth. Reality is too great to be comprehended in only one way. I do not know the whole, complete Truth. I still have much to learn. True spirituality involves humility. God is so much bigger than my small concept of God. Even God's revelations of truth only dimly reveal "The Truth." "We see through a glass darkly." To worship or absolutize revelation is idolatry. Only God is absolute.

I am repeatedly amazed at how similar the three religions are. One way this has become real for me is listening to sermons in mosques, synagogues, and churches. I instinctively analyze those sermons for their theology. Change a few words in many of the sermons preached in the mosque in Athens, Ohio, and you have a solid conservative Baptist sermon. There are many parallels between Calvinist theology and conservative Islamic theology. On Friday, May 15, 2009, I worshiped in the mosque in Athens. The sermon was about praising God in response to difficulties and hardships. Two days later, on May 17, I worshiped with an African-American congregation in Athens. The Christian sermon was almost identical in substance to the sermon in the mosque. One day I asked a Palestinian Muslim what is needed for peace. He said, "We need broken hearts before God." I asked him how we can get broken hearts. "By completely depending on God," he replied. A Jew or a Christian could have spoken those words.

Although there is a commonality in expressions of faith, the ways people experience faith and come to God vary greatly, from the subtle to the dramatic, from the gradual to the sudden, from the emotional to the rational, from informal to liturgical, from explicitly religious to secular, from quiet to boisterous. The differences between religions are not as great as the differences within each religion. Consider the liberal/conservative divide in all three religions. This is illustrated by my finding Jewish and Muslim thinkers that more closely express my beliefs than do some Christians. There is no one way when it comes to experience, yet there is but one God.

Most people of faith live out their faith within very narrow boundaries. It is interesting to observe the wide spectrum of those narrow boundaries, all of which have a small portion of The Truth, along with some untruth and distortions. Everyone has a narrow slice of The Truth. The problem comes in our not knowing how small our slice of The Truth really is, in not realizing how little we know, in making our little truth the Ultimate Truth, and in failing to see the truth other people see. Sometimes each side in a fight for truth has only partially grasped the truth, and is actually defending the same truth.

There is a story of a group of blind people describing their images of an elephant after having touched an elephant. The one who had touched the tail described the elephant as similar to a rope. The one who touched the side of the elephant compared an elephant to a wall. The one who had examined a leg of the elephant compared an elephant to a big pillar. All of these observers were correct, but they were describing only part of the elephant. Each of us, either as individuals or as religions, sees only a small part of The Truth. God grant us the humility to realize that the truth we see is only a small part of The Truth. If we could get beyond our arrogance and self-centeredness, we could learn so much from others who have different views of The One Truth.

It is exciting to observe all the different ways people respond to God's initiative in reaching out to us. Even within each of the three Abrahamic religions, there is much variety in how people respond to God, both liturgically, theologically, and in practical everyday expressions of faith in God. There are many ways to worship God, but only one God to worship. This is expressed in the Negro spiritual, "Wade in the Water." "Some say Peter, some say Paul, there ain't but one God made them all."

Spirituality is not necessarily good. Not all roads lead to Rome. Some roads lead to destruction. There are evil spiritualities. Materialism, greed, militarism, self-centeredness are spiritualities in opposition to God. Those who are seeking to accumulate the wealth of the world for themselves are operating out of a false spirituality. I often encounter people in all three religions who it seems are not listening to the same Spirit that I know. I have experienced worship with all three religions in which I sensed a bad spirit in the worship. In churches, in mosques, and in synagogues, I have heard sermons that blessed violence, condoned bigotry, and called for exclusiveness.

I am not a relativist. I believe it does matter what we believe and how we live. Some ideas are false, some better than others. Not all religions and philosophies are equally valid and true. There is Truth, even though we may see it only dimly. We are not blindly stumbling in darkness and occasionally bumping into some small truth. God's revelations through the prophets in every age have truth, depth, and amazing consistency. There is much in all three religions that I abhor: the violence, racism, closed-mindedness, ethnocentrism, and bigotry, but there are strands in all three religions that I believe to be of God's Spirit, to be true, holy, and good. If it comes from God, it is good.

There is a Jewish story of a person who entered a synagogue but did not know how to pray. He simply confessed to God that he did not know how to pray, and said, "Since I know only the letters of the alphabet, I shall repeat them and You can compose from them the prayers I should recite." It is the condition of our hearts, not what we say, that is important.

How can we discern whether God's Spirit is present? The answer is rather simple. Is there love? Is there justice and peace? Are people experiencing healing, reconciliation, and community? There are people in every religion, and people who profess no religion, who are obviously filled with God's Spirit. Those who oppress and exclude are not following God's Spirit.

We discern the presence of God's Spirit by discerning whether the fruits of the Spirit are in evidence. If the fruits of the Spirit are present, we can know that God is present. The fruits of the Spirit mentioned in Gal 5:22–23 (love, joy, peace, patience, kindness, goodness, faithfulness, gentleness, and self-control) are the infallible signs that God is present and active. We cannot create those fruits. They are gifts from God, no matter where we find them, no matter if the people are religious or nonreligious. The fruits of the Spirit are evidence that God is at work in people's lives. The next time you see evidence of these fruits in other people, give praise to God. How can we reject anything that is true and holy and from God? If I am hungry, it does not matter to me of what religion the person is who feeds me.

I agree with the message of a sign along a highway that reads, "Without God there is no love." If true, that means when atheists love, that love comes from God. The fruits of the Spirit are gifts from God's Spirit, no matter where they are found. According to the Bible, anyone "who loves is born of God and knows God."[48] An atheist who knows love knows God.

For me, to say that God is one is more than an intellectual affirmation. I know in my heart and in my guts that God is one, that I encounter the same God in churches, synagogues, mosques, alone in nature, and in countless other places where I experience an overwhelming sense of

48. 1 John 4:7.

God's presence. There is a consistency to those experiences. They direct me to repent, to praise, to love.

I remember spending a night in 2005 with a Muslim family in a cave in the South Hebron Hills. Issa, the father of the family, said, "There is not a Jewish religion, a Christian religion, or a Muslim religion. There is one God and one religion. We are not separate." I sensed a oneness of Spirit with those Muslims that night. Issa said that Jesus was present with us in that cave. I also sensed that as we broke bread and drank tea together. We truly celebrated communion together.

I must rejoice in and honor any positive human response to the call of God's Spirit, any desire to respond to God, even if it is from people I disagree with, or even disrespect. God will hear the cry of even the worst sinner, the most despicable people. God is not limited by my narrow little concepts. God is concerned with the heart, not with correct formulas. There are many varieties of responses to the working of God's Spirit, yet also an amazing similarity in those varied responses. God is one. God has many children, but children of the same parents relate to their parents in different ways.

I have spent much time in Palestine accompanying school children to protect them from Israeli settlers who frequently attack school children. Often the children question us team members about our faith. Are we Muslims or Christians, do we fast, do we pray? The questions come not only out of curiosity, but also out of a real love and concern for us. They want to know, bless their souls, if we are in right relationship with God. They want to know if we were going to heaven or hell. I think about the purity of their hearts, about their sincere love for God, and for us.

Does God not honor the sincerity of their hearts? Yes, I know that we can be sincerely wrong. I am sincerely wrong about many things that will be revealed to me either before or on the Day of Judgment. Some of the ways in which I am wrong may even have tragic consequences. What we believe is important. Some beliefs lead to peace; some lead to war. Some beliefs bring us together; some separate us. Some liberate; some enslave. It is important that I continue to examine myself, seek the truth, and repent of my wrongs, but I cannot believe that God will condemn me for being sincerely wrong.

From the Jewish Scriptures we have these words: "A broken and contrite heart you will not despise."[49] This Scripture reminds me of Amni Jaber, the illiterate matriarch of the Jaber family with whom I have lived in Hebron. Five times a day she does her Muslim prayers. Each time, at the end of those prayers, still kneeling, she opens her hands toward heaven and pours out her heart to God. I find it deeply troubling that anyone would think that God does not hear her prayers because she has not uttered what they think are the correct religious formulas. What arrogance, what disrespect for God, to say that God will cast into hell anyone who does not agree with me. Who am I to judge anyone? I can only plead for mercy.

There are many Scriptures in all three faiths that contend that God will not hear the prayers of those whose hearts are evil, who oppress the poor, who deceive others, who engage in violence. The Qur'an says God will exclude the oppressors.[50] On the Day of Judgment, each individual will be judged by their deeds, not by their tribal or religious identities. A broken and contrite heart God will not reject. It is our hearts that God sees first, not our doctrinal systems.

IS MONOTHEISM A PROBLEM?

The Freedom From Religion Foundation states in an advertisement, "There is no greater source of strife, hatred, terrorism, bloodshed, persecution, or war than religion."[51] It has been claimed that monotheism is the root cause of most of the world's problems, because of its linear view of history, its single focus that excludes other possibilities, and its violent god. It is claimed that the issues of power, control, authoritarianism, violence, and oppression flow out of the belief in oneness and unity in the cosmos.

First, it must be acknowledged that monotheists have been at the center of many of the world's problems. Monotheism has been used in oppressive ways. All three Abrahamic religions have had extremely violent and oppressive expressions. There is much to be ashamed of in all three religions.

49. Ps 51:17.
50. Qur'an 2:124.
51. *The Nation*, Sept. 25, 2006, 5.

A more liberating view, we are told, is a belief in diversity. Polytheism, not monotheism, points toward freedom. Yes, there is a wonderful history of nonviolence and egalitarianism in ancient polytheistic traditions, but the same can be said of sublime expressions of humanitarianism and equality in the three Abrahamic religions.

Polytheistic religions also have had brutal expressions. Much of human history has been brutal. If there are many gods, is there not an inherent possibility for war and conflict among the gods? The mythology of polytheism is full of stories of wars among the gods. Would it not be more honest to say that both monotheism and polytheism can be used either for liberation or oppression?

Monotheism affirms the ecological principle that everything is connected, that reality is one, that there is unity and order in the universe, something close to the Muslim concept of *tawhid*, the belief in oneness and unity in God. We live in a unified, integrated universe. Even the word "universe" contains the concept of unity.

The human body is a metaphor for the oneness of the universe. Although the human body has many members and displays an amazing amount of diversity, the human body is a unity, is one, and no member can exist apart from the rest of the body. No part of a healthy body is at war with the rest of the body. The same is true not only for the interconnectedness of and harmony between and balance within everything on earth, but also for the whole universe. These are expressions of the divine unity. Yes, there is an incredible amount of diversity in the universe, but consider also the order, harmony, and balance in and between everything.

This unity is expressed both in the creation of all that is, and the holding together of every atom, living being, and solar system in the universe. This unity is a sign (not proof) of the oneness of the God who created the universe. That all this unity could be an expression of chance is preposterous. If various parts of the cosmos came from different causes and different origins, it would indeed be highly unlikely that all those parts would fit together so perfectly as they do. Scientists describe the order in the cosmos, but they cannot explain it. It is God who creates cause and effect.

The Abrahamic tradition calls us to a holistic understanding of reality. For me, seeing order and unity in the universe points toward peace. The belief that love is the central reality in the cosmos calls us to nonviolent lifestyles. To understand the cosmos as creation rather than as a machine leads to awe, wonder, and respect. As I watch people paying homage to the gods of militarism, consumerism, and sex, with all the accompanying enslavements and suffering, I am grateful for a vision of a Reality that transcends our pettiness, a Reality that calls us to something better.

My atheist friends tell me that the very concept of God implies authority, control, and submission. They believe we can be free only by rejecting God. But I remember the oppression inherent in the great modern atheistic political experiment called Marxist Communism, hardly a kinder and more gentle history. Stalin and Mao were not nonviolent saints. Atheists also need humility. European secular nationalism was just as oppressive and violent as monotheism, and resulted in two world wars.

Monotheism accepts God as the only supreme authority in the universe. There is no hierarchy in the cosmos. Some planets do not rule over other planets. Some solar systems do not rule over others. Only God has the authority to rule. All other domination is usurpation of God's rule. People are to be subservient to none but God. The order of the universe is harmony, balance, and cooperation, not oppression. Oppression is the result of sin, of rebellion against God's rule. Oppressors do not accept God's rule, do not submit to God's authority. If they accepted God's rule, they would not be oppressors.

Secularism, education, and democracy are touted as the true paths to freedom. Look at the horrible legacies of secular humanism over the past few centuries with its history of colonialism, genocides, world wars, oppression of women, and destruction of the planet. While the twentieth century was the most educated and arguably the least religious century, it also was the most violent century. The Enlightenment and the Age of Reason had a vision of rationality bringing universal salvation for all people, an arrogant view, which led to imperialism. The Nazi government came to power democratically in secular, highly educated Germany. The Holocaust was rooted in both Christian anti-Jewish bigotry and secularism with its rejection of God. Many of the oppressive regimes of the twentieth century were secular. The government of the United States is supposedly secular and democratic, yet as of this writing, the United States is the most militarily aggressive nation on earth. Secularism has not kept its promise. Secularism has left us with spiritual emptiness.

Postmodernists rightly critique the shallowness of modernism. Modernity has meant order, control, and exclusiveness. The postmodern points to diversity, freedom, inclusiveness, and participation. The

Abrahamic religions call us to accept an order that comes from God rather than an order we try to create, submission to God rather than our seeking to be in control, and diversity rooted in God's creation. We need a holistic worldview that accepts also the spiritual dimensions of reality.

Monotheism and the concept of submission to God are criticized for forming the basis for oppression. I see it the opposite way. To be a servant of any human being is to be unfree, but to be a servant of God is to be truly free. I can say to any oppressor, "I know who has real authority, and it is not you." To give our loyalty to God is to deny loyalty to any nation, race, class, or any human institution. To bow down before the Creator of the universe is to refuse to bow down before any human authority. Submission only to God means that we cannot worship any authority other than God.

Instead of forming the basis for hierarchal social organization, Abrahamic monotheism can be the basis for decentralized, democratic decision making. Since creation is good, we need not fear chaos or need to be in control. Since all reality is held together by God's love and mercy, we can trust democratic decision-making.

An even less attractive alternative is to see the individual person as the ultimate authority, as the central social reality. As Margaret Thatcher, the former Prime Minister of Great Britain, put it, "There is no society, there are only individuals." The history of me-first, rugged individualism is not a history I respect. In individualism we owe nothing to anyone, we need nothing from anyone, and we are not accountable to anyone. Life is organized around self, with its egoism, self-centeredness, and alienation.

Political conservatives emphasize individual freedom as more important than the common good, understanding freedom to mean the liberty to do what ever I want to do. This leaves out both God and the good of my neighbor.

Few would want the state, society, or religious institutions to dictate to us what is true, but neither is truth to be decided individually and privately. The question of Truth is not a matter of personal preference, a worldview rooted in capitalist consumer choice. I get to decide what flavor of toothpaste I prefer. When applied to the question of religious truth, the problem is huge. To agree to Truth being privately discerned is to accept the equality of all beliefs, and the denial of revealed truth. The three Abrahamic religions see Truth rooted in revealed scripture and discerned in community.

Individualism, with its accompanying corporate control, violence, and dehumanizing consumerism, does not honor the dignity of each person. A basic flaw in individualism is that the dignity of the individual is separated from roots in community. Our dignity and freedom are found in relationships, in solidarity, cooperation, and community. Society does not function best when people care only about self and forget about the common interest. The community is responsible for its members. The highest commands are to love God and neighbor. We are all connected with each other through our Creator. No one is an island. We were made for community: community with God, with other people, with all of creation. I am not the final arbiter of what is true and false. I am not God. Truth, love, and community are more important than the individual. All our actions need to take into account their effect on others. Everything is connected. I cannot hurt someone else without hurting myself.

The monotheistic religions have raised the importance of the individual. Because God created each person, each person is important, is responsible to God, and becomes God's representative. The dignity and worth of each individual person, along with the affirmation of human rights, are rooted in God and to be respected. This is the opposite of individualism, in which the individual is ultimate and accountable to no one. In monotheism, humility replaces arrogance. Instead of standing alone, we all are connected by God's love. Biblical and Qur'anic faith call us away from self-centeredness to a life of generosity, especially toward those not of my clan.

ᗒ THREE ᗕ

A Short History of Jewish/
Christian/Muslim Relations

How Christians, Muslims, and Jews relate to each other today is rooted in a history about which most of us know little. The story includes much pain. People of all three religions have suffered deeply from breakdowns of relationships between the three religions. Unless we can hear and recognize the pain in the other, our relationships will not go far. It is important to look at where we have come from in past relationships between the three faiths, not to reopen old wounds, but to take a more open-minded look at our past.

There actually is a rich history of cooperation between the three religions, rooted in our common history, shared values, and common faith in God. It is quite significant that when Abraham died, the Bible says that his sons Isaac and Ishmael buried him.[1] That means there was some kind of reconciliation between Isaac (the father of the Jews) and Ishmael (the father of the Arabs), and that there is no biblical basis for hostility between Jew and Arab. Abraham was the father of both. Technically, Abraham, Hagar, and Sarah were not Jews, Muslims, or Christians. They are the parents of all three religions. Why not affirm and celebrate the unity we already have in being children of Abraham, and in our common faith in the Oneness of God?

1. Gen 25:9.

JEWISH/CHRISTIAN RELATIONS

Forty percent of all Jews who lived in the twentieth century were murdered. Six million Jews were brutally killed in the concentration camps of World War II. The atrocities of the Holocaust did not happen in a vacuum. They were the culmination of sixteen centuries of Christian bigotry toward Jews. The Holocaust was perpetrated by Christians. Christians need to take at least 95 percent of the responsibility for the broken relationships between Christians and Jews.

The tragic schism between Jews and Christians did not need to happen, and we do not need to perpetuate it.[2] Early Christianity was a Jewish movement, a Jewish sect. There was nothing anti-Jewish about early Christianity. Jesus and Paul were Jews. Most first-century Christians were Jews. Early Christianity was but one stream within Judaism. The early Christians worshiped in the temple and synagogues and did not see themselves as separate from the Jewish community. They did not see themselves preaching a new religion. John Howard Yoder argues that the only thing that separated the followers of Jesus from the rest of the Jewish community was the question of whether the messianic age had begun with Jesus.[3]

There is nothing un-Jewish about considering Jesus to be the Messiah. Jews throughout the centuries have looked forward to the coming of the Messiah and even proclaimed various persons to be the Messiah. Some Jews proclaimed Bar Kochba to be the Messiah. Some Jews proclaimed the seventeenth-century Shabbetai Zvi as Messiah. During the latter part of the twentieth century, many Lubavicher Jews believed that Menachem Mendel Sneerson was the Messiah. Most Jews totally rejected this, but Jews still recognized those Lubabvichers as fellow Jews. They simply disagreed. So why can't Jews and Christians affirm a common faith and simply disagree on whether Jesus was the Messiah?

Practically all of Jesus' teachings are to be found in the Hebrew Scriptures. Some Christians try to use Jesus' rejection of violence to draw a line between Jesus and Judaism, but there is nothing in the New Testament to indicate that Jews rejected Jesus because of his nonviolence. Jesus was affirming, not rejecting his Jewish identity when he called for love of enemy. The Jews of his time did not see this as un-Jewish. In fact,

2. My argument here is heavily dependant on the ground-breaking work of John Howard Yoder in his book, *The Jewish-Christian Schism Revisited*.

3. Ibid., 48–49.

even Jesus' statements in Matthew that "Of old it was said, but I say unto you" are prefaced by Jesus saying he came "not to abolish but to fulfill the law and the prophets."

Christians wrongly interpret Paul as rejecting both Jewish legalism and Judaism itself. Until the end, Paul saw himself as part of the Jewish community, and as Torah observant. Paul did not reject the Torah. Jesus and Paul condemned not Judaism, but rather certain tendencies in Judaism, especially the corrupt establishment. Paul argued that since we cannot follow every detail of the law, our only hope is to depend on the mercy and grace of God, something almost every Jew at that time would have affirmed. Practically no Jews in the time of Paul rejected God's grace or believed in salvation through works. Jews understood Torah as grace. Paul did not advocate the abolition of Judaism in favor of a new Christian faith, but saw the Christian community as the fulfillment of Judaism. Paul in Romans 11 insists that God has not rejected the Jews, and that they are still part of the covenant.

Paul saw the coming of the messianic age as a time of the nations coming to worship the one true God and being gathered into a new community. In Ephesians 2 and 3, Paul saw the Christian message including a vision of reconciliation between Jew and Gentile, with the dividing wall (culture, politics, religion) between the two broken down, with a resulting new humanity. The barriers between the "ins" and the "outs" are gone. There is nothing to keep us apart. Jews and Gentiles ate at the same table in the new community, shared their resources, and respected their differences. Paul had experienced living proof of the possibility of reconciliation between Jew and Gentile. Paul's vision of a new humanity developing out of the reconciliation between Jew and Gentile was not a contradiction of Judaism, since first-century Judaism actively sought Gentile proselytites.

Neither Jesus, Paul, or the early Church rejected Judaism. Neither did Jews reject Christians. Christians continued to be welcome in the temple and in synagogues. There were tensions, but they continued to fellowship together. There are questions in the New Testament as to whether one has to be a Jew in order to be a Christian, but never is it suggested that one cannot be both.

Conflict between Jews who did or did not accept Jesus as Messiah is evident in the New Testament. This conflict even became violent at times, as in the stoning of Stephen, the first Christian martyr.[4] Although this conflict was later used to support anti-Jewish bigotry, the conflict between Jews who followed or did not follow Jesus should be seen as a family fight between Jews, not a basis for racism.

Although there was tension, the real schism began only in the second century when some Christians wanted to separate from the Jewish community and then some Jews began to reject the followers of Jesus. Ignatius of Antioch was very anti-Jewish and around 110 CE had tried to separate Christianity from Jewish practice. The split was encouraged by Justin Martyr's writings against Jews (150 CE). For centuries, however, groups of people existed who maintained a Jewish/Christian identity, proof that it was possible to be both. These Jewish Christians, sometimes called Ebionites, are central characters of the New Testament and continued their communities in the Arab East after being driven out of Palestine by the Hellenized Christians.

It was much later that Christians saw the split as inevitable, because of the belief of some that Christians had replaced Jews as God's people and that Jews were no longer people of God since the old covenant was abrogated by a new covenant (supercessionism). Some Christians began to argue that since Jews rejected Jesus, God has rejected Judaism, and replaced Judaism with Christianity. This idea provides much of the basis for Christian anti-Jewish bigotry.

I heard a sermon in 2007 in which the preacher claimed that with the destruction of the temple in Jerusalem in 70 CE, the separation of Christians from Judaism was complete, which saved Christianity from being destroyed by the Judaizing heresy. The implication is clear: Judaism is not a valid religion. That was not the belief of the early Christians.

When I was a pastor of a church in Akron, Indiana, back in 1963–65, I once suggested to other pastors in the town that we sponsor a Seder (Passover meal) to help our congregations understand the Jewish roots of our faith. The pastors gave a hostile response and told me that no Jewish ceremony is valid, because Jesus ended all that. No early Christian would have agreed with those pastors. Thankfully, now many churches have Seder meals to explore their Jewish roots.

In the process of separating from its Jewish roots, Christianity was transformed from the Jewish faith of Jesus into a Hellenized mystery

---

4. Acts 7:54–60.

religion of finding salvation by worshiping a divine Jesus. As Christians turned to Greek pagan thought forms, they rejected the wisdom of their Jewish roots. In the process, Christians turned to imperial rulers not only for security, but to accomplish their religious goals. This process took a huge step forward when Constantine made Christianity the official religion of the Roman Empire. We can respect the attempts of early Christians to relate their faith to Greek culture, but we do not need to be bound by their synthesis.

In opposition to the Nazi attempt to separate Jesus and Christianity from Judaism, Christians can embrace their Jewish heritage.

With the rise of the Christian empire, Jews became a persecuted minority. No longer were Jews and Christians minority groups struggling with each other. Now Jews were on the bottom. Judaism no longer was a legal religion. Beginning with Constantine, Christians forbade Jews from living in Jerusalem. Christians continued to berate the "unbelieving Jews." Often Christians forced Jews to choose between baptism, expulsion, or death.

The murder of six million Jews did not happen in a vacuum. It was rooted in 1600 years of Christian bigotry toward Jews. Anti-Jewish bigotry was rooted in the church and mainly perpetrated by the church. As a Christian, I must come to terms with the horrible history of Christian persecution of Jews. Therefore I am spelling out a bit of that story in hopes that Christians will find repentance for this stain on Christian history.

John Chrysostom (ca.349–407) preached, "The synagogue is worse than a brothel . . . it is the den of scoundrels and the repair of wild beasts . . . the temple of demons devoted to idolatrous cults, . . . the refuge of brigands and debauchees, and the cavern of devils." He also wrote, "Debauchery and drunkenness had brought them to the level of the lusty goat and the pig. They know only one thing, to satisfy their stomachs, to get drunk, to kill and beat each other up."[5] Bernard of Clairvoux considered Jews to be lower than beasts. Peter Abelard, however, was one person in the Middle Ages who condemned the whole tradition of Judeophobia.

The most persistent libel of Jews was the accusation of Jews being responsible for killing Jesus. Actually, it was the Romans. The Jewish people

5. Quoted in Hay, *Europe and the Jews*, 25–29.

were not and are not responsible for the death of Jesus, and neither are the Italians, the modern descendants of the Romans. The plot to murder Jesus was hatched in secret by a Jewish power elite that was afraid of popular Jewish support for Jesus. This power elite saying, "His blood be on us and on our children,"[6] does not apply to all Jews who have ever lived. Sadly, this libel is still alive and well. Jewish high school students in liberal Athens, Ohio, are still sometimes called Christ killers. A new, recent twist on this theme, turning the accusation upside down, is Jewish settlers in Hebron confronting international peace activists, saying, "We killed Jesus and we will kill you too."

With the beginning of the Middle Ages, Jews would experience a thousand years of unrelenting, bloody persecution from Christians. The Christian Holy Week became a special time of fanning anti-Jewish feelings, including encouraging congregations to take vengeance on Jews for having killed Jesus, and claiming that Jews used the blood of Christians in making their Passover bread. In Toulouse in the Middle Ages, each year at Easter they would drag a Jew into the Church of St. Stephan and slap him in the face in front of the altar.

Generally the popes opposed some of the more serious attacks upon Jews, but supported the idea that Jews were to be hated and kept in servitude to Christians. Pope Innocent III issued an edict giving limited protection to Jews, but did not accept the legitimacy of Jews or Judaism. Innocent III wrote a letter to the French hierarchy stating that "Jews must live in perpetual slavery 'because they crucified the Lord.'"[7] The Fourth Lateran Council in 1215 declared that both Jews and Muslims needed to wear distinctive dress to identify themselves as Jews and Muslims.

Life became even more difficult for Jews beginning with the crusades. The first crusade in 1096 began with the slaughter of ten thousand Jews in Western Europe, which culminated in the massacre of Jews in Jerusalem. The second crusade began with the call to first kill Jews in Germany, which resulted in numerous massacres.

The Reformation brought no relief to Jews. Martin Luther recommended that all Jewish property be confiscated, their synagogues destroyed, and that all Jews be expelled from Germany. Luther said, "Verily a hopeless, wicked, venomous and devilish thing is the existence of these

---

6. Matt 27:25.

7. Hay, *Europe and the Jews*, 76.

Jews, who for fourteen hundred years have been, and still are, our pest, torment, and misfortune. They are just devils and nothing more."[8]

The first step for Christians in Christian/Jewish relations is for Christians to confess and repent of our whole history of anti-Jewish bigotry. There is no good reason to continue the disastrous Christian bigotry against Jews. In the second half of the twentieth century, partly in response to the Holocaust, Jews and Christians did begin dialogue and cooperation.

CHRISTIAN/MUSLIM RELATIONS

Many Christians have a deep fear of Muslims. One day in Hebron, I led a tour of the city for a group of American Christians. Part of the tour included a visit to the Ibrahimi Mosque. One member of the group refused to go into the mosque because she said, "Islam is a demonic religion. The mosque is filled with demons."

The roots of Western Christian bigotry towards Arabs go back at least to the Roman occupation of Arab lands. As is common, to rationalize their cruelty, occupiers dehumanize and create negative stereotypes of the people they occupy. The story of Ishmael in the Bible[9] has been used to confirm and support Western Christian bigotry towards Arabs.

At the time of Mohammad, the Arab East included maybe 15 million Christians and less than 200 thousand Jews.[10] The Meccans knew Christians and Jews. Several of Mohammad's relatives had converted to Christianity before Mohammad began receiving revelations. The second person after his wife to confirm the revelations Mohammad had received was a Christian (Waraqah ibn Nawfal), a cousin of Mohammad's wife. One of Mohammad's wives (Maryam) was a Christian.

Much has been written about how these relationships helped shape not only Mohammad's perceptions of Judaism and Christianity, but also his own theology. Actually, Mohammad had no concept of founding a new religion. He understood his message as the same as that of Abraham, Moses, and Jesus.

---

8. Ibid., 167.

9. Gen 21:8–21.

10. Courbage and Fargues, *Christians and Jews Under Islam*, 6.

The Christians in Arabia at the time of Mohammad were Mono-physites, Nestorians, and Jewish-Christians, groups considered heretical by both Rome and Constantinople. It is these "heretical" Christians that Mohammad encountered, and it is from them that he received his impressions of Christianity. Hans Küng argues that Mohammad received most of his understandings of Christianity from Jewish-Christians who lived in Arabia and had never accepted Hellenized views of Jesus.[11]

Muslims have lived side by side in peace with Christians and Jews for over a thousand years, and in many cases intermarried. Shared social values and lifestyles made co-existence easy. Both Christians and Jews quickly adopted Arabic (or Turkish) as their language.

Muslims are commanded in the Qur'an to seek dialogue with Jews and Christians.[12] Except when the People of the Book attack Muslims, Muslims are commanded to live in peace with the People of the Book.[13] Tradition says that Mohammad's last words were, "Be kind to the People of the Book." This is illustrated by a story about Mohammad, whose Jewish neighbor in Medina demonstrated his hostility to Islam by dumping his refuse in front of Mohammad's house each morning. Mohammad patiently bore this for a long time until for several days there was no refuse in front of Mohammad's house. Mohammad inquired as to why, and learned that his Jewish neighbor was sick. Out of love for his neighbor, Mohammad took food and visited his neighbor. Later, the Jewish neighbor converted to Islam.

When a delegation of Christians visited Mohammad in Medina, Mohammad invited the Christians to stay in the mosque and to conduct Christian liturgy in the mosque. Over a hundred of Mohammad's followers, including his daughter, left Mecca during a time of persecution and were welcomed by the Christian king of Abyssinia (Ethiopia).

As Islam spread, the conquered peoples had four choices: convert to Islam, agree to submit and pay a tribute to the Muslim rulers, fight, or leave. In order to rule these vast areas, the Muslim conquerors were dependent on the support of the people they ruled. Too often people forget that for the most part, Muslims did not force their subjects to become Muslims.

11. Küng, *Islam*, 494–97; Watt, *Muslim Christian Encounters*, 6. For a detailed history of Jewish and Christian relationships with Muslims, see Küng, Watt, and Courbage and Fargues.

12. Qur'an 3:16.

13. Ibid., 60:8.

For example, although ruled by Muslims for almost 500 years, most of the people of the Balkans remained Christian. Still today, after 1400 years, religious minorities continue to flourish in most Muslim lands.

The Christian and Jewish communities that survived throughout the Muslim lands did so by their ability to dialogue and cooperate with Muslims. Some scholars claim that at the beginning of the crusades, the majority of people in the Middle East were still non-Muslims. Half of all the Christians in the world had come under Muslim rule. After the crusades, Muslims were in the majority.

Tolerance was the official policy of Islam. The Qur'an says, there shall be no coercion in matters of faith.[14] As the Jewish historian, Bernard Lewis, put it, "In most respects, the position of non-Muslims under traditional Islamic rule was very much easier than that of non-Christians or even of heretical Christians in Medieval Europe."[15]

Non-Muslims who accepted Muslim dominance in return were granted protection, but had second-class status, which included paying a poll tax for each non-Muslim. Muslims argue this tax was a substitute to the compulsory yearly tithe (*zakat*) paid by Muslims, and payment for the protection Muslims provided to non-Muslims. Although their freedoms were restricted, they were to be protected from persecution. Although this may sound offensive to modern ears, Bernard Lewis points out that, "Second-class citizenship, though second class, is a kind of citizenship. It involves some rights, though not all, and is surely better than no rights at all. . . . A recognized status, albeit one of inferiority to the dominant group, which is established by law, recognized by tradition, and confirmed by popular assent, is not to be despised."[16]

During the same period in Christendom, non-Christians had practically no rights at all. It must be said that neither Roman Catholicism nor Reformation Protestantism contributed to or supported the development of democracy and human liberty. Both supported the policy of the prince determining the religion of his subjects. It was sectarian Christian groups like the Anabaptists who made a theological case for political and religious freedom.

14. Ibid., 2:256.
15. Lewis, *The Jews of Islam*, 62. Also see Courbage and Fargues.
16. Lewis, *The Jews of Islam*, 62.

While Western Christianity has been in perpetual conflict with Islam, Eastern Christianity has had a much more peaceful relationship with Islam.[17] The predominant view of Eastern Christians was to see Islam as another heresy to be resisted by the church. Patriarch Sophronius, who negotiated the surrender of Jerusalem to the Muslims in 636, saw the victory of Islam as God's punishment for the unfaithfulness of the Christian community. After surrendering Jerusalem to Caliph Omar, he invited Omar to pray in the Church of the Holy Sepulcher. Omar refused to enter the church building, fearing his more zealous followers might have wanted to turn the building into a mosque. The surrender agreement included a covenant that gave Christians freedom of religion and full control of Christian holy sites.

Medieval Christian attitudes towards Muslims were most negative in lands where there were no Muslims. European Christians saw the rapid expansion of Islam in the Middle East, across North Africa, and into Europe itself as a threat. Since European Christians for the most part professed loyalty to and identified with the Roman Empire, they considered any threat to that empire as a threat to the Christian faith. For some Christian groups, however, including groups considered heretical by Rome, the coming of Islam meant liberation from the domination of Rome and also Constantinople.

There was much cooperation between Muslims, Jews, and Christians in the past. In some cases, as in the Basilica of St. John in Damascus, Muslims and Christians worshiped in the same building up until the crusades.[18] Bernard Lewis points out that al-Ghazali (1059–1111), the great Muslim theologian, wrote a chapter in one of his books that is very similar to something written by the near contemporary Jewish philosopher, Bahye ibn Paquda. Later scholarship has shown that both the Muslim and the Jewish works were based on a work written by a Christian.[19] Caliph Harun al-Rashid (786–809) built Baghdad into a city of unparalleled splendor under the direction of Christian architects. Christian scholars took the Greek Classics to Baghdad.

Being conquered is not the worst thing that can happen. Many people throughout history have been conquered, survived, and often thrived

17. For a short history of the conflict between Christianity and Islam, see Murcholish Madjid, *The True Face of Islam*, 67–77.

18. Courbage and Fargues, *Christian and Jews Under Islam*, 109–11.

19. Lewis, *The Jews of Islam*, 57.

after being conquered. Modern Germany and Japan come to mind. For the most part, Christian and Jewish communities flourished from Persia to Spain under Islam, except for North Africa where the Christians either converted to Islam or migrated to Southern Europe. Relations were usually harmonious, but sometimes became violent from both sides. Much of the violence came from either Christian or Muslim groups wanting to retake land they considered rightfully theirs from the other side, or from power struggles between various leaders.

Neither Muslim respect for the People of the Book nor Muslim rules of warfare were always observed. Bad things happen when there is domination and occupation. But what is often forgotten is that Christians and Jews quickly rose to prominent positions in the new Islamic states and became important civil servants. Muslim rule in the lands they conquered was accomplished by hiring the native people to be the administrators for the Muslim rulers.

Stereotypes and prejudices developed on all sides. Christians experienced Islam as a heretical sect bent on domination and control. Muslims saw Christendom as hopelessly primitive, uneducated and lacking in culture, since education and literacy were not valued in medieval Europe as in the Islamic world.

It wasn't long before theological polemics began to be exchanged between Christians and Muslims, with Baghdad and Damascus being important centers for intellectual exchange. This involved not only rivalry, but also important exchanges of ideas. John of Damascus (675–749), who was not interested in interfaith dialogue, was quite influential in the history of Christian polemics against Islam. The political power struggles between the Islamic and the Byzantine empires colored perceptions on both sides. Later, Christians depicted Mohammad as the anti-Christ who indicated the approaching end of the world. A whole literature developed describing Mohammad as a psychopath whose dead body was eaten by pigs. There also were stories of Mohammad being baptized shortly before his death. Dante (1265–1321) assigned Mohammad to the twenty-eighth level of hell in his "Inferno." Sadly, many modern images of Islam are rooted in those medieval stereotypical images of Mohammad and Islam.

Although Orientalist scholarship of the nineteenth and twentieth centuries was an improvement over previous Christian writings on Islam, it still took a condescending view of Islam and the Muslim world, and has been seen by critics as subservient to colonialism. Much of more recent

Western writing has focused on political, militant Islam as a threat to Western civilization.

The Muslim invasion of Europe brought the roots of the fifteenth- and sixteenth-century Renaissance, which was stimulated and fed by the philosophical and scientific contributions of the Muslim world. The Muslims brought libraries, learning, philosophy, mathematics, and enlightenment to Europe, which literally was in the Dark Ages.

Muslims from North Africa conquered almost all of Spain in 711. For over seven hundred years, there was Muslim rule in Spain. The Muslim conquest of Spain was one of the most important events of the Middle Ages for Europe. Since *al-Andalus* (Muslim Spain) represented what many Muslims refer to as the golden age of Islam, it was through al-Andalus that much of the learning and culture of the Muslim world passed into Europe. The Muslim influence on Spanish culture and language was profound.

Al-Andalus was at the cutting edge of world culture during the Middle Ages, at least partly a result of the creative theological, philosophical, and cultural exchanges between Muslims, Christians, and Jews which took place in Spain. There was much cooperation and interaction between the people of the three religions, including intermarriage. Christians and Muslims shared a mosque in Cordoba. Even Spanish Christian and Jewish architecture had a heavy Muslim influence. Later, Christian conquerors of Muslim cities in Spain were amazed at the beauty and grandeur of the Muslim cities, something they had never seen.

Life in *al-Andalus*, although creative, was not perfect. It was not the kingdom of God on earth. There was oppression and persecution coming from both Muslims and Christians. Much of the strife centered on whether Christians or Muslims would control any particular area that was in dispute. For most of the time, Christians controlled northern Spain. Sometimes Muslims fought in Christian armies and Christians fought in Muslim armies.

The period known as the golden age ended when Almohads (1156–1269) ruled Spain. These strict Muslims believed they had the only truth and imposed a strict rule, including persecution of both Christians and

Jews. Most Andalusian Muslims did not accept this and many moved to northern Christian areas where they were welcomed and seen by Christians as tools in the Christian re-conquest of Muslim areas.

The Christian re-conquest of Spain started in the eleventh century, coinciding with the crusades. Christian armies slowly pushed back the Muslims in Spain, capturing Cordoba in 1236, and by 1250, only the Islamic emirate of Granada remained under Muslim rule. In 1492, the year Columbus sailed the ocean blue, Granada, the last Muslim province in Spain, fell to the Christians when King Ferdinand's military defeated the Muslim emirate of Granada. The Catholic victors enslaved many Muslims and ordered the rest and the Jews to convert or leave. The Inquisition ended cooperation between the three religions in Spain.

A major turning point in Christian/Muslim relations was the crusades, which stretched over four hundred years, leaving bitter memories that exist to this day. The crusaders captured Jerusalem in the first crusade in July 1099, resulting in a horrible massacre of Jews and Muslims, and also native Christians. The crusaders slaughtered sixty thousand Muslims around the area of the *al Aksa* Mosque, leaving blood three feet deep in places. No Jew or Muslim was allowed to remain in the city. When Saladin re-conquered Jerusalem in 1187, he allowed Christians to remain in Jerusalem, and invited Jews to return to Jerusalem.

One reason for the failure of the crusades was lack of support from Arab Christians who were living peacefully with their Muslim neighbors. Why should they support the crusaders who were extremely violent and immoral? Local Arab Christians even helped the Muslims drive out the crusaders.

The purpose of the crusades was not only to defeat the Muslims and retake the Holy Lands for the Roman Church; but also to defeat the Byzantine East. This included invasions of Eastern Europe, capturing large areas for the Catholic Church. It was during the crusades that Poland, for example, was conquered and forcibly changed from Orthodox to Roman Catholic. In 1204, the Crusaders conquered and plundered Constantinople, the center of the Eastern Church. This weakening of the Byzantine Church and the resulting horrible image of Christianity opened the way for most of the people in the whole area of West Asia to turn to Islam, which was seen as the way to peace. After the beginning of the crusades, the position of the non-Muslims in Muslim lands deteriorated. The persecution of Eastern Christianity by Rome, both before and during the crusades, led to the demise of the Eastern Church in the Middle East and the triumph of Islam.

One cannot help but draw the parallel of the earlier crusades to to-day's new crusade of Western nations against the Muslim world, which is discrediting even legitimate Western and Christian interests. America's invasions of and attacks on Muslim countries are striking a major blow to Christianity in Muslim countries. As in earlier crusades, repeated calls are put out for Christians to fight the treacherous enemies of Christianity. Sound familiar? It is rather obvious that any Christian who supports the current crusade against Islam has never adequately understood or re-pented of the earlier crusades.

There was a minority of European Christians who did not support the crusades. One was Francis of Assisi, who questioned Christians going to Muslim lands to kill Muslims. He knew a better way. Francis had been a preacher of peace and his followers were known for their ability to mediate feuds between Italian cities. As a pioneer in interfaith dialogue and as a precursor to Christian Peacemaker Teams, he made a nonviolent pilgrim-age to the Muslim lands to extend a hand of friendship to those he had been told were his enemies. During the fifth crusade, on June 24, 1219, Francis headed for Egypt to visit the sultan and convert him to Christianity. Francis believed in converting Jews and Muslims, but not by force.

He went to Damietta, an Egyptian Muslim city surrounded by cru-saders who were preparing an assault on the city. Because of the moral debauchery he witnessed among the crusaders, he decided he first had to preach repentance to the Christians. When he spoke out against an assault on the Muslims, he was shouted down and called a coward.

On August 29, the crusaders attacked and fell into a trap planned by the Muslims. The crusaders chased the Muslims who fled to the waiting Muslim army. Five thousand crusaders were killed and another thou-sand captured. While brutal fighting continued, and against the advice of crusader authorities, Francis risked death and headed toward the Muslim city. Two Muslim soldiers arrested and beat Francis and his companion. Death was a real possibility, for the sultan had offered a big reward for the head of any Christian. However, the soldiers accepted Francis' request to see the sultan.

Francis preached to the sultan and urged him to become a Christian. The sultan, Saladin's nephew, Malik al-Kamil, was impressed with Francis' spirit and invited Francis to be his guest for a week of dialogue. The sultan rejected the advice of his counselors that Francis be beheaded for trying to convert Muslims. Tradition says Francis accompanied the sultan to a mosque for prayers, saying, "God is everywhere."

We do not know that Francis converted anyone to Christianity that week. He was unable to bring peace, but Francis was a changed man as he left the sultan. He received a new understanding and love for Islam, and became clearer in his rejection of war. Francis realized that he had to change his image of Islam. Not only Christians believe in God.

The sultan was deeply impressed with Francis and wrote a letter giving Francis safe passage in the Muslim world. It is said that the sultan commented to Francis that if all Christians were like Francis, there would be no conflict between Christians and Muslims. The sultan became known for treating Christian prisoners humanely, and later, without a battle, the sultan was willing to negotiate the surrender of Jerusalem to the crusaders as part of a truce.

The crusaders in the thirteenth century hoped to convert the Mongols to Catholicism. They hoped the Mongols then would attack Islam from the east and together with attacks from the west, totally defeat Islam. That never happened. Instead, the Mongols converted to Islam and the Mongol empire, as all empires eventually do, began to disintegrate. Christians in the East who supported the Mongol invasion then suffered terribly from Muslim reprisals.

Toward the end of the crusades and the disintegration of the Seljuk Turkish Empire, the Ottoman Turks came to power, expanding their empire westward into Europe, establishing their rule by 1390 in Albania, Serbia, Bulgaria, and Northern Greece. In 1453, the Ottomans conquered

Constantinople. The Ottomans continued their westward expansion and by the early 1500's their rule reached as far as Vienna.

The Orthodox Patriarch in Constantinople (now Istanbul) swore his loyalty to the Ottomans exchanging protection from Rome. Christians in the east were protected by the new Ottoman rulers, and in many places thrived.

Empires are violent and oppressive. The Ottoman Empire was an empire. The surprising aspect of the Ottoman Empire is not that it was oppressive, but that it also showed an amazing amount of toleration for other religions. There were forced conversions to Islam, but Christianity and Judaism flourished under Ottoman rule. After four centuries of Ottoman rule, the Christian population had tripled and the Jews doubled their numbers.

As commonly happens in wars, tolerance broke down during World War I. When war broke out between the Ottomans and Russia, the Armenians suffered horribly because they were seen as allies of Russia. With the fall of the Ottoman Empire in 1914, a long history of multi-confessional cooperation was obliterated by the new secular Turkish government. The resulting deportations and massacres of Christians and the population exchanges of Muslims and Christians between Greece and Turkey following World War I are sad examples of religious bigotry replacing religious cooperation. Today, there are few Christians or Jews in Turkey. It is important to recognize the cooperation that had existed and build upon that tradition.

The view from Western Europe was much different. European Christians feared the Turks in a similar way that Americans feared communism in the twentieth century. This helps explain the fanatical reaction to the Anabaptist movement during the Reformation. The Anabaptists, like Francis, believed in simply following the teachings of Jesus, which include nonviolence and love for enemy. Both Roman Catholics and Protestants not only saw this as heresy, but as treasonous capitulation to the evil Muslims. Followers of Jesus were and are considered as naïve appeasers, because they are unwilling to kill to maintain any empire.

Throughout this whole period there were European Christian scholars who argued that the Qur'an was compatible with the Bible if studied in the right spirit. Sadly, this was a minority perspective. Thomas Aquinas wrote his *Summa* partly as a response to Islam, especially Muslim Aristotelian thinkers, with the goal of showing Christianity to be superior to Islam,

Judaism, and other religions. Most Christians took the position of making war against and defeating the Muslims. The result was a long history of polemics in all three faiths, harsh critiques of the other religions, and defenses of one's own religion. The polemics solved no problems, brought no understanding, and resulted in horrible oppression and bloodshed. Richard Fletcher put it well in his important history of Christian/Muslim relations: "The relations between Christian and Muslim during the middle ages were marked by the persistent failure of each to try to understand the other."[20]

During the period of the crusades, the Roman Catholic Church was mostly hostile to Islam. For example, the Catholic Church in Italy banned the use of Arabic numbers until the 1300s because the church believed the number zero carried spiritual danger. Yet even during the centuries of the crusades, there was much dialogue, negotiation, and actual working together of Muslims and Christians, especially in Palestine, Sicily, and Spain. Christian Europe was deeply impacted by the intellectual and technological superiority of Islamic civilization at the time. That relationship was then broken and only now is being reestablished, through war, immigration, commerce, and thankfully, interfaith dialogue.

There have been times in Muslim history when "pious" authorities sought to purify Islam, which included revoking innovations and turning to less compassionate interpretations of Islam. Often this included restricting the freedoms of non-Muslims. Whether Muslims, like any society, were tolerant or intolerant of religious minorities was greatly influenced by whether or not Muslim societies felt threatened or secure. Much of Muslim persecution of Christians occurred when Christians cooperated with or supported the enemies of Islam, i.e., the crusaders or Mongols, and more recent Western invasions of Muslim lands, i.e., Iraq.

Another cause of Muslim persecution of minorities was competition for power and influence among the minorities who tried to turn Muslim authorities against the other minority groups. An example of this is Christians importing Western anti-Jewish attitudes to the Muslim world.

With the discovery of the Americas, the rise of the Renaissance in Europe, and the beginning of scientific exploration in the West, the West turned its attention away from its obsessive fear of Islam. At the same

20. Fletcher, *The Cross and the Crescent*, 158.

time, Islam under Ottoman domination became ingrown and closed to progressive thinking.

During the 1800s, many Europeans and Americans made pilgrimages to "The Holy Lands" and brought back stories of despicable, degenerate Arabs who needed to be civilized and converted to Christianity. These stories circulated widely in newspapers and became the basis not only for increased Christian missionary activity in the Middle East, but also calls for Western military intervention, occupation, and colonization, which then fed into the Zionist call for Jews to return to reclaim everything from the river (Nile) to the river (Euphrates), an idea that fit well with Western colonial interests and with Christian Zionism, which understood Biblical prophecy to say that God would use the modern state of Israel, combined with Western military and economic power, to bring in the kingdom of God and bring history to its conclusion.

There were many calls in the 1800s by Western Christians to remove all the Muslims from the Middle East. Many Western pilgrims were offended by the presence of Muslims, and even Catholics and Orthodox Christians, in the Holy Places, believing the Holy Places should belong to the Protestant West. These feelings of resentment were soon expressed as hatred and resulted in calls to remove the "infidel" intruders from the places that "belonged" to Western Christians. There was little interest in understanding the Muslim world.[21]

In addition to memories of the crusades, the central and defining reality for Muslim perceptions of the West in the past two hundred years has been the invasion of Western colonialism, the destruction of the Ottoman Empire, and European domination of the Muslim world from Morocco to Indonesia. At the end of World War I, the entire Muslim world was dominated by the Christian world. European colonial powers ruled every Muslim country except Saudi Arabia, Yemen, Turkey, and Afghanistan. No Khalif had ever ruled over as many Muslims as did King George V. European colonial control was brutal, bringing rapid modernization and westernization along with economic and military control. Repeatedly Western interests have intervened to block democracy in the Muslim world. Christian missionaries ran many of the social institutions. There continues to be much resentment in the Muslim world not only for the crusades, but also for colonial rule.

21. See Fuad Sha'ban, *For Zion's Sake*.

Actually, many Muslims see the crusades as the beginning of European colonialism. Some have even seen the French invasions of North Africa, begun in 1830, as the ninth crusade and the founding of the state of Israel as the tenth crusade. With the rise of the "Christian" West and its military and economic power, the decreasing power of the Muslim world in the nineteenth and twentieth centuries, and Western imperial exploitation of Muslim countries, anger, nurtured by humiliation, has grown in the Muslim world. This anger was fueled by the cooperation between minorities in Muslim countries with foreign powers: for example, Armenians working for Russians on the eastern border of Turkey or Coptic Christians working for the French in Egypt. When Christian communities in the Muslim world became identified with the enemies of Islam, they suffered. Invasions by Christians, from the crusades to American invasions, have had devastating effects on native Christian populations, as for example the recent decline of the Iraqi church.

By the second half of the twentieth century, Muslims around the world were throwing off the shackles of colonial rule. Yet still today, Western colonial powers are resisting the reemergence of Islam, and continue to try to reassert Western dominance, militarily, economically, and culturally.

A major issue for Muslims is the decline of the Muslim world, the Israeli defeat of Muslims in 1948 and 1967, and Western domination of the Muslim world. Traditionally, Muslims have seen themselves as victorious and expansionist. Muslims have given many answers as to the cause of this decline. Reactionary Islamists claim that the decline is due to failure to strictly follow traditional Islam, and only a rigid return to "authentic" Islam will change Muslim standing in the world. This partly explains the rise of extremism.

The relationship between the "West" and Islam took a major turn after the attacks on 9/11, 2001. Deep suspicions came to the fore and greatly increased the fear and hostility between the West and Islam. These hostilities were not new. They were revived.

In a lecture on September 14, 2006, Pope Benedict XVI quoted a fourteenth-century Byzantium emperor, stating that there was nothing new or good in Islam, that Mohammad's teachings brought things "evil and inhuman," that Islam was spread by the sword. This caused a storm of protest in the Muslim world, including violence against Christians and church buildings, partly proving the validity of the Pope's remarks.

How tragic. The Pope had no moral authority to condemn Muslims for using violence in the spread of religion, given the long history of papal use of and blessing of violence against Muslims and the use of violence in spreading Catholicism. There is only one thing that the Pope had the moral right to say to Muslims, and that was to apologize for the atrocities against Muslims committed by so-called Christians.

The Pope gave a weak apology saying he was sorry for the pain his remarks caused, but he did not apologize for his arrogance, for his insensitivity, or for what Catholics have done to Muslims.

The response of some in the Muslim world was equally pathetic. To respond violently to criticism or mockery of one's faith is totally unacceptable. Neither God nor my faith needs defending. Instead of being defensive, we can restate and explain our faith, answer and challenge the criticism, propose dialogue, and reach out to those who in their ignorance denigrate our faith.

Part of the tension between Muslims and Christians is rooted in the Muslim experience of Western missionaries accompanying Western colonizers. Muslims experienced these missionaries as arrogant and disrespectful, seeking to subvert and weaken Islam rather than seeking dialogue and constructive relationships. Before Christians can witness to Muslims, they first need to comprehend how offensive Christian symbols like the cross are to some Muslims and Jews. For Muslims, the cross symbolizes the crusades, the mass murder of Muslims by Christian fanatics. Even the word "crusade" means "war of the cross."

Today, Roman Catholics, Orthodox Christians, and mainline Protestants tend to take a more moderate attitude toward Islam. Today it is Protestant fundamentalists who are most hostile to Islam. Catholic and Orthodox relations have been colored by the daily interaction of their members with Muslims in the Middle East. Palestinian Christians say they are Christian by religion and Muslim by culture.

American-Muslim history began in the slave ships bringing millions of African slaves to America. It is estimated that one fourth of those slaves were Muslims. Both George Washington and Thomas Jefferson included Muslims in their vision of a free, democratic society. Jefferson was proud of his efforts in passing Virginia's Statute for Establishing Religious Freedom in 1786, which included freedom for "Mahometans." [22]

Morocco, a Muslim country, was the first country to recognize the independence of the United States. The 1787 Treaty of Friendship and Cooperation between Morocco and the United States forms the basis for the longest unbroken treaty relationship of the United States with any other country. The first oversees military engagement of the United States was in cooperation with Morocco against Barbary pirates ("From the halls of Montezuma to the shores of Tripoli").

The Washington Monument was paid for in part by the Ottoman Sultan in Istanbul, the figurehead of all Muslims at the time. Islam is part of the American heritage. In January 2007, Keith Ellison of Minnesota became the first Muslim to serve in the United States Congress. He swore his oath of office on a Qur'an once owned by Thomas Jefferson.

The first attacks by Americans against Muslims began in the early 1900s when General Pershing conquered and massacred the Muslim Moro people in the southern Philippines, violently turning much of the Philippines Christian. The history of American Muslim relations has gone mostly downhill since then.

Today, the "war on terrorism" has become a cover for a massive Western attack on Islam. Muslims are called the worst, fanatical, genocidal maniacs the world has seen since Hitler. Muslims, we are told, will tolerate no dissent and want to kill every Christian and Jew. We hear this rhetoric of a new crusade from right-wing Americans. These distortions are used to build support for Western desires to control Middle Eastern oil.

For those who believe we need enemies, now that the Communist empire has disappeared, what better enemy than Islam? It is unknown, mysterious, and frightening. And it serves as a wonderful justification for military spending, wars, and imperialist ambitions. Westerners can project our fears, our frustrations, our anger, on the Muslims.

---

22. See Sylviane Diouf, *Servants of Allah: African Muslims Enslaved in the Americas.*

JEWISH/MUSLIM RELATIONS

Jews and Arabs looking back to Abraham have seen each other as cousins, descendants of Ishmael and Issac. Hagar, Abraham's other woman, the outcast slave, becomes a symbol of redemption as matriarch of both Arab and Muslim culture. Jews and Arabs have had a similar Semitic religious and cultural heritage, and strong economic ties based on trade between Canaan and Arabia dating back until at least the time of Solomon. There are repeated references to Arabs in the Hebrew Scriptures. In addition to the Judeo-Christian heritage, there also is a rich Judeo-Arabic and Judeo-Islamic heritage.

The Qur'an demands tolerance and respect toward Jews. Mohammad himself was deeply influenced by his Jewish friends. One of Mohammad's wives was Jewish. The Jewish communities in Arabia date back to a major migration in the sixth century BC from Palestine to Arabia, after the fall of Jerusalem in 586 to the Babylonians. There was a large Jewish community living in Medina when Mohammad moved there from Mecca. Mohammad immediately drafted a constitution to protect the rights of the Jews living in Medina, including the freedom for both groups to practice their religion. Mohammad considered the Jews in Medina to be part of one community of believers along with the Muslims. Much of the second *Sura* in the Qur'an is a lament over the breakdown of that covenant. Negative comments in the Qur'an about Jews are related to tensions that developed between Muslims and Jews in Medina.

The anti-Jewish bigotry found today in some of the Muslim world was not present in former centuries. That bigotry has Christian roots, is a recent import from the West, and is fueled by Israeli/Palestinian interactions. Much of Muslim anti-Jewish literature is translated from European works. Laqueur states that much of modern Muslim bigotry against Jews "originated with Orthodox and Catholic Christian communities, frequently with the support of European consular agents who were usually French or Greek. For example, in the nineteenth century there were a few cases of Muslims accusing Jews of ritual murder, a Christian accusation formerly unknown in the Muslim world. In parts of the Ottoman empire where Christian communities did not exist, such incidents did not occur."[23] The massacre of 67 Jews in Hebron in 1929 was instigated and abetted by British forces. Palestinian Muslims in Hebron saved the lives of many of

23. Laqueur, *Changing Face of Antisemitism*, 194–95.

their Jewish friends. I personally know some of those Muslim families. Until recently, Muslims saw Christians, not Jews, as their main threat.

Despite tensions between Jews and Muslims in Medina, most Jews welcomed the spread of Islam in the early centuries of Islam. Jews saw the rise of Islam as liberation from Christian domination. At the beginning of Islam, the largest concentration of Jews was in what is now Iraq and Iran, where they suffered oppression from Christians. The Jews of Iraq and Iran welcomed their new freedom and status under Islamic rule.

The Jews of Palestine also welcomed the Muslims. Under Muslim rule, Jews could again live in Jerusalem, something prohibited by Christians. Palestinian Jews had suffered greatly under the persecution of Heraclius I in the 630s. Some traditions even claim that Palestinian Jews delivered Hebron and Caesarea to the Muslim invaders. The same was true for Jews in North Africa.

Many Jews look back to Muslim Spain as the golden age of Judaism. Jews had lived in Spain at least since the destruction of the temple in Jerusalem in 70 CE. More Jews lived in Spain during the Middle Ages than in all the other European countries combined. Christian persecution of Spanish Jews had begun already by the fourth century, but greatly increased during the time of the Visigoth kings, Recared, Sisebut, and Chintila. King Egica ordered Jews to become slaves.

It is not surprising that Spanish Jews welcomed the Muslim invasion in 711.[24] Persecution of Jews stopped after the Muslim conquest of Spain. There was a large migration of Jews to Muslim Spain. Spanish Jews for the most part flourished under Muslim rule. The Muslims put Jews in positions of authority. The Spanish Jews learned philosophy, science, and literature from the Muslims. The Jews, to a great degree, assimilated into Muslim culture, adopted Arabic as their language, and flourished. The great Jewish philosopher, Maimonides, was Spanish.

In the thirteenth and fourteenth centuries, Spanish Jews suffered severe persecution from Christians. When Muslim Granada fell to the Christians, the surrender agreement included a provision that all of Granada's Jews had to either convert to Christianity or leave Spain. Rather

---

24. Perez, *History of a Tragedy*, 8–12.

than leave Spain (and Portugal) to avoid death, many Jews converted to Catholicism, at least outwardly, but continued to secretly practice Judaism. These "New Christians," as distinguished from "Old Christians," are also referred to as "Crypto-Jews" and were a major focus of the Spanish Inquisition, another sad story in the history of Jewish/Christian relations.[25]

The year 1492 marked the end of coexistence between the three religions in Spain. The Spanish Inquisition, which had begun in 1478, put the final touches to Muslim and Jewish life in Spain. Spain was the last nation in Europe to expel its Jews. Between two and five hundred thousand Jews left Spain, in addition to the Muslims. That was the end of Spanish Judaism.

The Jews that did convert to Catholicism continued to be suspect, and were the main victims of the Spanish Inquisition. For generations, these "New Christians" experienced discrimination, persecution, and even sometimes massacres from the hands of the "Old Christians." Thousands were burned at the stake.[26]

Until the last century, Muslim lands were safe havens for Jews. While much of Europe was persecuting the Jews, Muslims welcomed European Jews. The Ottomans took in many Jews from Europe in the late Middle Ages and from France and Russia in the eighteenth century. When the Jews were driven out of Spain, the Ottomans welcomed them. Some Spanish Jews moved to Muslim Hebron. There is still the *Qurdoba* School in Hebron. I know a Jewish woman who lives in Jerusalem. She is the fifteenth generation of her family to have lived in Jerusalem after having been expelled from Spain. I have an Israeli friend whose family moved to Israel from Turkey. His family had moved to Turkey from Spain.

During the Middle Ages, the majority of Jews lived under Muslim rule. Those Jews were much more educated and progressive than the Jews of Christendom. Most of Jewish creativity during the Middle Ages occurred in Muslim societies. The Jews of the Muslim world adopted Arabic as their language and became integrated into Arab culture, producing a Judeo-Islamic culture in contrast to the Judeo-Christian culture of Europe.

25. See Bodian, *Dying in the Law of Moses*, and Perez, *History of a Tragedy*.
26. See Alpert, *Crypto-Judaism*.

Generally, Jews fared better under Muslim rule than under Christian rule, although there were instances of pogroms, forced conversions, and of Jews needing to wear distinctive dress under Muslim rule. Until the founding of the state of Israel, Jews had an advantage in Muslim lands, because there was no political group in the world that had become identified both with Jews and with the enemies of Islam.

The interaction between Jews and Muslims often was creative for both religions. In addition to Islam's Jewish roots, through dialogue and Jewish conversions to Islam, Jews influenced the development of Islamic thought. Examples would be the influence of Jewish law (*Halakah*) in the development of Islamic law (*Sharia*), and the Islamic influence in the development of Jewish theology. The Hebrew language was strongly influenced by Arabic during this period.[27]

The situation became worse for Jews in Muslim lands during the nineteenth century. Bernard Lewis lists reasons for the decline, including falling educational standards in the Jewish communities, the decline of Muslim power, European imperial expansion into Muslim lands, local Christian bigotry against Jews, and Jewish cooperation with Western powers.[28]

Until recently, most Christian writings about Islam were negative and polemical. It is interesting to note that nineteenth- and early twentieth-century European Jewish scholars praised and identified with Islam. The architecture of many synagogues in Europe and America was deeply influenced by Islamic architecture. Jews were proud of the Jewish roots of Islam and the respect shown to Judaism by Islam, a respect they did not experience in the Christian world. These Jews saw Arabs as fellow Semites and Islam and Judaism as kindred religions. Jews wrote the first sympathetic European scholarship on Islam.[29]

A major problem in the relationship between the three religions is the state of Israel and its occupation of the West Bank and the Golan Heights, in addition to all the ways that Occupation has affected international

27. Lewis, *The Jews of Islam*, 75–90.

28. Ibid., 169–71.

29. See Kramer, *Jewish Discovery of Islam*.

relations, not only in the Middle East, but the whole world. No dialogue with Jews can be honest without addressing this subject.

The beginning of Zionism and Jewish colonization of Palestine brought a strong reaction, but most Muslims distinguished between Zionism and Judaism, pointing out that Jews and Muslims had always lived peacefully together. It is common to hear older Palestinian Muslims talk about their past friendships with Jews and express fear that because of the Occupation, their grandchildren will grow up to hate Jews. That is happening. Israeli identification of Zionism with Judaism makes it difficult for most Muslims to distinguish between the two. Modern Muslim Judeophobia is rooted not in anti-Jewish bigotry, but rather in their experiences of Israeli persecution of Arabs.

Sadly, Judeophobia is on the rise in the Muslim world, fueled by Israeli oppression of Palestinians. Many Muslims see America as a puppet of Israel. Every day Muslim television shows scenes of Israelis and Americans killing Muslims. The Israeli/Palestinian conflict has become a Jewish/Muslim conflict.

Although many pro-Israel people unfairly label any criticism of Israel as anti-Semitic, I have also become aware that some people do camouflage their anti-Jewish bigotry in anti-Zionist rhetoric. I regularly try to confront this bigotry.

Since the founding of the State of Israel, Jewish communities severely declined in the Arab countries, due to emigration to Israel. The blending together of Jews from Christendom with Jews from Islamic lands is an important struggle in the state of Israel, a struggle related to the larger relationship between the three religions. The many tensions in Israel include not only the three religions, but also tensions between these two groups of Jews in Israel.

On January 10, 2004, a friend and I visited a Jewish settler family in the Kiryat Arba settlement just outside Hebron. Our conversation with this right wing family was intense. Before we left we were served cookies. When I told them that the cookies tasted almost exactly like cookies I had eaten that morning in a Palestinian home, they responded by telling me that the mother of the family had come to Israel from a Muslim country and they were not surprised that the cookies tasted the same. She had come from a Muslim culture.

Jewish fear of Muslims also is on the rise. Israelis live in daily fear of suicide bombings or other attacks from Muslims. Many Jews have succumbed to Islamophobia, but not all. I heard Rami Elkannan, an Israeli from Bereaved Families, give a moving speech to a group of Palestinians. He said that when a suicide bomber killed his daughter, he had the choice to either seek revenge or seek peace. He chose to seek peace. Much credit needs to be given to progressive Jews who are seeking dialogue with Muslims and opposing Jewish oppression of Muslims. Jews do not need to prolong the eviction of Hagar from Abraham's tent.

≫ FOUR ≪

A New Look at Interfaith Dialogue

FOR MUCH OF HISTORY, people of different religions existed somewhat separate from each other. We now all live in a global village. In our modern world of global communication and transportation, it is common for people to interact daily with people of different religions. We are all interconnected. It is becoming increasingly common to have family members who follow a religion other than one's own. Interfaith relationships are discussed around dinner tables. There no longer is an option of whether or not we relate to people of other religions. The question is how we relate to them.[1]

The issue of tolerance is not theoretical. Any study of the past two thousand years produces volumes of evidence of how bigotry leads to discrimination, persecution, and death. I personally know people in all three religions who have killed someone from another religion. Massacres, mass graves, and genocide are witnesses to intolerance.

Religious people hold the key to world peace by the way in which we interact with each other. In many places in the world, dialogue between religious groups has been crucial in reducing violence between religious communities. Religion can separate us, or it can reconcile and unite. Our common enemy is bigotry, oppression, and violence, not some other religion.

---

1. For an excellent introduction to and guide for interfaith dialogue, see Abu-Nimer and Shafiq, *Interfaith Dialogue: A Guide for Muslims.* This book does much more than present a Muslim basis for dialogue. Long lists of helpful guidelines and suggestions for dialogue are presented, along with a history of and current examples of interfaith dialogue.

Most people probably will never engage in intense interfaith dialogue or relate to more than one religion. It is not realistic to expect most people to have the depth of involvement in other traditions that I have been privileged to have. On the other hand, it is important for everyone to recognize the interconnectedness between all people, and the special interconnectedness between people who believe in a loving God.

A Muslim student from Saudi Arabia at Ohio University told me that he rejoiced that in the midst of degenerate American culture, he had learned to know Christians who also sought to obey God. I know a Muslim, who while a student at Ohio University, regularly worshiped with an evangelical Christian congregation in Athens. He continues to be a practicing Muslim, and is grateful for the contribution that congregation made to his relationship with God and the broadening of his perspective.

Jewish and Muslim students cooperated in getting kosher/halal foods in the dining halls at Ohio University. In addition to Muslims and Jews sharing the same food, each time Jewish and Muslim students encounter each other at the kosher/halal kiosk, they can be reminded of the commonality of faith that Jews and Muslims share.

In places where there is a mix of ethnic and religious groups, there is the challenge of developing a sense of the common good in which all groups feel some sense of participation and ownership. Simple neighborliness, cooperation, and civic mindedness are options available to all of us. This can include anything from being friendly to the people of other religions who live in your neighborhood, to supporting equal rights for all, to working together for common causes to make a better world. Few people would object to working together with someone from another religion to build a neighborhood park, to support a family with severe health issues, or to help improve local schools. These activities require no discussion of faith, no wrestling with difficult issues, but can go a long way to building healthy relationships and peaceful neighborhoods. Who would disagree that this is preferable to suspicion, animosity, or violence in our neighborhoods? On February 5, 2010, an interfaith coalition of Christians, Jews, and Muslims in Athens, Ohio, organized an event of rice and beans, and music, to raise money for earthquake victims in Haiti.

I was on a hospital ward when an emergency developed with one of the patients on the ward. About fifteen or twenty medical personnel, doctors, nurses, aids, rushed to the room, rolling emergency equipment down the hall and into the room. I am sure those emergency workers knew nothing about the religion of the patient, and didn't care at that time. I also am sure there was a diversity of religious commitments among the staff. The first concern was to save the life of the patient, irrespective of religion.

Many people work with people of other religions on their jobs, they encounter people of other religions at the grocery store, and their children attend school with children of other religions. Because of these interactions, increasingly, special events like weddings and funerals include a wide diversity of peoples. Recent Christian funerals and weddings I have attended have included Jews, Muslims, Hindus, Sikhs, Buddhists, atheists, neo-pagans, and secularists. These celebrations make a clear witness to the faith of the people planning these celebrations, make no compromise in the expressions of that faith, but also include the people of other religions on the level they want to be included.

On July 1, 2007, Abhishek Singh, a graduate student from India at Ohio University, was struck and killed by an automobile driven by a drunk driver in Athens, Ohio. On July 19, the university hosted an interfaith memorial service commemorating the young student's life. Abhishek was a Hindu. The memorial service included statements, music, scriptures, and prayers from various religions, including Sikh, Hindu, Muslim, Jewish, and Christian. I sensed God's presence and rejoiced that people had called the attention of the Ohio University community to God.

In the fall of 2002 I did a week-long speaking tour in Iowa, speaking in churches and university settings. A Muslim friend from Somalia drove me to the airport in Columbus. A Hindu friend, in whose home I stayed for the duration of my preaching mission, met me at the airport in Iowa. Jews, Muslims, Christians, and Hindus, and others, came to hear me speak. I had an especially strong sense of God's Spirit during that whole trip.

There is little value in having dialogue about dialogue. Neither is interfaith dialogue reserved for academics and religious professionals. It can happen on many levels, be planned or spontaneous, formal or informal. I know many people in all three religions who are reaching out to people of other religions. I think of a Jewish woman who reaches out to Muslim university students in her town, Christians who share their places of worship with people of other religions for their gatherings, as well as Muslims who seek friendship with Jews and Christians. I rejoice when I see Jews in the mosque or Muslims in the synagogue in Athens.

In May, 2009, my wife had surgery for cancer. One of the things that sustained and encouraged us was the prayers of Christians, Muslims, Jews, pagans, and many unknown friends and supporters. At the point of praying for Peggy, theological differences were unimportant.

On August 29, 2008, Israeli peace activists organized a trip for Palestinian children from the South Hebron Hills to visit the zoo in Tel Aviv. This exposed the Palestinian children to Israeli Jews in a non-threatening, non-oppressive context. The children expressed fear when they saw an Israeli wearing a kippah, but learned that not all Jews are to be feared.

When dialoguing with others, some people focus on differences while others focus on things in common. There is something important in both approaches. Both similarities and differences should be acknowledged. Focusing on our commonalities is most important. I was listening to a right-wing radio talk show in 2006 whose host was very bigoted against Muslims. A Muslim called in and made comments about pornography, which impressed the talk show host, who then commented, "Maybe this could be a bridge to bring together America and the Muslim world."

I often hear people say, "I have nothing in common with that person." Sometimes I ask, "Does he have two eyes? How many ears does she have?" and suggest we have much in common with everyone. We all have the same Creator, breathe the same air, and live on the same planet. Some people seem to regularly draw lines and circles to exclude and separate others, while some people keep drawing larger circles to include others. When someone does something we do not like, too often we work to avoid or exclude that person. A more interesting option is to reach out to that person, to seek the transformation of that person into a better person. I remember taking an unpopular stand on a controversial issue in Athens. One person became very angry with me and for a long time refused to talk to me. In response, I reached out in friendly ways to that person for six months before the walls came down and we could again talk with each other.

It is fine to disagree. We do not need to agree with everything and everyone. But how do we disagree? There are creative and destructive ways to disagree. Increasingly, when I am in groups or with individuals with whom I disagree, instead of confronting them with my disagreements, I find myself asking questions about our points of disagreement. My showing interest in understanding their perspective breaks down defensiveness and often opens doors to productive discussion. When people on the other side of issues have the opportunity to explain their views to me, and I am able to listen, a relationship has been established which can go a long way in dialogue.

The answer to disagreements is not separation from the people with whom we disagree, but rather to deal openly with our disagreements and seek understanding, if not agreement. Dialogue is about building bridges. To accept unity only with those with whom we agree is cliquishness. It is to deny unity as a gift of God, as a work of grace. To be truly open to God is to seek truth, no matter where it leads us, no matter what the cost. Disagreements can lead to repentance and new life.

Our own prejudices and fears can be a major barrier to dialogue. If Christians view Islam as repressive, violent, anti-women, or evil, dialogue will be difficult. If we accept media stereotypes of Islam, dialogue will be difficult. If Muslims see Christians and Jews as infidels, dialogue will be difficult. If Jews see Christianity and Islam as perversions of Abrahamic faith, dialogue will be difficult.

It is important to remember that none of our religions are mono-lithic. There are wide varieties of views and Scriptural interpretations in all religions. We find what we look for. We are more likely to find integrity, love, justice, and goodness in the world if we expect to find it. We see what we expect to see. I have not been disappointed in my trying to find something of God and genuine faith among people of other religions.

Dialogue will come to a quick end if I compare the best of my reli-gion with the worst of your religion. All of our religions have strengths and weaknesses. I want to avoid confusing the practice with the essence of the other religion, or twisting the texts of the other religions. It is help-ful to make the most generous interpretations possible, to see another religion as members of that religion see that religion. There is no place for degrading or demonizing the other.

Dialogue requires a lot of patience and forgiveness. Because of igno-rance and insensitivity, not malice, many things will be said and done that will sound offensive to people of other religions, especially when sensitive issues are touched on. It is essential that we trust the good intentions of our dialogue partners when they ask what may seem like dumb questions, make implications that seem totally unfair, or state views that are offen-sive to us. We need openness, humility, and love, something very different from tolerating each other, ignoring each other, or talking past each other. Our conversations can be tempered with love, mercy, and grace.

Dialogue can happen on many levels. It can be cultural/social. Each May in Athens, Ohio, there is an international street fair. The main street is closed, and people from many countries sell their foods while cultural presentations occur on the stage in the street. The hope is that people will learn something about other cultures.

On November 23, 2007, about 25 Quakers from the Athens Friends' Meeting attended Friday Prayers in the mosque in Athens. This visit was a response to Muslims earlier visiting the Friends' Meeting. The sermon in the mosque was both a straightforward presentation of the essentials of the Muslim religion, and a sensitive attempt to reach out to and affirm the validity of the Quaker faith, including stories of early Muslim/Christian relationships. This was followed by sharing of pies and cider brought by the Quakers. This visit has now become an annual event.

We can simply get to know each other. One approach for people who already have some knowledge of the other religion is to share what it is in the other religion that I find most attractive. What in our own culture do we feel is destructive and to be avoided? How do we raise children? Questions of justice, war, and violence can be important topics.

We can go beyond talking about our beliefs about God to sharing about our relationship with God. A deeper level of sharing occurs when people open their hearts to each other. I like to ask people very personal questions about their faith. I ask people about their prayer life, their fears and doubts, their hopes. This opens doors and deep sharing often is the result.

Dialogue will never go very deep without listening to each other's pain, of which there is plenty in Abraham's family. Listening to each other's pain is difficult, especially when I also am hurting. Even more difficult is to listen to the pain of the one I feel hurt me. Too often I have cut myself off from people who were abusing me. Especially powerful are the stories of the coming together of Israeli and Palestinian families who lost loved ones to violence from the other side.

Dialogue is not always possible. Sometimes doors are shut. The time must be right.

INTERFAITH DIALOGUE BEGINS WITH FAITH

At its best, interfaith dialogue begins with faith. Interfaith dialogue is hampered when participants are unclear in their own faith. The more clearly I understand what I truly believe, the more ready I can be to dialogue with people of other religions. The stronger my faith is, the more open I can be with other people.

Some people's faith is extremely fragile, a faith these people fear cannot withstand any challenges. They are afraid that if even one minor detail of their belief system were proven false, the whole structure of their faith would crumble. Since faith involves the deepest parts of our being, to talk with others about faith can be seen as a threat to one's faith. Interfaith dialogue can challenge us to the core of our being. If I do not hold tightly to my faith, could I lose my faith and everything fall apart? Will I be left with no foundation in my life, with nothing remaining certain? Even worse, could I lose my salvation?

These fears have not been confirmed in my life as I open my heart to Muslims and Jews. I am learning that God is faithful. God has not only sustained me, God has deepened my faith. I am no less a Christian now. Rather than seeing other religions as a threat, we can see dialogue as an opportunity to learn more about God's truth and will for us.

Rather than lose our identity in dialogue, we can find a deeper understanding of the roots of our faith. Because of the deepening of faith I have experienced, it would be impossible to turn back, to close my eyes and heart, to reject what God has shown me. There is more to fear in becoming rigid and closed than in being open to learning from others. To reject spiritual growth is to close oneself to God's Spirit. To turn back would be spiritual suicide. God is so much bigger than I have ever imagined. The little, narrow concept of God I learned to know as a child has now expanded to seeing God as the Lord of the Universe, the God of all Nations, the Spirit who enlightens hearts everywhere, the God who cannot be contained in my small concepts.

It seems to be a common human tendency to become closed and defensive when we encounter new ideas that at first seem to contradict some of our cherished values. Instead of listening, we immediately judge and reject the new idea, begin building our arguments, and rehearsing our responses. A much more interesting way to live is to be curious, to ask people with whom we disagree why they think the way they do. If nothing more, we may learn better ways to respond to them by understanding their views. We also may learn something that will deepen our own understanding. Arguing with people out of our own ignorance is hardly a sign of wisdom.

I am constantly amazed at how curious children are, but by the time we become adults it seems much of that curiosity has been crushed. I never quite understand why many people have so little interest in learning about anything outside their little world. Dialogue is rooted in curiosity. Why do other people believe as they do?

We do not need to be defensive. We can respond to other religions with fear and hostility, as did the Apostle Paul before his conversion, or we can step out of our comfort zones and make ourselves vulnerable even on the turf of "the other." We can be open to new ideas, learn from them, and mature in our thinking. Religion can be used as an excuse for closing our minds, or it can open us to new possibilities. The starting point for dialogue is respect, humility, and an eagerness to understand. Instead of seeing others as a threat, we can see them as people created and loved by God.

I have learned that God can be trusted. I can let go, take risks, step out in faith, knowing that God will be there on the other side of dialogue. Holding tightly to my religion indicates a lack of faith in the sovereignty of God. When we think we have the truth, we have abandoned the mystery of God.

Most of the people who oppose interfaith dialogue have never experienced interfaith dialogue. If they had experienced the power of God's Spirit in encounters with other people of faith and been transformed by that encounter, it is unlikely that they would oppose what they now oppose. This ignorance can be simple not knowing, or it can be the result of closed-mindedness. Closedness to dialogue can be a result of a failure to love our neighbors.

An American friend of mine was traveling in a Muslim country during Ramadan. To be polite, he fasted while he was there. To his surprise, his Muslim acquaintances not only appreciated his gesture, but indicated this caused them to reconsider their stereotypes of Westerners. One Muslim said to him, "I wonder if we can show as much respect to the customs of others as you have shown."

Opposition to interfaith work often comes from a right-wing political agenda, often involving hatred of or oppression of another religious or racial group. Sometimes interfaith activity is seen as a threat to some people's privilege and power. Often religious statements against dialogue are a cover for support of morally questionable stands, such as war, racism, sexism, imperialism, and other oppressions. Some people use religion to support the structures of oppression, while others see in their faith a call for liberation.

The biblical Jonah did not support interfaith dialogue. He hated non-Jews and certainly did not want God to forgive and accept the people of Nineveh, now known as Iraqis. In the end, he did go to Nineveh, preached, the people repented, and just as Jonah feared, God accepted the people of Nineveh and Jonah went into a deep depression. Jonah failed to accept the graciousness of an all-loving God. There is nothing in the story to suggest that the people of Nineveh first became Jews before God accepted them.

It is not only conservatives who are closed to dialogue. People on the left also build ideologies that are used to oppress and control people. Especially insidious is when the rhetoric of liberation and overcoming oppression replaces love and is used as an excuse to maintain privilege and power over others. In its absolutism and lack of humility, even attempts to undo oppression can become oppressive towards people who do not completely buy into the "liberated" ideology. Those whose mission in life is to dominate and control others can use liberal undoing oppression rhetoric as well as anything to accomplish their goals. People use ideology as a rationalization for being closed to dialogue, when the real issue is maintaining privilege and power. "They are racists or sexists, and since we are good and they are bad, we cannot dialogue with them."

There are closed system ideologies on the left, right, and the middle, religious and secular. Either one completely agrees with the promoters of those ideologies or one is labeled as bad, and excluded. The absolute truth of those ideologies is not to be questioned. Dialogue is impossible and seen as a waste of time, if not collaboration with the enemy. Repeatedly these ideologies are used to exercise power over other people, to isolate and discard people, and to serve as the basis for prideful self-righteousness and judgmentalism.

There are issues in many groups that are too controversial to be discussed. Even among some of my liberal friends, there are topics that are not open for discussion. This is sad, especially when it occurs among religious groups who claim to be open to God's Spirit. For interfaith dialogue to have integrity, the difficult questions must be faced. How could Christians dialogue with Hindus without dealing with the caste system, or Hindus not bring up Christian support for colonialism? Christians must face the Holocaust and the whole history of anti-Jewish and anti-Muslim bigotry. Muslims must be willing to talk about suicide bombers and op-pressive aspects of Muslim societies. Jews must face up to Israeli oppres-sion of Palestinians

I have a passion to dialogue not only with the "moderates" of other faiths, but also the "extremists," and have put a lot of effort into listening to right-wing Israeli settlers, Hamas and Islamic Jihad, and the religious right in Christian circles. Too often people seek out the least devoted people in other religions with whom to dialogue. Often the more chal-lenging dialogue will happen with those who are most different from us and most deeply rooted in their traditions.

Sadly, much of Jewish/Christian dialogue has agreed to silence re-garding the state of Israel and its persecution of its Palestinian inhabitants. One Christian leader told me that although he supported the Palestinians, he could not speak out for Palestinians because he was trying to cultivate relationships with the Jewish community. That feels dishonest and conde-scending to me. I want the Jewish community to know that what they hear from me is sincere. I do not want to play games with or mislead anyone. Much of Jewish/Christian dialogue is rooted in Christian guilt feelings for the long history of Christian anti-Jewish bigotry. To redeem themselves of their complicity in the persecution of Jews, now some Christians have become complicit in the Israeli persecution of Palestinians.

There is a Jewish story of students reconciling after disputing with each other. Rabbi Mendel of Kotzk was upset that they had reconciled so easily and said, "Controversies in the name of Heaven spring from the root of truth. A peace without truth is a false peace."[2] It is imperative that we both hold on to the truth and affirm the possibility that those with whom we disagree may also have valid insights.

I attended an interfaith public forum where the five speakers started with excellent five-minute opening statements. The stage was set for a marvelous dialogue, but the rest of the program was a series of short monologues from both speakers and the audience. There was no dialogue, no probing questions to deepen understandings between the various faiths, no exploring points of agreement and divergence. They were not listening to each other. Comments did not build on what was said before.

In other dialogues, the participants listened to each other, shared their faith with each other, and drew close to each other with empathy

2. Friedman, "Hasidim and the Love of Enemies," 46, in Polner and Goodman, eds., *The Challenge of Shalom.*

and understanding. I remember being part of a two-week gathering of Palestinian and Israeli teenage girls in which there was both trust and honesty. I was amazed at how well both the Israeli and Palestinian girls were able to articulate their pain and fears, how each group was able to listen to the other. There were tears and some angry outbursts, but everyone listened as those girls developed a close bond.

Academic discussions between people who do not know each other are severely limited. We can go beyond the verbal. A deeper level of dialogue involves building relationships. Dialogue involves listening with all our heart, soul, mind, and strength. It means opening our minds and souls to new ideas. It means becoming vulnerable as we accept the inevitability that we will be changed by our encounter with other faiths. It means asking and trusting God to lead us to deeper levels of truth and understanding.

Someone suggested that when we dialogue we should all put our holy books on the table between us. In response to this suggestion, another person suggested that we put our holy books behind us, indicating that our holy books inform us, but do not stand between us. Another person said, "Let's forget about dialogue and just talk with each other."

When I hear the beautiful, sublime Muslim call to prayer, I open my heart and allow those words and sounds to penetrate to the depths of my being. Each time I open myself to that profound call to prayer, I am changed, transformed, lifted out of my own self-centeredness to a deeper awareness of God's presence. When I am in Muslim cities, I lie awake each morning, waiting for the call to prayer to come over the loud speakers. When the call begins, my heart leaps with joy. I want to praise God. Each morning my soul affirms the words of the morning call to prayer, "It is better to pray than to sleep." From the window of my hotel room in Amman, Jordan, I saw a church steeple and a minaret two blocks away, and listened to the church bells and the call to prayer. I rejoiced in seeing those two buildings standing side by side, and prayed in both of those buildings.

We cannot listen if we are afraid to change. Although scary, the change we experience in prayer and dialogue is nothing to fear. It is to be welcomed. Change, although sometimes painful, brings liberation and great joy.

For Christians, interfaith dialogue must begin with the cross, making ourselves vulnerable to others, confessing to them Christian sins of bigotry, arrogance, and violence toward other religions. Christians must be ready to hear and absorb the pain and anger people in the other religions feel toward Christians, and be clear that we are ready to die for our Muslim and Jewish sisters and brothers. I admire the way Israeli peace activists are able to listen to the pain and anger of Palestinians.

Whenever over the past twenty or more years I have spoken to groups of Muslims or Jews, I have started by apologizing to them for the horrible history of Christianity under which Jews and Muslims have suffered so deeply. I apologize not only for the history, but also for the horrible atrocities "Christians" continue to perpetrate on Muslims and Jews. Asking for forgiveness, however, has little real substance if it does not include giving up my power over the ones I offended. We are all in need of God's mercy, but it cannot be on our terms. Each religion in its relationship with other religions can begin with apologizing for the horrible things people of their religion have done to the other religious groups. People in each of the three Abrahamic religions have much to be ashamed of.

I remember a meeting of peace activists with Muslims in the mosque in Athens, Ohio, toward the end of the Gulf War in 1991. When it came my turn to introduce myself, I looked at the one Iraqi in the room and apologized to him for what my country had done to his people. His response was to apologize for the pain caused by the Iraqi government. I sensed no defensiveness as we continued our discussion. Trust had been established.

David W. Shenk, a global missions consultant with Eastern Mennonite missions, tells the story of engaging in a formal dialogue with a female Iranian Shia theologian in a theological forum in Germany. When he made a presentation on the meaning of the cross, the woman responded in anger, saying, "I have never before known that the cross has anything to do with love or forgiveness. We Muslims experience the cross as an instrument of violence. The Christian movement as we experience it is a violent movement." Shenk responded with tears as he asked for forgiveness for the way the church has distorted the gospel. After lunch the Muslim woman responded. "The last two hours have been the most significant minutes of my life, for never before have I experienced a

Christian asking a Muslim [for] forgiveness. This has opened my eyes to a Jesus I never knew existed."[3]

A major barrier to dialogue is ignorance of other religions, and in many cases ignorance of one's own beliefs. Often the first step in dialogue must be one of both learning more about one's own faith, and study of the other religions. For some, the starting point will need to be intra-faith dialogue, dialogue within the religion between groups who have widely divergent views of their own religion. Can we talk with people with whom we disagree within our own religion?

Another barrier is to have gained some knowledge and then think we know everything about another religion. Dialogue must begin with humility and an eagerness to learn. As I learn more about Islam and Judaism, I realize how many of my conceptions of those religions have been incomplete or even wrong. When Peter, the Jewish Christian, was called to witness to the pagan Cornelius, he first needed to be humbled and transformed before he could witness to this Gentile who already had a deep faith in God.[4]

Tom Segev, a well-known Israeli journalist, tells the story of sitting around a big table, eating with a conservative Mennonite family in Lancaster County, Pennsylvania. He was having a light conversation with the family when a young boy at the table asked this Jewish man if he believed in Jesus. Tom didn't know what to say, but simply responded by saying, "No." For some minutes there was an awkward silence. No one knew what to say. The conversation then went to some safe subject.

This family was not prepared for interfaith dialogue, and may not even have been prepared to share their faith with this "nonbeliever." How sad. A wonderful opportunity for a significant conversation was lost, a conversation from which everyone could have benefited. They may not have known enough about Judaism to talk about Judaism with Tom, but they could have asked questions. They could have asked Tom about his impressions of Jesus, about how he sees Jewish-Christian relationships,

---

3. Krabill et al., *Anabaptists Meeting Muslims*, 454–55.

4. Acts 10:1–48.

or something about his understanding of Judaism. How many of us are prepared and eager to share our faith with others?

For dialogue to happen, we must move beyond our ignorance and misconceptions of the other religion. Muslims do not worship Moham-mad. The very thought of worshiping a human being is anathema to any Muslim. Christians do not believe there are three gods, or that Mary is part of the Trinity. Christians do not worship the cross and Muslims do not worship the Ka'ba. Jews are not hopelessly mired in legalism.

A common Muslim perception is that Christians have very low moral standards. This is partly due to the images portrayed by Western media and the confusion of Western with Christian values. Sadly, most Muslims fail to make a distinction between the Christian faith and Western values. But many Christians also fail to make that distinction. I have had Muslim university students ask me why Christians teach that men and women can sleep together whenever and with whomever they want. It would be good for Christians to take this misconception seriously and try to be clearer about Christian moral standards. It is true, in general, that Western Christians do not take the Commandments very seriously. In fact, they abhor commandments of any kind. Westerners want to be "free."

The misconceptions people have of Islam are many, and are perpe-trated by Western media. Many Westerners continue to believe the distort-ed Medieval European perceptions of Islam. Probably the most common stereotype is seeing Islam as violent and vengeful. It is interesting that Christians would bring this charge against Islam, since Christians have been much more violent in the past 1400 years than Muslims have been.

I have heard many Christians claim that Muslims do not believe they can have a personal relationship with God. Yet the Qur'an says God is closer to us than our jugular vein.[5] Muslims believe that no priesthood or any other intermediaries are needed in our relationship with God.

There has been a long history of Christian misconceptions of Judaism. A common misperception is that Jews live in bondage to the law, something we will consider later in the next chapter. Another mispercep-tion is that Judaism worships a vengeful God, while Christians worship a God of love. This is simple bigotry. There is much in the Jewish Scriptures about God's steadfast love. Jews also have a sense of God's love and pa-tience. Christian Scriptures also include texts concerning God's anger and

5. Qur'an 50:16.

judgment upon sin. I have been deeply moved by the deep sense of God's love and grace I have sensed in all of my participation in worship in the synagogue in Athens.

Too often the most negative aspects of the three religions are pitted against each other. A beautiful example of moving beyond old debates is found in a statement, "A Common Word between Us and You," put out in 2007 by The Royal Aal al-Bayt Institute for Islamic Thought in Jordan, calling for understanding and unity between Muslims and Christians. The statement quotes the Qur'an forbidding having any partners with God, and interprets this as calling us to "complete and total devotion to God," to reject all forms of idolatry, and connects this with the biblical call to love God "with all your heart, with all your soul, with all your mind, and with all your strength." Muslims have traditionally used the command to not have any partners with God as a debating point with Christians about the Trinity. This ecumenical statement does not resolve that debate, but moves beyond that debate to interpret those Scriptures in new, creative ways. Even if we are correct in our interpretation of a portion of Scripture, if we are stuck in our correct interpretation, we are unable to move forward.[6]

Mohammad sent a letter to a Christian king. He started the letter with, "In the name of the God of Abraham, Isaac, and Jacob," a beautiful attempt to reach out to the Christian and connect with him on his terms. Dialogue is about building bridges of peace and understanding. None of us know what those bridges might mean in the future.

DIALOGUE VS. PROCLAMATION/ WITNESS/CONVERSION

A serious critique of interfaith dialogue comes from those who believe that our main focus in relating to people of other religions should be witnessing to those people in the hope that they will convert to my religion. From this perspective, dialogue misses the point. Dialogue is seen as shallow and shortsighted. One conservative Christian told me that he was willing to cooperate with people of other religions on activities such as service projects, but he could not engage in dialogue with them. He could only declare his faith to them.

---

6. See the entire statement at http://www.acommonword.com/.

Around November 25, 2008, the world media carried stories of Pope Benedict arguing that interfaith dialogue is impossible for Christians, that true dialogue puts "one's faith in parentheses." Instead, the pope welcomed intercultural dialogue in which the cultural implications of religious differences can be discussed. The pope is to be commended for his support for this dialogue, and his own reaching out to other religions.

The pope also was right that interfaith dialogue is not like political dialogue or negotiations, where each side gives a little. Interfaith dialogue includes issues of truth and revelation, but that does not mean we cannot have deep dialogue about the deepest aspects of our faith. When I engage in dialogue I do not put my faith in parenthesis, but rather engage my faith in the deepest ways possible.

God's Truth needs no defending. It is inclusive and open to everyone. It is the little "truths" and dogmas that we create that need defending, that we think cannot be opened to unfettered dialogue. The pope's rejection of dialogue about the deepest aspects of his faith stands as a severe indictment of the dogmas of the Roman Catholic Church.

To argue that dialogue and cooperation can occur only in regard to secular issues is a huge concession to secularism. If only secular perspectives can form the basis for our interfaith relationships, then our faith perspectives become irrelevant to our relationships, a huge concession indeed. Why would we not relate to each other on the basis of our faith? Our common concerns grow out of our faith. Modern secularism is a challenge to all people of faith. We have an immediate tie to people of other religions precisely because of their faith in God.

I do not need to reject the truth of my religion in order to accept the truth in other religions. Each religion has its own sets of truths, but is it not possible for people both to engage in dialogue and humbly affirm their distinctive truths? If we can accept the legitimacy of the other person's religion, we are well on the way to fruitful dialogue. Christians can continue to affirm that "Jesus is Lord," that Jesus is "the way, the truth, and the life." Muslims can continue to affirm that Mohammad is the seal of the prophets. Jews can continue to affirm God's covenant with Israel and God's unique revelation in the Torah. We can continue to witness to each other about our distinctive understandings of God's truth. We can trust that one day God will clear away the fog from our eyes and all of us will see the Truth in a more complete way.

Our distinctive affirmations are an essential part of interfaith dialogue. We do not need to water down our faith to accommodate others. To say that all religions are the same can be a barrier to true dialogue, as is being too ready to compromise for the sake of unity. Those who say, "I support all religions," usually do not support any religion. To take relativism seriously, to believe that all religions and philosophies are equal, is to deny the possibility of opposing racism, sexism, or any other ism. Some values are superior to other values.[7]

Anyone who has experienced God's love and grace, and has caught a vision of God's kingdom, will want in some way to share that good news and invite others to participate in God's reconciling work. I have the right to proclaim to others, however, only as I am open to listening to and learning from them. This openness can help prevent our proclamation from becoming arrogant and oppressive. In true dialogue we are open to gain new insights from others. Unless we are open to change, we are not open to dialogue. We can still engage in conversation, discussion, and debate without being open, but not in dialogue. In true dialogue we become open to learning from the other. Dialogue is a sham if the faith of other people can have no value or meaning for me. In true dialogue we affirm the dignity of the other person and trust that God's Spirit can speak to us through that person.

Too often have I listened to people of different persuasions trying to convince each other that they have the Truth. These conversations do not convince the other person to convert. If anything, they make it more difficult for someone to convert to the other religion. They only convince each person that the other person is closed, narrow-minded, and wrong. Proclamation, and not only dialogue, must include respect. For conversion to another religion to take place, one must find something deeply attractive in the other religion. Inflammatory polemics are not helpful.

I met a man who had done a lot of spiritual searching and was well read on religious issues. I was eager to talk with him and learn from him, but our conversation quickly became a monologue with him going on and on about why his religion was better than all other religions. I quickly lost interest in the conversation, even though there was much I could have learned from him. I wanted dialogue, not monologue.

---

7. For two contrasting Christian perspectives on interfaith dialogue, see Hick and Knitter, *Myth of Christian Uniqueness* and D'Costa, *Christian Uniqueness Reconsidered*.

When people tell me I am going to hell because I do not agree with their theology, I am not impressed or attracted to learn more about their faith. I get tired of people trying to convert me. I want honest dialogue between equals, not condescending implications that they have the Truth and I am ignorant. I resent anything done as a strategy to get me to convert. I want to be respected as a person, to have interest shown in my journey, my struggles, my doubts.

A young woman approached me during a peace demonstration in Washington, D.C., and began witnessing to me. Ironically, she apparently assumed I was not a Christian since I was demonstrating for peace. She began by asking if I was a Christian. It was not the answer she wanted when I told her I was a Christian. She then asked if I was born again. I disappointed her again when I said yes. She then asked if I had experienced the baptism of the Holy Spirit. "Yes," I said. Then she trapped me. She asked, "Have you spoken in tongues?" I said, "No," which finally gave her the opening she was seeking. She began, "If you will receive Jesus into your heart . . . ," and gave me the speech she had prepared for every poor sinner she would meet that day. I would have welcomed her talking to me about my faith, my need for repentance, my need for God, but she had not listened to me. She had no clue about what to say to my spiritual need.

Witnessing does not mean converting other people. Conversion is the work of God's Spirit, not our work. Our task is to witness to our faith and to show love to others, to share experiences of God's work in our lives in ways that can be helpful to others.

Those who try to convert others have legitimate concerns. There is one Truth to which we all are called. Dialogue is more than a game. Dialogue will be shallow if we have nothing of conviction to share in the dialogue. If there is no Truth, why waste the energy? We can enter dialogue with firm convictions and at the same time respect the convictions of others. All three religions have the God-given mandate to share the revelation they have received with the rest of the world. If our faith is real and vibrant, why would we not want to share it with others?

There is an important place for proclamation in dialogue, but before that can be effective, I must first understand the people I am speaking to, and have spent enough time listening to others to have earned their trust. Only then can I speak to them. This process of listening and understanding can be manipulative, but it need not be. Any attempt to understand needs to be genuine.

Because of my belief that God can speak through anyone, in every encounter with other people, I must be open to the possibility that God is speaking to me through that other person. Because of this, I must always listen carefully to everyone, being eager and open to learn from others. Dialogue is first about my own conversion.

Interfaith dialogue and proclaiming our faith are not separate or contradictory activities. In fact, neither is valid without the other. There is no contradiction between proclamation and dialogue because they are two sides of the same coin. In dialogue we share what we believe most deeply. There is a difference between standing for what I believe to be true and imposing that on others. We must be open because we could be wrong, because we are not God, and because we trust the future to God. To coerce is to lose faith in God's power. Those who would impose their faith on others are wrong both because they do not trust God enough, and because they do not believe the specifics of their own faith deeply enough.

Of course, I have goals, hopes, and expectations for dialogue. There will be convictions, concerns, and values I will want to communicate. I want increased understanding that can lead to justice and peace. I want everyone to open their lives to God's presence, to follow Jesus and the prophets. I want everyone to accept the love of Jesus. I have a commitment to developing nonviolent responses to conflict. I have something to say to people who use religion to justify violence and oppression. The best proclamation, I have learned, is through dialogue. When I speak to groups of people, I do have something to communicate, but I spend most of the time in dialogue.

I am often asked if in all my work for peace I talk to other people about their relationship with God, if I witness to them about Jesus. I try to do that every day. Hopefully, my life is the most important witness I make. Do my friends see God's Spirit in my life? Do they see Jesus in who I am and what I do? Sadly, many people do a lot of talking about God, but their lives do not support their talk. Do I love my Jewish and Muslim friends? Do they know I love them? Do I love them enough to die for them? Francis of Assisi said, "Preach the gospel always. And when necessary, use words." Our actions speak louder than our words.

Active peacemaking, calling people to nonviolent resistance to the powers of evil, is a central part of what evangelism is about. Making the nonviolent Jesus visible to the world certainly is evangelism.

I often directly ask people about their relationship with God, about what is happening in their souls, about what spiritual struggles they are experiencing. I try to direct conversations toward a more spiritual direction, to reflect theologically on the subject of our conversation. Often I do this by raising theological questions. For example, when I encounter racist oppression, I often point out to my friends that racism is a denial of the oneness of God. Recently while participating in a peace vigil, a man questioned the wisdom of my beliefs. At the end of our dialogue, I told him that I based my views on Jesus and encouraged the man, who had a Christian background, to take Jesus seriously and follow him.

I often pray with people. After a Muslim friend shared some important personal struggles with me, we spent a deep time of prayer with each other. I then encouraged him to spend more time in informal prayer (du'a) in conversation with God. He later told me that his expanded prayer life was important for him. If another person draws closer to God, what can I do but rejoice?

Some may overreact to people trying to convert people of other faiths and be too hesitant to share their own faith. I have found Muslims in particular, not only eager to share their faith, but equally eager for Christians to share their faith with them. Muslims respect openness about one's faith. I have repeatedly been invited by Muslims to convert to Islam. I have usually felt honored by those invitations. How could we not be open, inviting, and eager to share and include others in the joy of our own faith?

From July 20–31, 2008, I was on a speaking tour in Indonesia, partly to promote the Indonesian translation of my Hebron Journal, which had just been published. It seemed like something of a miracle that Muslims would invite and organize a speaking tour for a Christian to preach to Muslims. I felt humbled by the challenge and the trust they had placed in me. I remembered how Christian, how Jesus-centered that book is. It was amazing that an Islamist publishing company would be publishing this book. On July 12, a week before I left to go to Indonesia for the lecture tour, I wrote these words:

What is my Christian witness to the Muslims I will meet? Obviously I will need to show respect and love to everyone. I need to listen, to be open. Hopefully the Light of Christ will shine through me. But that does not answer the question. How can I make an explicit Christian witness? What will it mean for me to speak to them as a Christian? How can I communicate the message of the gospel? I think of my evangelical friends and what they would want me to say. They would want me to focus on Jesus. "What an opportunity," they would say, "to call Muslims to Jesus."

I hope to speak to the Muslims as a Christian. Although I identify with all three religions, to speak to them only as a fellow Muslim would be to deny them the possibility of a deeper and broader dialogue. I want to talk about Jesus. Jesus is very important in my life. At the same time, I know that God is already at work in the lives of those Muslims in Indonesia. Humility is the starting point for the dialogue.

I lectured in universities, schools, and mosques, and met with activists, which resulted in intense dialogue. There were interviews with many journalists. In some of these interviews, our interaction changed from interview to deep personal sharing about our faith in God, about trusting in God.

I talked about my relationship with Islam, about praying with Muslims, about the influence of Islam in my life, but usually did not identify myself as being a Muslim. I spoke as a Christian. It seemed better that they see me as a caring Christian than as a caring Muslim, that they see something good in the Christian faith.

For a long time I have felt that my relationship with the Muslim world has been a preparation for something in the future. I still do not know what that is, but it is clear to me that all of my relationships and preparation were a wonderful asset in my ability to communicate with Muslims there. I know how to speak the Muslim language, just as I can speak the Christian language. Although I spoke there as a Christian, I often used Muslim language, using Muslim words and concepts. The response of Muslims was overwhelmingly positive.

After I spoke, often a number of people identified themselves as Christians. Christians were included in most of my speaking events. Many of them were deeply involved in dialogue and social action with Muslims. I asked them if what I said was a problem for them. They repeatedly said that they appreciated very much what I said, that what I said needed to be said. I felt supported by the Christians who heard me speak. That was quite encouraging for me. I went to Indonesia concerned that I not upset the Christian community or do anything to weaken their witness. I really did not want to say anything that would be a problem for the Christians there. I pray that what I said will help bridge the divide between Christians and Muslims.

The events in which I participated included explicit Christian witness. Mizan Press put a short statement from Franz Magnis-Suseno, a famous Indonesian Catholic, as a blurb on the front of my book, emphasizing my commitment to love. One Christian, Paulus Widjaja, a Mennonite, moderated one of my speaking sessions. A professor who moderated one session started by reading a quote from Ron Sider on the meaning of the cross. I also talked about the cross as God's answer to sin and discussed my understanding of the atonement. Each session was an exercise in Christian/Muslim dialogue.

Nonviolence was one of the major issues that emerged in our dialogue. Although most of those I talked to were open to or accepted the importance of nonviolence, those who argued with me used mainly political, pragmatic arguments. The same is true for Christians who reject nonviolence. Their basic arguments are political, not Scriptural or theological.

Quite a few times during my speaking tour of Indonesia, I heard anti-Jewish bigotry expressed. Every time I confronted it head on, arguing it is not Islamic, that it was imported from Christians, and that they should resist it. I said the Jews were also created by God, are Abraham's children, and are to be respected. I quoted Prophet Mohammad, "Be kind to the people of the Book."

I answered questions about Christian Zionism and fundamentalism. I said that the heresy of Christian Zionists is that they believe that the center of God's redeeming work in history is the nation state of Israel. I then suggested that for Christians the center of God's work is the church, the Body of Christ, for Muslims it is the Ummah, and for Jews the people of God, concepts that are essentially the same.

My trip ended with an overwhelming sense of gratitude to God for being allowed to serve God, for the opportunity to engage in dialogue. My soul was full of praise to God. Nothing can compare with the joy of serving God. But who am I, such a poor and unfaithful servant, to serve God? Ilhamdililah. Praise be to God. I really do want to give the praise to God.

With much historical justification, Muslims tend to see Western Christian missionary activity as a plot to weaken Muslim culture and make it more susceptible to Western goals to subdue and control the Muslim world. Missionaries then are seen as co-conspirators, along with global corporations, entertainment media, and military threats. A different image was Mennonite missionary work in Somalia (1960–80), resulting not so much in Muslims converting to Christianity, but in Muslims becoming better Muslims, Muslims who became followers of Jesus. Some of those Muslims are still called "Mennonite Muslims."[8] In my peace work among Muslims I experience transformation of persons and communities as we share the sufferings of oppressed people in the middle of horrible violence.

It is interesting how secular Western society has taken up the evangelistic mission to convert people, not to God, but to secularism. The new revised secular mission to Islam is to modernize and secularize Muslim society. The goal is not to argue with religious understandings of truth, but to render them obsolete and irrelevant.

Evangelism, witnessing, and sharing our faith are important. We can tell our stories. We can share our pain and become witnesses to the pain of others, and to the healing that can take place in people's lives. We can share the light we have received. We can counter falsehood with truth. Evangelism becomes a problem only when it gets mixed up with arrogance, manipulation, conquest, domination, and imperialism. We denigrate our faith when we share it out of arrogance.

We all need to be sensitive to others' fears and legitimate concerns. Something has probably gone wrong if a community of faith feels attacked and threatened by outside evangelists from another religion. None of us want that for our communities. Sometimes persecution of converts comes out of bigotry and closedness, but often persecution is a result of a community feeling threatened by evangelists.

Jews have in the past 1900 years not been evangelistic like Christians and Muslims, although in earlier times they did seek proselytites. It has been claimed that Judaism was the first great missionary religion of the Mediterranean world.[9] An Orthodox Israeli friend confided in me that

8. Krabill et al., *Anabaptists Meeting Muslims*, 424.
9. Torrey, *Jewish Foundation of Islam*, 22.

there is one great commandment that modern Jews have ignored: the command "to be a light unto the Gentiles." It could be an exciting process to re-explore what this commandment might mean in our modern world.

FREEDOM TO CHANGE RELIGIONS

It is essential that people have the freedom to change religions. Any religious system that does not allow people to leave is a prison. If people remain in their present religion only because they are forced to, horrible damage is done to their souls. All barriers to seeking truth must be removed. There is no legitimate justification for keeping people ignorant. Actually, with modern means of communication, it is becoming increasingly difficult to keep people ignorant.

The theological basis for religious freedom is rooted in the belief that each of us is accountable to God for our actions, which presupposes freedom. Belief is not free without freedom to accept or reject that belief. How can we freely worship God without being free? The Qur'an, like the Hebrew and Christian Scriptures, supports and encourages free intellectual inquiry. It is discouraging to learn that free inquiry at various times has been discouraged by elites in all three religions who wanted to protect their power. The Abrahamic Scriptures value knowledge and critical thinking, not ignorance.

The Muslim teaching of no force in religion must include the positive freedom to study and choose without any fear of punishment. The only punishment threatened for apostasy in the Qur'an is in the next world. The Muslim concept of religious freedom is rooted in the Qur'an, in the constitution implemented in Medina, and in the treaty Mohammad made with the pagan rulers in Mecca, which allowed Mohammad and 2,000 of his followers in year seven of the Hijarh to make a pilgrimage to Mecca. This treaty recognized the right of people to freely teach and practice their religions. We should note that neither the church in Rome or Constantinople at the time supported freedom of religion for non-Christians.

For me, coming out of my Anabaptist tradition, freedom of religion is rooted in adult believers' baptism, in my responsibility to choose the forms of my relationship with God. My parents, my culture, my government cannot make that decision for me. We cannot force anyone, because ultimately only God can give inner guidance to people.

There are people in every religion, who for many different reasons, cannot find spiritual peace in the religion of their parents, but do find fulfillment and meaning in another religion. These conversions often involve much pain for all involved, but it is possible to rejoice whenever someone has found a new and deeper relationship with God. Sadly, people often pay a high price for converting to another religion. They lose inheritance, family ties, everything. Sometimes they face death. It is troubling that anyone would be punished for seeking to draw closer to God.

A personal example may help illustrate the need for freedom and grace. I do not go around saying, "Praise the Lord." Somehow, the phrase triggers something negative in me. Maybe I heard it misused too often. I received a gift of grace in my life when I was introduced to the Arabic word, "Ilhamdililah," which means, "Praise God." Muslims, and Christians in the Muslim world, use the word repeatedly. I immediately fell in love with the word and it soon became an important part of my devotional life. Now I say the word, "Ilhamdililah" at least a hundred times every day. But I still have problems with the phrase, "Praise the Lord." Thank God for grace.

I personally know of people who have converted from each of the Abrahamic religions to one of the other religions. I have been present when conversions to Islam, Judaism, and Christianity were celebrated. Why not rejoice when someone has found a new and deeper relationship with God? To come to know God through a religion other than the religion in which one was born is not apostasy. Coming to know God is something to be celebrated.

A person who converted from Christianity to Islam told me he never knew about a personal relationship with God until he became a Muslim. Something went wrong in his upbringing. It is a common belief among Christians, as with Muslims, that one can have a personal relationship with God. But that was never communicated to him. He found what he was looking for in Islam, even though it was all around him in his Christian community. We can rejoice that he found this relationship with God.

IS JESUS THE ONLY WAY?

Jesus said, "I am the way, the truth, and the life. No one comes to the father except through me."[10] What does that mean? Whatever it means,

10. John 14:6.

it does not say that only Christians can have a relationship with God and go to heaven. This is only one of the many references in John's Gospel to I AM statements of Jesus. Was Jesus claiming to be God, or was he identifying with the I AM that Moses encountered in the burning bush, the Creator and Sustainer of the universe, the I AM who encounters people of faith everywhere? How can anyone come to God without encountering the great I AM? Brian Arthur Brown put it this way:

> Abraham experienced the "I AM" and was accounted righteous because of his response. Moses heard the "I AM" and what transpired became the core code of Hebrew religion. Jesus articulated the "I AM" and embodied the messianic principle to the extent that his followers feel fully justified in calling him the Messiah. Finally, Mohammad bore witness to the "I AM" in reporting the revelation concerning the burning bush in the Qur'an where he recites the words of Allah: "I AM the Lord" (10:10) and again "I AM Allah" (28:30).
>
> Rather than being exclusive, the "I AM" texts are supremely inclusive. No matter what name people use for the great "I AM," if they worship the "I AM," they are worshiping God.[11]

There is no other way to God except through encountering the great I AM.

Christians see the I AM embodied and manifested in the life of Jesus. Early Quakers identified the Light of God that enlightens every person with the Light of Christ. That Presence, that Power that some people refer to as the Living Christ, is available to all people. All that is needed is humility, openness, and trust.

If it is true that only through Jesus can we have a relationship with God, then when a Muslim or a Jew finds a relationship with God, the Christian can simply rejoice in the work of Jesus Christ in that person, even though that person does not use the name of Jesus. Why would a Christian not affirm that the atoning work of Jesus applies to all humanity? My wife's uncle used to tell the story of a Nigerian animist, who after becoming a Christian, said that he had known Jesus for a long time, but that he had never known his name before.

This idea is a "stumbling block" for many Jews and Muslims, an area that needs more dialogue. Since Christians do not agree on the meaning of this, the dialogue can be helpful also for Christians.

11. Brown, *Noah's Other Son*, 199–200.

First we need to convince Christians that Jesus is the way, the truth, and the life. One Sunday I visited an evangelical Christian congregation. The sermon was "Jesus is the only way." The preacher made a big point of saying Jesus is the only way, but said little about that way, that truth, that life. As he preached I kept glancing at the American flag to which the congregation had just pledged allegiance. They had just prayed for U. S. soldiers at war, but not for the soldiers of our "enemies." Did they believe that Jesus is the only way? The pastor later told me that in spite of what Jesus said, he would kill anyone who threatened his family and he would kill anyone his government asked him to kill. Apparently he did not believe Jesus is the only way, or even the best way. How high one's view of Jesus is depends on the extent to which one accepts Jesus' Lordship over every area of life.

Jesus' teaching about the Good Shepherd in John 10 is often used to argue that Jesus is the Shepherd and that there is no other way into the fold except through Jesus. If this is true, it does not necessarily exclude non-Christians from knowing and following the voice of the Good Shepherd. In fact, Jesus says, "I have other sheep that are not of this fold; I must bring them also, and they will heed my voice. So there shall be one flock, one shepherd."[12]

This reminds me of my work in the Palestinian village of At-Tuwani. The Israeli military had prevented Palestinian shepherds from grazing their sheep on their own land. With international accompaniment, a dozen or more shepherds each day would combine their flocks in order not be isolated out in the hills, and go on land where they had not been allowed to graze for as much as six years. At the end of each day, the shepherds would call their sheep, and all the sheep would follow their own shepherd, and go home. Each sheep knew its shepherd. Any person, no matter what religion, who knows the voice of the Shepherd can follow that voice. Yes, there is only one true Shepherd. Anyone who follows the voice of thieves, of imposters, of oppressors, is being led to destruction. The voice of God leads to life.

One of the questions I have wrestled with during the past 20 years is how can I proclaim the good news of Jesus to Muslims and Jews. How can I articulate the gospel in ways that can speak to Muslims and Jews, in ways that they can hear? I want them to understand my Christian faith.

12. John 10:16.

The answer is not for Christians to pick off a few individuals here and there and make Christians out of them, and in the process increase suspicion between the three religions. I can rejoice in the spiritual rebirth people experience in converting from one religion to another, but I doubt that increased competition between the three faiths is a good answer.

On September 14, 2008, Peggy and I spoke to the Chiques Church of the Brethren in Eastern Pennsylvania about our peace work in the Middle East. Afterward, concerns were raised in the congregation about whether we do evangelism, and whether we believe Jesus is the only way. The congregation ended up inviting us to come back and continue the conversation. On October 22, we returned to Pennsylvania and met with about 75 members of the congregation for an open and intense discussion of their concerns. We complimented them for their openness and honesty in sharing their concerns with us, and for their willingness to talk through their concerns. Too often, people have concerns, but refuse to openly discuss them. We ended up having an intense, honest, and loving discussion of these contentious issues. We tried to listen carefully to their concerns.

We began with a discussion of evangelism, explaining to them that we do not proselytize, but that we see everything we do as pointing people to God's love expressed in Jesus, and witnessing to God's redemptive activity in the world.

We then turned to the question of whether Jesus is the only way, presenting some of the Scriptures and theology spelled out in this book, demonstrating that throughout the Bible, both non-Jews and non-Christians are described as people of deep faith. We affirmed that it is through that Reality that Christians see incarnated in Jesus that we are saved.

We did not all agree. Some in the congregation believe strongly that only Christians can be saved. But we engaged in honest dialogue in a loving spirit, and who knows how God will use that dialogue.

MIXING RELIGIONS?

A common concern people raise when the subject of inter-religious dialogue is mentioned is syncretism, the mixing of religions. There is a legitimate concern that dialogue can result in a watered down, lowest common denominator, vague, new religion. That is not the subject of this book. I have no intention of compromising my faith for the sake of anything, nor do I want others to compromise their faith. Integrity is essential to dialogue. Without integrity the whole enterprise becomes mush. We can move beyond both triumphalism and relativism.

There are dividing lines between religions, boundaries of experience, theology, and practice, that are expressions of deep wisdom, boundaries that are simply different and do not mesh easily with other boundaries, boundaries that also are important and need to be respected. Take away those boundaries between two religions and something vital will be lost in at least one of the religions. Each religion is an expression of deep truths given by God. Each community can affirm a unique relationship to the Truth, rooted in a unique revelation. Those truths are too important to be blurred. Examples would include understandings of God, salvation, ethics, etc. Often those distinctions are sharper and clearer within each religion than between religions. For example, my Anabaptist heritage is too important to compromise away to mainline Protestantism or evangelicalism.

I totally reject blind mixing of religions and philosophies with seeming disregard for truth or consistency. There may be many paths to the one Truth, but there is one Truth, even if our understanding of that Truth is always quite partial. Although it has often been compromised, there is a devotion to truth in the Abrahamic religions. Syncretism easily tolerates contradictions and has little concern for Truth. Syncretism is incorporating new elements that contradict and compromise the integrity of a religion. The result usually is a bland, tasteless civil religion. A critical spirit is not appreciated in syncretism.

Some religious organizations advertise themselves as being open to all religions and sometimes include the symbols for twelve or more religions in their logos. I admire their openness and spirit of tolerance, but I always wonder about their commitment to any standards of truth. All paths to God are not equal. It is too simplistic to say, "We are all saying the same thing." We are not all saying the same things. This is not real dialogue, nor is it very interesting.

To relativize our faith is to deny the possibility of real dialogue and leaves us with mere tolerance, which can be another form of Western arrogance rooted in the Enlightenment. It may mean seeing secular values as superior to religious faith. It is also a form of imperialism to see other religions as Christian when they are not Christian. The idea that all religions are equal and essentially the same is a threat to dialogue, because since we all believe the same thing, there is no "other" with whom to dialogue and nothing to dialogue about. Relativism is a sophisticated way of refusing to recognize the integrity of the other. All religions are not the same. Why would I want to dialogue with any group that has no claim to uniqueness?

For a balanced perspective, we need an understanding of both particular and universal truth. The Abrahamic religions affirm both the particular and universal, therefore we cannot sacrifice the particulars of our faith for the sake of dialogue, which in effect would seriously depreciate the value and integrity of dialogue. Even the universality of God is weakened, for God is understood through particular revelations and experiences.

There are true and false religions. All religions are not equal. There is the true and the false within all religions. Some values, some understandings of God, humanity and salvation are to be resisted. There are theologies within the Christian church that I find abhorrent. I wrestle with to what degree I can work with elements within each of the three religions that are patently false, hateful, racist, sexist, etc.

Syncretism actually makes interfaith dialogue more difficult. For any of us to share our faith with integrity, we must first disentangle and separate our faith from all the perversions that are attached to it through the marriage of religion with empire and culture. Dialogue will be difficult if our faith is mixed with nationalism, patriotism, racism, materialism, or any other form of idolatry, because these isms muddle the heart of our faith. These isms lead to condescending views of people who share different beliefs. Often what many people identify as essentials of their faith are actually modern ideas that are not part of our original religions. When the spiritual arrogance of believing I am superior to other people is added to the mix, dialogue becomes nearly impossible.

One Sunday morning after preaching in a church in Ohio, an elderly man, who had been in the military during World War II, expressed his deep displeasure with what I had said in my sermon. After spending some time listening to his concerns, I asked him what I had said that he thought contradicted the message of Jesus or the New Testament. Quite angrily, he replied, "I don't care about Jesus or the New Testament. I believe in defending my country!" Apparently for this man, the violent defense of his country was more important than any commitment to the Christian faith. His mixing anti-Christian attitudes with his Christian faith made dialogue difficult. When political philosophy trumps our religious beliefs, we are in trouble. What does any religion have to say to others if that religion is captive of any secular power or ideology?

The issue is not mixing religions. There is much mixing of religions in the Bible. Both Babylonian and Greek religious views had important influence on Biblical thought, for example. Even The Ten Commandments have roots in other Near Eastern religions. There is a strong Jewish and Christian influence in the Qur'an. All three Abrahamic religions have deep roots in paganism, but they are not a mishmash of these influences. They are the result of intense dialogue with the pagan world, a dialogue guided and influenced by God's Spirit, just as we hope God's Spirit influences our dialogue.

There are distinctives in each religion that are precious and need to be respected. What a loss it would be if the three Abrahamic religions were compressed into one new religion. Each religion has its own integrity and uniqueness that must be respected. The question is, how can God speak to each of the three religions through the other religions? How can Jews and Muslims come to accept the truth revealed in Jesus? How can Muslims and Christians rediscover their Hebraic roots in Judaism? How can Jews and Christians come to accept the revelation that has come through Mohammad? This does not mean a mish-mash, lowest common denominator combination of the three religions. It could mean people in all three religions finding increased depth and integrity in their own faith, along with close relationships and respect between the three religions.

I have heard of a man who practices five religions. He has a small room in his house for each religion. Whenever he is in one of those rooms praying, he is sure to have the doors closed to the other four rooms, because he does not in any way want to mix religions. I respect the concern, but when I say that I am a Muslim, Christian, and Jew, I am not saying that I have three religions. I have one faith. My life is not divided into separate compartments. When the early Christians daily went to worship in the Jewish temple in Jerusalem, they were not practicing two religions. They had one faith.

There are many ways, but only one true way. It is narrow and requires commitment, intentionality, and sacrifice. It means choosing, discerning, claiming truth over falsehood. We do not just go with the wind. There is one way, one truth, one God.

≈ FIVE ≈

Similarities and Differences in the Three Religions

I T SHOULD NOT BE surprising to find striking similarities in the poetry, prayers, and writings of different religions. One should expect similarities if various writings are inspired by the same Spirit. This does not mean acceptance of everything in all religions. Not all religious writings and views are from God. One can find disgusting views expressed in all religions, including some of the vindictive and sexist views expressed in the Bible and the Muslim Hadith. Discernment is needed in all matters of faith.

From both personal experience and historical study, it is clear to me that people in all three religions have experienced the transforming power of God's grace. People respond in various ways to God's work, yet there are many common threads in those responses. Sometimes people may use very different words to express their faith, maybe even language that sounds contradictory or offensive to people of other faiths. But on closer examination, often behind those different theologies lie the same profound truths. It is also possible to use similar words with very different meanings.

For example, I do not believe in reincarnation. But I can see in the doctrine of reincarnation the truth that everything we do has eternal consequences (karma), something I also believe. Thus, although I do not believe in reincarnation, I accept the truth inherent in the doctrine. We reap what we sow. The judgment of God is sure. We cannot escape the consequences of our actions. It is eternally important that we live justly, love tenderly, and walk humbly with our God.

Many times in worship among all three religions I hear words of deep faith and meaning that would sound offensive to people in the other religions, yet those words are true. Each of us sees truth from our own narrow, shallow perspectives. Consider the words to an evangelical Christian hymn: "What can wash away my sin? What can make me whole again? Nothing but the blood of Jesus." Many people, not only Muslims and Jews, would find these words offensive and untrue if taken literally. But if the blood of Jesus is interpreted as a symbol of God's grace, then the words of the hymn are true. Nothing but the grace of God can save us. Interfaith dialogue requires sensitive listening and understanding. Many times both sides in an argument are right, but are speaking only part of the truth. When we come in our dialogue to basic differences, we can still affirm the truth implied in the doctrines with which we disagree. It is important not to forget our differences, but even more important to understand those differences.

To properly understand the doctrines of any religion, one must ask what questions or conflicts those doctrines were meant to answer. For example, Paul's writings on justification by grace are related to the conflict between Gentiles and Jews in the early Church and are relevant to interfaith relationships today. The doctrine of justification by grace is Paul's answer to racism and exclusivism. One must also ask about the social and philosophical context out of which those doctrines emerged. Revelation is God's response to specific social contexts. We know that various chapters of the Qur'an were related to specific situations faced by the early Muslim community.

I am learning that in many cases where on the surface there appears to be a contradiction between something in the Qur'an and in the Bible, upon closer examination, these texts do not need to be seen as contradictory. For example, the Qur'an says in Surah 112, "Allah is one. He begets not, nor was he begotten." As a Christian, I have no trouble accepting this important part of the Qur'an. This text does not need to be seen as contradictory to John 1:1, which proclaims that the Word has become flesh, or to John 3:16, which calls Jesus the only begotten son, which can be understood as one of a kind. All Christians would reject the idea that God had sex with Mary who then bore God's son. Christians do not understand sonship and the incarnation so literally.

It is not necessary for Muslims to reject the idea of the Word becoming flesh. Although this is controversial, some commentators have suggested that the Muslim belief that the Word became flesh in the Qur'an is not that different from the Christian idea of the Word becoming flesh in the man Jesus. No Muslim would advocate worshiping the Qur'an, and neither would most Christians worship the flesh of Jesus. Dialogue between Muslims and Christians on this issue could be very creative for both religions.

Another point of contention between Christians and Muslims over the centuries has been the crucifixion of Jesus. Muslims have denied that Jesus was killed by crucifixion, an idea central to Christian thinking.[1] Some Muslim commentators accept that Jesus was crucified.[2] Muslims have theological reasons for believing Jesus could not have been killed by crucifixion. It is inconceivable for Muslims that God could allow God's Messiah to be killed. Since Muslims believe that God is all-powerful, defeat for God is a theological impossibility. Thus Muslim denial of the crucifixion is actually an affirmation that Jesus is the Messiah, and a statement of faith that human sin cannot destroy the Word of God.

There is a possible resolution to this seeming contradiction, without changing either Muslim or Christian understandings of God. Maybe the Qur'an is right in claiming that Jesus was not killed by crucifixion. This is confirmed by a closer reading of all four Gospel crucifixion stories. To be killed by crucifixion took agonizing days of a slow death. Often death came after more than a week of agony. The Gospel accounts say that after a few hours, "Jesus gave up the ghost." They did not kill him. Jesus gave up his life. This is confirmed by Jesus' statement in John 10:18 where Jesus says he will lay down his life. "No one takes it from me, but I lay it down of my own accord." Both the Qur'an and the New Testament are correct. How profound! Jesus gave up his life for us. That has much more meaning than Jesus being killed.

The similarities between the three Abrahamic religions are striking and need to be repeated over and over. This should not be surprising when we recognize that all three religions are branches of the same tree. The early Muslim community included Jews and Christians who helped weave the Jewish and Christian traditions into the formation of Islam.

---

1. Ayoub, "Islamic Christology," 91–121.

2. For references, see Robinson, *Christ in Islam*, 120–22.

Similarities include the oneness and greatness of God who is the Creator and Lord of history, belief in an orderly, moral universe, the rejection of idolatry, the importance of relationship with God, the importance of faith, the affirmation that faith affects all of life, understandings of morality, personal piety, charity, the essential equality of all humanity (social justice), our accountability to God for what we do, the last judgment, and the final victory of good over evil. That is a lot of agreement.

All three religions look back to Moses' experience with the burning bush, when he was encountered by a reality that shook him, transformed him, and in turn shook and transformed the world with the spread of ethical monotheism.

Bernard Lewis points out that, in spite of severe persecution, Judaism in the past two thousand years flourished only in Muslim and Christian lands, possibly because of the close relationship of Judaism with its "two successor religions." Judaism did not fare well under Hinduism, Buddhism, and other religions.[3]

Each of the three religions needs the other two religions for its renewal. The potential contributions of the other two are so great that any renewal without these contributions will be less than it could be. Through dialogue with the other two religions we can be reminded of neglected insights of our own religion. Christianity came from Judaism and can be enriched by rediscovering its Jewish roots. Rediscovering its roots also can enrich Islam, a child of both Judaism and Christianity. Muslims can learn from Judaism and Christianity's longer experience of dealing with modernity. It is impossible for Jews to ignore their Christian and Muslim children. The blood of Abraham still flows in the veins of Jews, Christians, and Muslims.

Sitting through Rosh Hashanah services in the fall of 2008, I was struck again with the similarity between the three Abrahamic religions. How, I wondered, could anyone be a Christian or a Muslim without accepting the Scriptures and the vision of the Jewish faith, which are foundational for Christianity and Islam? Christians and Muslims have much to learn from Judaism. The Hebrew Scriptures are an essential root of both Islam and Christianity. The concept of Torah, the grace of living a life of conformity to God's law instead of cultural conformity to the world systems, can liberate us from slavery to contemporary culture. We can

3. Lewis, *Jews of Islam*, IX.

all benefit from a new recognition of God as both Creator and as Lord of history, the God who brought Israel out of Egypt, the God who acts in history, who demands righteousness and social justice. Many people have identified the essence and contribution of Judaism with ethics. Jews traditionally have had a deep sense of right and wrong, and a vision of a new social order of peace and justice. Judaism includes a deep wisdom of how to relate to the rest of God's creation. Many of the laws in the Torah teach respect for God's creation.

Judaism reminds us of the sacredness of God's name. Too often the name of God has become commonplace for Christians and Muslims, occurring daily in the speech of many, with little apparent meaning or respect. The name of God is bantered about everywhere, by believers, unbelievers, and atheists alike. Often God's name is used in self-serving ways, to support and bless our own self-centeredness and pride. For Jews, the name of G-d (YAHWEH) is too sacred to even pronounce. Can we learn to be silent before God?

Christians and Muslims have much to learn from Jewish biblical scholars, which can lead to new and deeper understandings of both the Bible and the Qur'an. By reconnecting with Judaism, Christians can learn how Christianity became separated from its roots. Christians can see Judaism as an essential connection to Jesus. Without understanding Jesus' Jewishness, Christians can transform Jesus into anything they want Jesus to be, as for example Nazis who rejected the Jewishness of Jesus.

Jews can see Christianity and Islam as fulfillments of God's promise to make Abraham the father of many nations, and rejoice, that through Muslims and Christians, Abrahamic monotheism has been presented to the whole world. Both Islam and Christianity can remind Jews of the universality of God. Jews can learn from Christian and Muslim reinterpretations of the Hebrew Scriptures.

Muslims and Jews have much to learn and their faith can be greatly enriched by a renewed interest in Jesus and the gospel. Muslims and Jews can learn from Christian emphasis on the presence and intimacy of God, the emphasis on love and forgiveness, the concept of nonviolent, self-giving love of neighbor and enemy, and hopes for reconciliation and redemption. Maybe it will be through the Qur'an and Islam that Jews will be able to take a new look at Jesus and Jewish messianic scriptures.

Since Islam is a reaction to perversions of Christianity, Christians can ask how Islam can be a corrective for Christian understandings of the gospel. Jews and Christians can learn from the Muslim emphasis on the transcendence of God, the importance of social justice, the unity of the sacred and the secular, the religious and the political, and the spiritual discipline in Islam. Jesus said, "Unless your righteousness exceeds that of the Pharisees, you cannot enter the kingdom of God." Could Christians use the word "Muslims" in place of "Pharisees"? Muslims pray five times a day, fast for one month each year, and live lives of devotion to God. Christians, especially, need to accept the challenges of Islam in their own religious lives.

In reconnecting to its Jewish roots and the challenge of Islam, Christians might rethink their marriage of church with oppressive social and political structures, the corrupting influence of Hellenistic pagan culture and theology, and the centralization of authority in a hierarchical church. Christians need to hear Muslim critiques of praying to God through any intermediaries. Dialogue with Jews and Muslims will force Christians to rethink who Jesus was.

The three religions need each other in their understandings of God. For Jews and Christians, God is like a father who cares for his children. God is like the prophet Hosea who married a prostitute to demonstrate God's unfailing love for us sinners. God is like a good shepherd who seeks the lost sheep. In the Qur'an, God is transcendent, an important message for those who want to create God in their own image.

Not all the differences between the three religions can be reconciled. Differences will remain. None of us is wise enough to know all the answers. Syncretism is not the answer. The integrity of each religion needs to be maintained. In no way should the identity of any group be collapsed into the others. Christianity is not a replacement for Judaism, and neither is Islam a replacement for Judaism and Christianity. All three religions were called into being by God and exist as the people of God.

Let's look at some difficult issues: Scripture, Jesus, grace, the cross, and the Trinity.

SCRIPTURE

One day I was carrying a Bible on the streets of Hebron, returning from having led a worship service for our team in a park. An Israeli soldier stopped me and asked to see my Bible. He opened the Bible to the beginning and started reading the book of Genesis. He expressed surprise that the words in my Bible were the same as in his Torah.

Jews, Christians, and Muslims are "People of the Book," in that their faith is rooted in Scripture. All three religions are based on and are responses to God's revelation, which in turn was interactive with what was happening at the time of the revelation. The codification of law and morality, as symbolized by the Ten Commandments, laid the foundation for much of human civilization. To some extent the ideals of the Scriptures of all three religions have been adopted by secular society: integrity, justice for all, equal rights for all people, the importance of literacy and education, freedom, tolerance, and peace. All these ideals are rooted in God's revelations through the prophets.

People gathering around a book and allowing that book to inform their lives, conduct, and loyalties gives that people cultural and spiritual integrity separate from political and economic institutions, effectively limiting the power of those institutions. The identity of that people transcends the limits of their own society. Justice, for example, is rooted in and understood through Scripture, not in the edicts of kings and empires.

A possible fruitful area for dialogue is the important differences in understandings of what revelation is. Revelation means unveiled, uncovered, discovered. For Muslims, revelation is something "sent down" (tanzil) from God, while for Jews and some Christians, revelation is God's acting in history. However, the Qur'an was not simply dictated to Mohammad. Often a revelation resulted in deep, painful searching on Mohammad's part to receive and understand the message. Mohammad was not simply passive. In the Bible, revelation comes through people inspired by God. The ultimate revelation for Christians is the Word becoming flesh in the man Jesus. Revelation is embedded in human personality and culture. The Bible is the story of God's self-revelation to people through the events of history.

The Bible and the Qur'an are not about us, but about what God is doing in the world, about God's seeking us, reaching out to us. Included in Jewish prayer books are these words about Scripture from Hillel the Elder.

> When Torah entered the world, freedom entered it. The whole Torah exists only to establish peace. Its first and last aim is to teach love and kindness. What is hateful to you, do not do to others. That is the whole Torah; all the rest is commentary.

The Bible and Qur'an are living books, continually inspiring new insights, new faith. For me, the authority of Scripture is affirmed by the depth, the power, and the truth I experience each time I encounter Scripture. The universality of any Scripture is affirmed in its being heard in the midst of our pain and struggle for liberation. Rather than frozen in time and space, Scripture is a living word that continually can speak to us with new power and authority. When people lock themselves into a particular interpretation of Scripture, they are placing more authority in their interpretations of Scripture than in Scripture itself. Commentaries can become more authoritative than the Scripture itself. Traditional interpretations of Scripture are not the last word, because God continues to speak to us through Scripture.

A significant problem between the three religions is the unwillingness of most people to take seriously and accept the legitimacy of the Scriptures of the other two religions. Jews do not accept Christian or Muslim scriptures. Christians do not accept the Qur'an, and although Christians in various degrees do accept the Jewish Scriptures, many have big problems in reconciling the Jewish and Christian Scriptures.

Muslims give lip service to the Torah, Psalms, and Gospels having been revealed by God, but do not take them seriously or wrestle with the problems of reconciling the Bible and the Qur'an. Muslims say they accept all the prophets, but they don't. Most Muslims accept only one prophet and give lip service to the other prophets. Their answer is simply to say that since the text of the Bible has been corrupted and the Qur'an is a complete revelation, why bother? Although the Qur'an refers to Christians and Jews changing the words of their faith, the Qur'an does not say that the Jewish and Christian Scriptures are corrupted and worthless.[4] That is a later Muslim interpretation and needs to be rejected. The Qur'an says that Christian and Jewish Scriptures teach essentially the same doctrines as the Qur'an, but that Christians and Jews have strayed from the truth of their Scriptures. Muslims must go beyond the brief descriptions of Judaism and Christianity in the Qur'an and study the Jewish and Christian Scriptures if they want to understand Judaism and Christianity.

Although untrue, some Muslims have told me that it is forbidden for Muslims to read the Bible. This is unfortunate, because it cuts Muslims off from an important part of God's revelation. The Jesus of Islam has been

---

4. Qur'an 2:75, 4:46, 5:13, and 5:41.

completely Islamicized, stripped of almost all of his teachings. Through the Christian Scriptures Muslims can come to a more complete understanding of Jesus. Islam would be enriched if it put more emphasis on the biblical themes of grace, love, and redemption. To give more credence to the biblical scriptures would be to truly embrace all of God's prophets and all of God's messages to humanity.

Too often Scriptures have been used to build walls and divide people, instead of seeing Scripture as common ground. Instead of questioning the legitimacy of each other's Scriptures, we can appreciate both the fascinating points of agreement and the diversity in understandings of the greatness and glory of God. There are statements in the Scriptures of each religion that are offensive to people in the other religions. The challenge for all of us is to try to understand the context and meanings of those offensive passages and to recognize that God's Truth is so much bigger than our small understandings. The Golden Rule of treating others as we want to be treated can be applied to our interpretations of other Scriptures. We can study how the people of any religion interpret their own Scriptures.[5] Each religion has limited its understandings of its own Scriptures by not learning from the Scriptures of the other two.

We can begin to solve the problem by studying each other's Scriptures and all be enriched in the process. I have found in my accepting the validity of all three Scriptures a complementary richness and depth that is more than one can find in any one of the Scriptures. During a Rosh Hashanah service in Athens, Ohio, on September 12, 2007, the rabbi quoted a passage about God's grace from the Qur'an in her sermon. I have heard quotes from the Bible in sermons in the mosque. That is moving in the right direction.

In December 2008, we read Psalm 80 in our team worship in At-Tuwani. When I heard words like, "Restore us, O God; let your face shine, that we may be saved," I thought of how the Palestinian Muslims in the village would hear those words, and how differently the nearby Israeli settlers would interpret the same words. Maybe an essential part of Scriptural

---

5. A good example of taking each others' Scriptures seriously is John Kalter's excellent book, *Ishmael Instructs Isaac: An Introduction to the Qur'an for Bible Readers,* which compares stories and characters common to the Qur'an and the Bible, showing both commonalities and differences in those Scriptures, and demonstrating how taking each others' Scriptures seriously can enhance the understanding of one's own Scriptures. A good example would be to compare the biblical and Qur'anic stories of Jonah.

interpretation is to consider how other groups, particularly groups we are in conflict with, would interpret the Scriptures we are interpreting. I wondered what it would mean for the settlers and the Palestinian villagers to study Psalm 80 together. People in all three religions too often use Scripture to support domination and oppression.

I recently read a Christian tract arguing that the moral and spiritual crisis in Christianity is the result of not believing in the absolute authority and inerrancy of the Bible. The author did not spell out what that means concretely. The author did not recognize that people with his belief tend to be more racist and more militaristic than the general U.S. population. Neither did the author point out the wide disagreement concerning the meaning of a literal interpretation of the Bible. Would a literal interpretation lead us to be pacifist or militarist? Should we kill rebellious children? Should we stone adulterers, as is commanded in the Bible?

Questions of the nature of inspiration and inerrancy of Scripture are deeply divisive within and between the three religions, and will need to be part of the dialogue at some point, but not the starting point. This raises questions of God's continued guidance, whether we can continue listening to God's Spirit, and be open to new truth. We need not fear the tools of textual, historical, literary, or linguistic scholarship in the study of Scripture.

All three religions have wrestled with the question of the relative importance of tradition and Scripture: the Torah versus the "Oral Torah," or Jesus versus church tradition, or the Qur'an versus the *Sunnah* and the commentaries. In Judaism, the *Talmud* and *Halakhah* replaced the Torah, in Catholicism, church law eclipsed Scripture, and in Islam, the Sunnah, the *Tafsir*, and *Shariah* have taken precedence over the Qur'an.

Christians feel the need to affirm the finality of God's revelation in Jesus in a similar way that Muslims affirm the finality of God's revelation in the Qur'an. This does not negate the possibility of further revelation, but for Christians, further revelation, if true, will not contradict the revelation we have in Jesus. The Qur'an refers to Mohammad as "the seal of the prophets,"[6] which simply means that Mohammad confirmed the validity of the previous prophets and that the Qur'an is authoritative. It does not mean that God is barred from continuing to speak to humanity.

6. Qur'an 33:40.

New revelations build on previous revelations. The Muslim understanding that drinking alcohol is contrary to God's ultimate purpose for humans and causes untold suffering does not need to be seen as a contradiction of the Torah or gospel, where drinking alcohol is permitted, but rather can be seen as taking the concerns of the Torah and gospel to new levels. Islam at first permitted drinking alcohol but prohibited drunkenness. In later revelations, God made it clear that all drinking of alcohol is prohibited. What a blessing it would be if all people of faith would accept this revelation.

In the same way, the revelation of God in people like Gandhi or Martin Luther King takes the concerns in the Hebrew, Christian, and Muslim Scriptures for justice, mercy, and forgiveness to new levels. We also can move to new levels by rejecting violence and bigotry. Exciting possibilities lie before us if we base our discernment of God's will in the Jewish, Christian, and Muslim Scriptures.

JESUS

Who was Jesus? This question has been especially divisive for the relationship of Christians with Jews and Muslims.

The whole history of Christian oppression of Jews and the extent to which that oppression involved the question of Jesus makes the question of Jesus a doubly difficult issue for Jews. Christians need to understand that when Jews do not want to hear the name of Jesus, it is because for many Jews, the name of Jesus means oppression. It is difficult for a Jew to accept that the Messiah came two thousand years ago, after which Jews suffered so deeply. They certainly have not experienced the redemption they would associate with the coming of the Messiah. The pain is so deep that many Jews accept that one can be both Jewish and atheist, but not both Jewish and Christian. Rejection of Jesus being the Messiah has become an essential issue for Jewish identity and survival.

In this new day, what would it mean for Jews to accept Jesus as a great Jewish prophet, to recognize his Jewishness? Can Jews see Jesus as a successor to Moses, who gave new meaning to Jewishness? There is much modern Jewish literature about Jesus, much of which emphasizes the Jewishness of Jesus in distinction to the Hellenized Jesus of the church. Martin Buber was a pioneer in Jewish reconsideration of Jesus. In his important book, *I and Thou*, Buber engages in profound dialogue with the message of the Christian Gospels. Buber looked to Jesus as "my great brother," and went so far as to claim that Jesus has an important place in the history of Jewish faith.[7] This book is a serious wrestling with the Christian gospel and its relationship to Judaism. Buber claims that Jews and Christians have much to learn from each other.[8]

Jesus is the bridge between Islam and Christianity. Jesus is the most revered person in the Qur'an. Muslims have no problem accepting Jesus as Messiah. In fact, there is more about Jesus in the Qur'an than about Mohammad. Muslims honor Jesus. Muslims believe Jesus was born of a virgin. The Qur'an says Jesus was the Word (*kahimatullah*) of God and the Spirit (*ruhallah*) of God.[9] Muslims believe Jesus will return to rule the earth. I have often heard Muslims say they believe Jesus will return soon. A Muslim friend told me that in his later days, his father often listened to the Qur'an on tape. He said that whenever he listened to Sura "Miriam," he could understand why Christians would worship Jesus. Mohammad recognized claims about Jesus that he never claimed for himself. Sufis have had a high view of Jesus as a perfect man who will bring all of humanity to God.[10]

The Qur'an says that God breathed his Spirit into Mary and Jesus was conceived.[11] Although there is not agreement on the meaning of these verses, it is clear according to the Qur'an that something unique and special happened in the conception and birth of Jesus. On that Christians and Muslims can agree.

The sticking point for Muslims is whether Jesus was the Son of God. For Muslims, to put anything equal to God is idolatry (*shirk*). As we said before, the Christian understanding of sonship is not about genetics or sex, but rather about Jesus' special relationship with God. In fact, many Christians believe that we all are God's children, all are the sons and daughters of God. Some commentators distinguish the two Arabic words for son, *walad* referring to offspring, and *ibn* signifying relationship. For Christians, Jesus is the ibn of God.

7. Buber, *Two Types of Faith*, 12–13.

8. For a short history of Jewish interest in Jesus, see Novak, *Jewish-Christian Dialogue: a Jewish Justification*, 73–92.

9. Qur'an 4:171; 3:44, 4:41.

10. For a comparison of the Jesus of the New Testament and the Qur'an, see Heikki Raisanen, "The portrait of Jesus in the Qur'an," 122–33.

11. Qur'an 21:90–91; 62:12.

Whatever the early Christians believed about Jesus, it is clear that they were monotheistic Jews who saw no contradiction between their belief in Jesus as Messiah and their monotheism. They did not consider themselves to be polytheistic. The idea of sonship meaning divinity was not part of early Christian thinking. That came later in debates about the Trinity. The term "son of God" as a reference to Jesus as Messiah (King) looks back to the Israelites referring to their kings as sons of God when they were coronated.[12] This had no hint of divinity for the Hebrews. The term "son of God" was a common title given to emperors and kings during the time of Jesus. Roman coins at the time of Jesus carried an image of Caesar and carried the inscription, "Long live the son of God." A sign with the title, "son of God" was attached to Jesus' cross to mock Jesus by calling him a political leader. When the early Christians called Jesus "the son of God," they meant that the Roman emperor was not the son of God, and instead they pledged their allegiance to Jesus. Calling Jesus "son of God" referred to his mission, not his divinity. The term can be equated to what the Qur'an calls Jesus' being elevated to God.[13]

Only later did Christians change it into "Son of God," to indicate divinity. If the term is used, it should be understood metaphorically, referring to Jesus' close relationship to God. It means that Jesus was dependent upon and in submission to God, his Father. The term also points to the authority Jesus received from God. Jesus had the authority to forgive sins, an authority that has also been given to us.[14] In Col 1:15–17, Jesus has a high role, the first of creation, but he is not God. Jesus is Messiah, Suffering Servant, Lamb of God, High Priest, Mediator between God and humanity, Son of Man, and Word of God.

The disciples of Jesus did not think of Jesus as God, but they were aware of the powerful and transforming presence of God in Jesus. Through Jesus, God's presence became real to them. They experienced God's love in Jesus. This experience was different than the philosophizing that came later as intellectuals tried to explain and interpret the reality of love becoming flesh. The experience of God in the man Jesus is central to Christian faith. But a Christian does not need to believe the philosophizing of fourth-century intellectuals. The incarnation of God's perfect love was unique in Jesus, but God's Spirit of love can also become real in our lives.

12. Psalm 2.

13. Qur'an 3:55; 4:158.

14. Mark 2:1–12.

Muslim views of Jesus are not that different from early Christian views. Ideas about Jesus being God came later out of a Hellenized church, after Christians had rejected Judaism. Maybe conversations between the three religions about Jesus could be more fruitful if we started with early Jewish Christianity.

Who was Jesus? First, Christians believe that Jesus was a man, totally human. He experienced the same struggles that we face. He was not a god, not someone without limitations, temptations, or doubts. He prayed to God, asked God for strength and guidance, and claimed that he could do nothing except by God's power.

Christians believe that in the man Jesus, God entered history in a decisive way. Jesus revealed the nature of God in a unique, authoritative way. This does not contradict God acting uniquely in forming the Hebrew people or through Mohammad. Christians believe and experience that God loves us unconditionally. That love has been revealed to us in the life of Jesus the Messiah. When we come to know the love of Jesus, we come to know God. The presence of God's Spirit empowers us to love as God loves us.

This is not a question of metaphysics. The Hebrew word "Messiah," or "Christ" in Greek, is a political term, like lord or king. Jesus, the Lamb of God, is a king who rules as a servant. To accept Jesus as Messiah is to follow him, to accept his teachings as moral imperatives. For Christians, ethics should be rooted in the person of Jesus. I believe that the teachings, life, and death of Jesus are normative for us today.

The Christian Scriptures see Jesus as more than a prophet. In Jesus we have something more than a word from God. In Jesus the Word became flesh. But what does that mean? People want to know what God is like. What can we know about God? Christians affirm that the clearest picture we have of God is what we see in Jesus. In Jesus we hear not only words, but see the living out of those words. The Incarnation points to the unity of Jesus' teaching and his life, what he said and did and who he was. In Jesus, the Word became flesh. The Word became something we can see, something we can imitate. The words, "the divinity of Christ," do not necessarily mean that Jesus was God, but that in Jesus we can see something of God, that God was in Jesus in a special, unique way. Christians believe that the Word of God is also incarnate in the church, but the church is not God.

Muhammad Legenhausen, in his preface to a fascinating Muslim book on Jesus, lays the basis for creative possibilities for dialogue about who Jesus was.

> To call Christ the Word of Allah is not to deify him, but to verify his status as prophet. Because of his high status as prophet, Jesus becomes a complete manifestation of God, one who conveys the message of God, one who can speak on behalf of God, and thus, the Word of God. Jesus becomes the Word of God not because of an incarnation whereby his flesh becomes divine, but because his spirit is refined to such an extent that it becomes a mirror whereby divinity comes to be known. The temple is holy not because of any inherent sanctity in the structure, but because it is the place of the worship of God.[15]

Jesus came with a universal message. Three times the Qur'an refers to Jesus as a "sign of God for all people."[16]

Part of the objection of some Muslims comes out of an objection to the Christian understanding of intimacy with God. Christians see themselves as children of God, "abiding in God and God abiding in us." Christians reject the idea of humans becoming God, but accept the idea of God's Spirit entering human life. The Qur'an says that God breathed his spirit into humanity.[17]

GRACE-LAW

Maybe the central story of grace for all three religions is God choosing Israel, not for any special merit Israel had, not because Israel had done anything important, not because Israel was special. In both the Bible and the Qur'an, it is clear that God led the Israelites out of Egypt in spite of their lack of faith, their complaining, and their readiness to worship other gods. In spite of their unfaithfulness, God never abandoned the Israelites. In the same way, God accepts us even though we are unacceptable. God shows mercy to us even though we have done nothing to deserve mercy. That is grace.

---

15. Qua'im, *Jesus Through the Qur'an*, 13. For another interesting collection of Muslim understandings of Jesus, see Khalidi, *The Muslim Jesus*.

16. Qur'an 19:21; 21:91; and 23:50.

17. Ibid., 32:7; 2:31; and 15:29.

What can babies do to earn the love of their parents? Nothing. The love of parent for a child is simply given. It is a gift. God's love for us is even greater.

Muslims sometimes claim that Judaism emphasizes law and Christianity grace, while Islam has the correct combination of law and grace. Christians commonly refer to the legalism of Judaism, yet have little understanding of how observant Jews understand the law. Often Christians use Jesus and Paul as examples of rejection of the law, and fail to realize the depth of their commitment to the law.

Paul rejected the idea that people can become righteous and favored by God by following religious regulations, an idea that soon turns into the racist idea that God loves my people more than other people, because we are better than other people. Paul does not reject following Torah as a legitimate spirituality, as long as it is not forgotten that salvation is by God's grace alone. Good people also need salvation. We all are dependent on God's mercy. Being good is not good enough. Most any Jew at the time of Paul would have agreed.

Another problem with law is to understand sin as external behavior that can be avoided and resisted. This shallow view can easily lead to pride and self-righteousness, because if I avoid certain behaviors I am good, or at least better than other sinners, and have no need of God's transforming grace. We can become completely oblivious of the depth of human alienation and bondage. All of us need to be transformed and given new hearts, to have God's law written on our hearts, to become new creatures in Christ.

One can often hear Christians say that Judaism is a religion of law, not grace, that Judaism is obsessed with trivia and details. But Christians miss the deeper meanings behind Jewish rules and regulations. Torah means not law to be obeyed, but teaching to be fulfilled in one's life, a life that comes out of love and devotion to God. Paul understood this when he wrote, "love is the fulfilling of the law."[18]

Consider the Jewish practice of not cooking meat and dairy products together, a practice derived from "building a fence around the Torah." The Torah forbids boiling a lamb in its mother's milk. To be sure they are not violating God's command, Jews do not cook or eat meat and dairy products together in the same meal. To be really sure they are not violating

18. Rom 13:8–10.

God's command, they have separate dishes and cooking ware for meat and dairy. This is called building a fence around the Torah. It is a way of showing the deepest respect for Torah. For Jews, observing the rules of Torah is not about earning salvation, but rather about maintaining their identity as God's people over against the pagan world around them. The law was visible proof that they belonged to God, not to Babylon. Torah is about living a liberated lifestyle.

Not wasting natural resources is a deep concern of mine. I try not to waste anything. I try to recycle everything. Recently I was at a dinner in which I ate three huge olives. I quietly put the seeds in my pocket, took those three seeds home, and added them to my compost pile. I know that saving the miniscule amount of precious nutrients in those three little olive seeds is quite insignificant in terms of global resources. But not wasting those three seeds by putting them in a landfill is incredibly important in respect to my integrity. If I cannot be faithful in something as small as a little olive seed, how can I expect to be faithful in something big, which might entail sacrifice or even suffering? It was not legalistic to save those three olive seeds. It was a tiny step toward responsible stewardship of the earth and recognizing God's ownership of the earth.

It is not legalism to develop cultural practices, such as not eating meat and dairy together or not eating pork, that are expressions of a deep faith. It is not legalism to put olive seeds in the compost pile. There is something profound in religion being a way of life. Throughout all of the Hebrew Scriptures there is a profound sense of God's grace and mercy. God is "merciful and gracious, slow to anger, and abounding in steadfast love and faithfulness."[19] In my experience of worshiping in Jewish synagogues, I have found not a rigid legalism, but rather a liberating sense of God's grace.

On the most holy day in the Jewish year, Yom Kippur, the promise of God's forgiveness and atonement is offered, even though we have failed in the previous year. The congregation is even released from all the commitments they made in the past year but did not keep. That is grace.

On the subject of law, Judaism and Islam are quite similar, both in the scope and meaning of law. Shariah and Halakah are quite similar. In fact, there probably was a strong influence of Halakah in the development of Shariah.

19. Exod 34:6.

There is no more of a problem with Muslim law (Shariah) being rooted in the Qur'an than in Western law being rooted in the Hebrew and Christian scriptures. There is a problem when law is used to promote personal power, oppress others, and deny mercy and grace. There is a problem when law becomes frozen in time, when law becomes our master rather than our servant, when punishment replaces mercy, and when law separates people instead of being a bridge between people.

After the first four caliphs, Islam turned to Shariah (law) as the center and basis of Islam. But is submission to Shariah the same as submission to God? There are aspects of Shariah law that seem to be misinterpretations of the Qur'an. Demanding the death penalty for saying anything negative about Islam (blasphemy) or changing one's religion (apostasy), and treating women as less than human are not true Islam. These are perversions of the Muslim vision of mercy, freedom, equality, and respect for all of God's creation. Christians and Jews have had the same problems.

A common misconception is that Muslims believe in salvation by works, that there is no grace in Islam. It is true that works are essential for Muslims, that on the great judgment day we will be judged by our works. Muslims put great effort into laying up treasure in heaven by doing good works, but they also believe in grace. Muslims claim that even Mohammad was not good enough to get into heaven. He also will enter heaven only by God's grace. Muslims are required to say God is "merciful and compassionate" (*ar rachman, ir rahiim*) at least thirty four times a day. Muslims repeatedly in their daily conversations refer to the goodness and generosity of God (*Allah karim*). Most commonly, Muslims use the word "mercy" rather than "grace."

Muslims do not talk much about redemption. For Muslims, the issue is repentance, followed by doing what is right and following God's commands. There is little talk of grace. Yet if you question Muslims, they will quickly tell you that it is only by God's grace that we can repent and turn to God. Christians would include the importance of accepting God's forgiveness. If we experience forgiveness, we cannot continue in our destructive paths.

In Islam, salvation is based on weighing our good and bad deeds, in having our good deeds outweigh our sins. As I look back on my own life, it is clear to me that I have done more harm than good in my life. I am in need of God's grace.

Grace is God accepting us even though we are unacceptable, God showing mercy to us even though we have done nothing to deserve mercy.

It is amazing how many people in all three religions deny God's grace, and think we humanly achieve salvation by believing and doing the right things. The belief that only people of my religion will go to heaven is a denial that we are saved by God's grace. I have met many zealous, sincere, religious people who appear to never have experienced grace. I know judgmental people for whom I never know if I have done enough for them to accept me. I have also met formerly rigid people who have experienced grace, who have mellowed, who have become open to God's Spirit, who now are filled with love. No matter how correct one's theology might be, if it is not rooted in grace, it is rooted in pride and is bad theology.

There is a story in the Qur'an (5:112–15) of the disciples asking Jesus to have God send down a table from heaven loaded with food to "satisfy our hearts." This story obviously refers to the Eucharistic table. God does send down a table for a celebrative feast. It is to that table of fellowship that all of us are invited.

There is a story of Mohammad meeting a man who devoted all his time to prayer. Mohammad's immediate response was, "Who takes care of him?" and then said that the people who supported the man were more righteous than the man who constantly prayed. There is another Muslim story of a man who had done nothing but pray all his life. When he arrived at the great judgment day, he announced that he had come for his reward. God said, "Send him straight to hell." The man cried out to God for mercy, whereupon God said he could enter heaven.

We will be judged not on our religious practice, but on our love for our neighbor. This is not to say that religious practice is not important. I find religious practice essential for my life. It helps me to love my neighbor. To pray five times a day is a gift.

I am grateful that I have no fear of meeting God. This trust grows out of my Christian faith. I know God's love and grace, and can act in trust in God's goodness. I do not need to live my life in fear of God sending me to hell. God's mercy has no end. With this confidence, I can have the freedom to do what I believe God is calling me to do.

I do not want to do anything in hope of being rewarded by God. That seems egocentric and selfish. I want to act out of love for God, out of gratitude for God's love and grace, and out of love for my neighbor. I do not ask, "Have I done enough to earn God's favor?" Tradition quotes Mohammad saying that in Heaven he will be found with the poorest and least rewarded people. I also want no rewards in heaven. I also want to be with the least. I am appalled when I see Muslims pushing to get in the front prayer line so that they can get a greater reward. Maybe they get the least reward of all.

Many times I think other people too rigidly follow the rules of their religions. I then thank God for grace and am grateful for my freedom. But if I am honest, I know that often my rejection of "legalism" is nothing more than taking the easy way out, and that I am rationalizing my spiritual laziness. I recognize that often I do not have the depth of discipline that my more "legalistic" friends have.

A big problem for Christians has been "cheap grace," justifying sin instead of justifying the sinner, seeking forgiveness without repentance. What is the meaning of atonement or redemption if it does not result in the transformation of people, changed lives, and obedience to God?

THE CROSS

The Jewish Scriptures look forward to the coming of a Savior. Jews and Christians believe in the necessity of a Savior while Muslims see no need for a Savior. Here is another possible area for fruitful dialogue between Christians, Muslims, and Jews. The Muslims are right. God is able to forgive sin. If we sin, we need to repent (have remorse for the sin, stop committing the sin, and make restitution if needed) and God will forgive us. For Muslims, it is as simple as that.

I remember a conversation with some Christians about Islam and Christianity. When I explained to them that Muslims see no need for atonement, that all we have to do is repent and God will forgive us, they replied, "But God is just." They were repeating the Western legal understanding of justice (borrowed from the Romans) that Western Christians have imposed on the doctrine of salvation. According to this theory, God is just. Our sin demands the penalty of death. Sin must be punished. Because God is just, God cannot forgive sin without the penalty being paid. God's righteous anger must be satisfied. There must be justice (revenge?). We, however, in no way are able to pay this debt. Even our death would not pay the price. Only Jesus, God's perfect Son, has the legal standing to pay the debt we owe. Jesus died in our place, satisfied

God's anger and the need for justice, and now we can be forgiven. I have often heard Christians say, "If Jesus had not died, we could not go to heaven." This is sometimes called the satisfaction or substitution theory of the atonement.

This understanding raises many serious questions. Does God need to be appeased before God can forgive? Does God need to hurt someone before God can love or forgive? Does God need to maintain his dignity? Do we need Jesus to protect us from God? Why did God need to pour out his wrath on his Son so that God could forgive us? Why is God restricted by some demand for justice and unable to forgive sin? Is God vengeful and petty? Why was Jesus able to forgive those who had hung him on a cross? Is God less able to forgive than a parent? Would any good parent torture their children eternally in hell for not being perfect? Is God responsible for having his son killed? Is God guilty of child abuse?

The Jewish understanding of God is a God of compassion, very different from the notion of some Christians who believe that God is unable to show any compassion except through the sacrifice of Jesus. Christian attempts to limit God must be rejected. God is able to forgive in any way God wants.

This theory is too simple. Jesus paid the price and we get a free ticket to heaven. As one person said to me, "The one and only reason that Jesus came to earth was to pay the death penalty for our sins." The only reason? This understanding of the cross provides no basis for ethics or how to live. It makes Jesus basically irrelevant to how we live.

Another serious problem with this theory, which was developed in the Middle Ages, is that it provides a theological basis for war and oppression. It is the basis for our criminal justice system. This theory neatly fits the world's understanding of power and justice, seeing violence as redemptive. If God demands vengeance, why shouldn't we? This theory is a primary basis for Christians to reject the message of the nonviolent Jesus.

This theory is wrong also in thinking God needs to be reconciled to us. No! God does not have a problem. It is our hearts that need to be changed, not God's heart. We are the ones who need to be reconciled (at-one-ment). We need to be saved from our sin, not from God's wrath. We are the ones separated from God. The problem is with us. It was human hostility that Jesus endured, not God's wrath.

A similar theory is the ransom theory. In this theory, Jesus' death is a ransom paid to Satan to free captive sinners. God was so weak that he had to sacrifice his Son to free captive sinners from Satan's grasp. Try to imagine that.

Muslims and Jews are right in rejecting these theories. Must we then also reject the cross and any idea of the atonement? I think not. There are other and better ways of understanding the cross.

A better interpretation of the satisfaction theory is that God is righteous and just, and so does take offense at sin, at injustice, and the waste of God's creation. God is offended not because God is petty, but because God loves and cares for creation. Sin and injustice cause suffering, including suffering for God. The message of the incarnation and the cross is that God takes on and absorbs the suffering caused by sin, thus removing any basis for retribution and violence.

Let's take a look at Jesus' ministry to see other possible ways of understanding the cross. Jesus preached the in-breaking of a new social order, the kingdom of God. Jesus resisted the powers of evil. He stood with the poor, healed the sick, and cast out demons, which created strong opposition. The two final straws that broke the camel's back were the raising of Lazarus from the dead and the cleansing of the temple. Here Jesus won two major victories over the power of death and stood in the way of the corrupt religious establishment.

It was the powers of evil that crucified Jesus, not God. It was not God's will that Jesus die. God's will was for repentance. Jesus could have called down legions of angels for protection. Jesus submitted to death rather than seek revenge. Jesus broke the cycle of revenge and retaliation. Jesus did not repay humanity for its violence against him. Rather, Jesus offered grace and forgiveness. The forgiveness Jesus offered on the cross, under extreme agony, was real forgiveness. Vengeance was not part of Jesus' atoning sacrifice. Jesus spoke a better word than the blood of Abel that cried out for vengeance.[20]

One need not accept the idea that God demands a pound of flesh to understand that Jesus did take on the sin of the world and even our sin. Likewise, God's demand for justice was satisfied, not by vengeance, but by God's making things right, by God's taking the initiative in restoring broken relationships.

We are estranged from God. Christians believe that in our alienation, it is God who comes to us. The Christian message of the cross is that God

20. Heb 12:24.

has come to us, has experienced our pain. God is not an insensitive father who sent his son to die. Rather, God Himself has come to us and borne our grief. We can see God's suffering in every rape, every murder, every act of oppression. Where is God, we ask? God is to be found wherever people suffer and are exploited. Christians understand Jesus' death as a symbol of God's love for us.

God's love grants us freedom. We are free to say yes or no to God. God respects that freedom even to the point of allowing us to destroy ourselves, which we are doing. So what can God do to save us other than overrule human freedom and zap us? God's willingness to forgive us makes little difference. To get our attention, to prove God's love for us, Jesus took on our suffering and laid down his life for us. If we understand this, what can we do other than turn to God in gratitude? Jesus resisted the evil of the world and accepted the suffering that would bring. Jesus demonstrated the depth of God's love.

Many people know they are living contrary to God's will. They are filled with guilt and hopelessness. They feel trapped. What can they do? The answer must come from outside. Someone must reach out to them, listen to, and absorb some of the fear, hostility, and hopelessness. That is real love. That is what God did in reaching out to us in Jesus. This is "good news" to all who have lost hope.

One of the wonderful proclamations of the Christian faith is that our sins are forgiven, and reconciliation with God is offered as a gift to us. There is no need for us to atone for our sins. That is finished. Although we may need to make amends for wrongs we have done to others, there is no basis for retribution. There is no need for us to worry about God's forgiveness, no need to fear God's judgment. Christians express this in many ways: our sins are covered, the power of sin has been broken, we are redeemed, we are restored to wholeness, we are reconciled, we are saved.

Christians believe that the death of Jesus was not the end. The powers of evil could not contain or restrain God's love. Jesus rose victorious over the powers of evil and death. Jesus defeated the powers of evil by making himself vulnerable to those powers. The powers of evil overstepped their boundary when they attacked Jesus, and were defeated. In Revelation 5, Jesus is portrayed as a conquering Lamb. It is the Lamb that will conquer evil and rule the world.

According to the book of Hebrews, Jesus' victory over death and evil was in his suffering and giving up his life. The power of the resurrection became real in the rebirth of community among the dispirited followers of Jesus who were given the hope and power to continue the work of Jesus. We are invited to share in that victory through our own suffering. We experience salvation by participating in Jesus' suffering, in following Jesus, in taking up the cross ourselves, in repenting from our participation in sin, and then living a life of love and service to others, even when that seems foolish and hopeless.

In contrast to a theology of the cross that Christians have used to persecute and kill Jews and Muslims, this theology of the cross is the Christian basis for nonviolent action. In the cross we see a new way to exercise power. Instead of dominating and controlling, we become servants. We make ourselves vulnerable. In the cross we see the cycle of violence and counter-violence broken. We see reconciliation. Jesus overturned the pretentiousness and arrogance of worldly power. Instead of dominating and controlling, we act as communities of love engaging in servanthood and nonviolent resistance. We are ready to die, but we will not kill. We see no one as our enemy. We seek understanding and reconciliation, not the defeat of anyone. Christians cannot forget the suffering of Jesus on the cross and its definition of the meaning of love.

The atonement becomes real for us as we follow Jesus and participate in his suffering and victory. We accept the call to take up the cross by making ourselves vulnerable to the powers of evil. God's ultimate way of overcoming evil is the cross, nonviolent suffering love. This is the basis for Christian nonviolent action.

I remember a conversation with a Muslim friend in which he tried to prove the Christian understanding of Jesus could not be true. A good father would not allow his son to be killed, he told me. Rather, he would kill the one attacking his son. I pointed out to my friend that at this point there was a major difference between Christianity and Islam. Rather than kill the attacker, I would want to put myself between the attacker and my son, be willing to die for my son, and try to reach that of God in the attacker's soul. I then tried to explain the meaning of the cross, the nature of God's love, our need for redemption, and why I was willing to risk my life to stand in the middle of the Israeli/Palestinian conflict.

While it is possible to interpret the Qur'an in a way that makes the crucifixion of Jesus possible, for Muslims, it is theologically difficult, based on the Muslim belief that Jesus was the Messiah. How, Muslims ask, can one who has been anointed by the power of God suffer and be humiliated?

God cannot suffer. But according to God's revelation in the Bible, God can and does suffer. God loves us that much. Imagine the power that could result if Muslims would accept this part of God's previous revelations. The cross is an affirmation of the power and sovereignty of God.

How can we square a good God with unearned suffering? The Muslim answer is that what ever comes, it is God's will and a sign of God's mercy. The Christian answer, rooted in the cross, is that God comes to us in our suffering and bears our suffering. This difference has resulted in a huge contrast between Muslim and Christian responses to suffering. Christians formed charitable orders and hospitals to care for the sick and suffering, something Muslims traditionally did not do. Muslims accepted the suffering. The cross calls us to stand with those who are suffering as God stands with us.

Both the Qur'an and the Bible state that God has taken upon Himself mercy and insures our forgiveness. The Messiah is the "Lamb of God." The very essence of God is self-giving love. That is the essential meaning of the cross. For me, the cross is not a religious icon, but the brutal form of capital punishment reserved for anyone who rejected the lordship of Roman authority. The cross is a symbol of resistance to the power of evil and the pride of military empire.

Mohammad's decision to turn the other cheek and accept humiliation at Hudaybiyah has parallels with the cross of Jesus and nonviolent action. His controversial and creative decision ultimately resulted in victory for the Muslims, and laid the foundation for further Muslim peace initiatives. This story is a profound basis for Muslim nonviolence.

An excellent Muslim example of taking up the cross is the Ghawi family in the Sheikh Jarrah neighborhood in East Jerusalem. On August 2, 2009, Israeli police evicted them from their home at 4:30 in the morning. Within a half hour, Israeli settlers had moved into their house. Immediately after Israeli police had evicted them from their home, the Ghawi family set up and moved into a tent on the sidewalk in front of their home, braving heat and cold, subjecting themselves to the hostility of the settlers and harassment from Israeli authorities, as a nonviolent witness to expose the injustice of Israeli settlers stealing their house. Every day, as settlers went to and from the Palestinian house, they had to walk past the Palestinian family they had dispossessed. I had the privilege of spending a week with the Ghawi family in their tent in December, 2009. The vulnerability of the Ghawi family was a powerful witness to those who visited the tent, and to people around the world who heard of their witness.

The only way I know of overcoming evil is through nonviolent suffering love, the cross. The only way I know of reaching a troubled person is to make myself vulnerable to that person. The only way I know of overcoming political oppression and economic exploitation is for us to make ourselves vulnerable to those powers, to stand in front of their tanks and bulldozers, to expose them for the corrupt, rotten powers they are. This becomes real for me as I engage in nonviolent direct action to resist the powers of evil. It is at the point that we are most vulnerable that we can experience God's power and God's victory. I have often been arrested in public actions against oppression. When I am handcuffed and taken to jail, I am completely weak and vulnerable. Yet every time I am handcuffed or sit in a jail cell, I feel an incredible strength

All three religions place great meaning in suffering. Even suicide bombers understand this, although they add their desire for others to suffer. The Suffering Servant theme is rooted in the Jewish Scriptures of Isaiah chapters 42, 50, 52, and 53. Muslims have an understanding of the value of unearned suffering, which they believe Allah will reward. Since the spread of Sunni Islam was so successful, Sunnis have felt less need to develop a theology of suffering. Shia Muslims, on the other hand, suffered repeated defeats and developed more of a theology of redemptive suffering. Will Sunnis, now with all their sufferings and defeats, also develop more of a theology of suffering?

Our struggle is a spiritual struggle. Because of the cross, Christians believe that the powers of evil already have been defeated and are not nearly as strong as they appear to be. The cross reminds us of God's breaking the powers that dominate and oppress us. Evil can be brought down and transformed by the power of love. We can work for liberation and reconciliation. This, I believe, is the biblical doctrine of the atonement, a doctrine that Muslims and Jews can accept.

Repentance and forgiveness are not enough. We also need redemption, a strong Jewish and Christian theme. Muslims are correct; God is not limited. God can simply forgive. Ritual sacrifice is not necessary, as affirmed by the Hebrew prophets, but forgiveness is not enough. We also need the healing power of God's love. It is through God's grace that we can resist the powers of evil and live a new life. Muslims need to look deeper and recognize our need for a Savior. In sermon after sermon in mosques, I hear the challenge to live in obedience to God, to live a moral life, to reject all sin, but I seldom hear the good news of God's saving grace that makes repentance and righteous living possible, that we do not have to rely only on our own strength. Too often, Muslim preaching comes across as shallow legalism, a works-righteousness with no grace. Although Muslims have an understanding of grace, studying Jewish and Christian understandings of grace could enrich Muslims. Muslims do recognize our need for God's salvation in their belief that without the guidance of revelation we would be in a helpless state.

We do need a Savior. We cannot save ourselves. How can we work for peace and reconciliation if we have not been reconciled? We need grace that comes from beyond ourselves. The answer to the human condition is God's transforming, saving grace made known in Jesus Christ. We must turn to God for salvation. We cannot save ourselves. Only God can save.

For too many people, repentance, forgiveness, and God's grace are not enough. They want revenge, a pound of flesh. They even attribute this vicious attitude to God. For Christians, the price for sin has already been paid. Jesus' sacrifice ends the whole sacrificial system. There is no need for further shedding of blood. War, capital punishment, and seeking revenge are rejections of God's saving grace. Jesus put an end to all vengeance and blood sacrifice.

A leader in a progressive organization I work with committed a serious breach of trust with the membership of the organization. I was surprised at the viciousness of the attacks and the lack of compassion for him. In response to my sharing my concern for the man, an atheist friend said to me, "Art, I expect you to say that. You are a Christian. You believe in reconciliation and redemption." Christians who believe Jesus' teachings are meant to be followed, partially base their ethics on the possibilities of redemption. For example, I reject capital punishment because I believe in the possibility of redemption.

Christianity has both a deeper understanding of sin and a stronger vision for the possibilities of redemption for those who do evil than does either Islam or Judaism. One does not need to accept the Calvinist understanding of the complete depravity of human nature to understand that humanity is enslaved and captive to sin. For Muslims, the human problem is more weakness than sinfulness.

Islam has a wonderfully clear vision of social justice, but much less emphasis on love. In my conversations with Muslims I miss a vision of redeeming love, hope for the redemption of evil people, of reconciliation, that I find in the Jewish and Christian Scriptures. It is not that this theme is not in the Qur'an. It is not that there are no Muslim pacifists, nor that Muslims cannot believe in nonviolent suffering love, but most miss the richness, the depth, and the radical vision of the sacrificial love of the cross.

It is difficult to talk with Jews about the cross. For Jews, the cross is the ultimate symbol of bigotry, pogroms, and oppression. For Jews, the cross means suffering and death. We need to be sensitive. Actually, the Christian understanding of the cross is rooted in the Hebrew Scriptures, in the Suffering Servant vision of the prophet Isaiah, in the concept of a God of love who suffers because of human destructiveness. The prophet Hosea told of a God who never gives up on wayward humanity.

Can we all agree that whoever Jesus was, death cannot have the last word about God's purposes? It was in humbling himself and becoming a servant that Jesus was victorious over the powers of evil. We also are called to take up the cross, humble ourselves, and become servants. In doing this, we participate in the salvation offered by Jesus. Salvation is not magical, not mysterious. But it does involve suffering. In the struggle for social justice, we will overcome through our willingness to suffer, through our willingness to endure more suffering than our opponents.

I long for the day when the cross will no longer be seen as an instrument of oppression to Jews and Muslims, but rather become a symbol of God's love and grace, a symbol of nonviolence, of humility, and of hope, but that will take a lot of repentance on the part of Christians. How can Muslims and Jews accept the cross when so many of them have been killed in the name of the cross?

THE TRINITY

The Christian doctrine of the Trinity has mystified not only Jews and Muslims, but also many Christians. How can God be three and one?

When Jews and Muslims reject the Trinity, they are expressing profound truths Christians need to listen to. Christians need to reaffirm the truths of the Hebrew Scriptures that were blurred by the early Christian interaction with Hellenistic culture. The doctrine of the Trinity came out of dialogue with Hellenistic culture. It was not part of the message of Jesus. Hans Küng argues that the "tremendously complicated Christological and Trinitarian constructions built with the help of Greek and Latin concepts" make understanding between Muslims and Christians almost impossible.[21]

There are various ways of understanding the doctrine of the Trinity. One understanding developed in the fourth century and currently a popular understanding, is that God is three distinct persons, yet one. This understanding is problematic in that it is not spelled out in the New Testament, and that it opens Christianity to the charge of having three gods. Actually, the doctrine of the Trinity was an attempt by early Christians to maintain their monotheism in relation to Hellenistic and Roman polytheism.

There is no hint in the Bible of God being three distinct persons. Someone said that if a thousand persons from another planet were each given a Bible and did nothing for ten years except to study the Bible, not one of them would come up with the idea of the Trinity. God is described in the Bible as Spirit, Father, Creator, Immanuel (God with us), Word, Wisdom, etc, but not as three persons. Each of these descriptive words says something about the oneness of God.

Although I personally think the doctrine of the Trinity is a philosophical construct foreign to the Bible and to modern thinking, and that it creates more problems than it solves, it is important for many Christians, does express profound truths, and cannot be ignored in interfaith dialogue.

Some Christians understand the Trinity as three different ways of experiencing or conceiving of God, similar to the ninety-nine names of God in the Qur'an, or the ten names of God in the Torah, which point to a wide variety of ways of conceptualizing God. The Trinity does not mean that God is three any more than Muslims would limit God to ninety-nine attributes. Both point to infinity. In this understanding, the number three is not important, but the concepts of God as Creator and Sovereign Lord, as God present with us (Incarnation), and as Guide and Comforter are essential.

Christians need to go farther than equate the Muslim understanding of God with the first person of the Trinity. Aspects of God understood in the second and third persons of the Trinity are also aspects of the Muslim understanding of God. Some Muslims have distinguished between the names of God, the attributes of God, and the actions of God. If we lose one or more of these aspects of God, we lose a holistic un-

21. Küng, *Islam*, 363.

derstanding of God and become unbalanced. The number three is not exclusively sacred, however.

The doctrine of the Trinity recognizes the greatness of God, but does not deny the oneness of God. Monotheism, or unity, does not negate multiplicity or diversity. Actually, the doctrine of the Trinity is an attempt to articulate the concept of diversity in unity. In both Judaism and Islam, God is referred to in the plural, because God is too great to be one. This is not an affirmation of the Trinity or a contradiction of the oneness of God, but a simple recognition that God is too great to be referred to in the singular. The doctrine of the Trinity carries some of this meaning by pointing to the connectedness of all of God's attributes.

Instead of a philosophical concept, the doctrine of the Trinity can be understood as relational. The doctrine of the Trinity points to relationships and community. Seeing God as not only transcendent, but also as having come to us in Jesus and present with us as the Holy Spirit, can lead to a lifestyle of caring and serving, to dialogue and respect. Out of this understanding of God come the concepts of love and servanthood that result in communities of faith that serve the needs of each other and the wider world.

⇒ SIX ⇐

Stories of Interfaith Solidarity

THE VALUE OF INTERFAITH dialogue is severely limited if it mainly involves academics discussing abstract issues unconnected with struggles for social justice. An exciting further step is to stand in solidarity with people of other religions in the struggle for social justice. Interfaith cooperation must include standing in solidarity with the oppressed, together resisting oppression, asking each other for forgiveness, and embodying in our relationships the seeds of the new social order for which we pray. It is important that rich Christians, Muslims, and Jews, with all their financial, political, technological, and military power, not become an alliance of the powerful over against the powerless, thus negating the heart of the three religions rooted in the biblical and Qur'anic calls for justice based on the oneness of God. Sadly, many Abrahamic people already have made alliances with injustice.

I remember the mass meetings during the Civil Rights Movement, when black and white, young and old, rich and poor, men and women, plus people of many religious persuasions came together in an incredible sense of unity. Our singing and praying was connected to facing the police dogs, the tear gas, the serious repression, and the knowledge that our lives were literally on the line. Faith became real. We turned to God as we learned to walk the talk.

It has been an inspiration and blessing to Peggy and me that whenever we take stands for justice, we can count on support from people not only in all three Abrahamic religions, but from people of many religions and perspectives. Literally thousands of people from many religions pray for us in our work.

There is a "peace process" that takes place in fancy resorts like Wye River, Sharm al Sheik, or at the United Nations, but there is another peace process that happens around demolished homes, in shepherds' caves, in people's living rooms, in demonstrations and vigils on the street. The real peace process happens when common people share their pain with each other and join together in resisting oppression and struggle for a better world. Much more exciting than academic discussions is for Jews and Christians to stand with Muslims when Muslims are under threat from Christians and Jews, or when Muslims and Christians reach out and support Jews when Jews are in danger. The most exciting dialogue happens not in academic conferences, but in the struggle for social justice, in together working to undo oppression. In many cases, these actions will not be popular.

During the massacre of 67 Jews in Hebron in 1929, many Palestinian Muslim families hid Jews in their homes and saved the lives of many Jews. I know many of these Muslim families and even though they now are suffering abuse from Israeli settlers, these Muslims continue to be proud of their families for the risks they took for Jews.

During World War II, both Protestants and Catholics in the French village of Le Chambon saved the lives of 5,000 Jews from extermination by the Nazis.

Farid Esack tells the story of a powerful interfaith experience in South Africa in 1984 when nineteen religious leaders from various backgrounds were arrested and jailed together. They experienced in the jail cells their common need for God and their common commitment to justice. As Esack tells it, "In eight hours, years of suspicion and mistrust were shattered."[1] In the three days following his inauguration as President of South Africa, Nelson Mandela visited a mosque, a synagogue, and a church as a symbol of his commitment to freedom for all. He appointed Muslims and Jews to important positions in his administration.

During the time in 1994 when Christians in Rwanda were slaughtering three quarters of a million of their fellow Christians, many Muslims intervened to save their Christian neighbors. By 2002, the Muslim population in Rwanda had doubled or tripled due to a large extent to the Muslim support of their Christian neighbors during the genocide.

1. Esack, *Liberation and Pluralism*, 37.

In December 2008, I met a Jewish couple in Bethlehem. They were working in solidarity with Palestinians. They had just returned from being part of a peace delegation to Iran where they had identified themselves as Jews. The man wore his kippah in Iran. The Iranian people warmly welcomed them as Jews. There are 20,000 Jews living in Iran.

It is exciting to join hands across the boundaries of race, clan, and religion in the struggle for social justice. It is in this crossing of boundaries that we are stretched and forced to grow. Seeking unity on moral, social concerns should be seen as just as important as unity on doctrine and worship. Issues of violence and war, economic justice, racism, and sexism can be significant starting points for seeking unity across divisions of religion, race, gender, or class.

When our CPT team learned in February 1997 that the Israeli military had placed demolition orders on 700 Palestinian homes in the Hebron area, we felt led to do a public fast for 700 hours (27 days). Each day we sat in a tent in downtown Hebron and were joined by Muslims and Jews, which resulted in intense dialogue between many factions in the Israeli/Palestinian conflict. Each day we had our Christian time of worship in the tent, which was open to everyone. The tent became a forum for people to share their pain, to tell their stories, and to talk with people on the opposite side of issues from them. Muslims, Christians, and Jews came together in a deep way. Lives were changed and people made new commitments to work for peace.[2] Abraham, Hagar, and Sarah, would have been happy if they could have seen their children coming together.

In December 1999, I was living with a Palestinian Muslim family whose home was regularly being attacked by Israeli settlers. The settlers were demanding that the Israeli military demolish the house and they then would start a new settlement there. The settlers also were threatening to demolish the house themselves. The situation was serious. Our team sent out an urgent action alert, asking people around the world to send messages to the Israeli and U.S. government asking that this home not be demolished. Members of one Mennonite congregation in Indiana sent at least 75 faxes to the Israeli government in support of this Muslim family. In situations like this, there is great potential for evil, but even greater possibilities for good. This Muslim family welcomed Jews to come and be a presence with them. Four Jews (two Israelis, one Canadian, and one American) came to stay with the family. Groups of Israelis came during

2. Gish, *Hebron Journal*, 121–35.

the daytime. As a result of this action, the Israeli government promised that the home would not be demolished and clamped down on settler attacks against the family.[3]

On February 11, 2000, there was a demonstration near Hebron to protest Israeli confiscation of Palestinian land. The action was based on Jesus' teaching that if someone who has power over you asks you to do something you should not have to do, sometimes as a form of resistance, you can do more than you were ordered to do to shame that person, like walking an extra mile. Or if someone wants to take your cloak, give him your underwear as well to shame him with your nakedness. Based on this idea, we came up with the idea of taking buckets of soil to an expanding Israeli settlement, telling the settlers that if they want more land, here, we would give them more land.

On that Friday morning, Jews, Muslims, and Christians marched to the Harsina settlement east of Hebron. Each person poured out their bucket of soil and made a short statement about the horror of stealing people's land. The message was, "Here, you are so greedy that you take the land of these simple farmers, here, we will give you more." Rabbi Arik Ascherman referred to the Biblical story in First Kings 21 of Naboth's vineyard when King Ahab stole the garden of Naboth, simply because the king wanted more.

In publicizing this action, I went door to door in Muslim neighborhoods with leaflets explicitly referring to Jesus' words, inviting people to this Christian planned action, and was warmly welcomed everywhere I went. In a common struggle for justice, when we make ourselves vulnerable to each other, we can authentically be who we are. We were not preaching abstract religious dogma, but were drawn together by our common struggle for justice.[4]

On January 9, 2004, a delegation of seven American Jews came to the West Bank for a solidarity visit with Palestinians. I was their guide for the two days they spent in Hebron. They wanted to be identified as Jews so that they could communicate to the Palestinians that some Jews care about their oppression. I took them to visit various Muslim families who were delighted to have Jews in their homes. We visited one family who has suffered deeply from Jewish settlers in Hebron, even though that

---

3. Ibid., 194–221.
4. Ibid., 233–37.

family had hidden and saved the lives of Jews in Hebron during the massacre in 1929. We visited families who had their land confiscated, families who had repeatedly been attacked by settlers, and families who had had their homes demolished. The group spent the night in Muslim homes. These Jews expressed their sorrow and embarrassment for what fellow Jews were doing to Palestinians. How profound! What is of more significance than to reach out to one's "enemy," to build bridges instead of walls, for "enemies" to eat together, sleep in each other's homes, and share their stories? The Palestinians were deeply grateful and honored that these Jews would come to visit them. The Jews were touched by the welcome, the hospitality, and love they received from Palestinian Muslims. The Jews told me how amazed they were that they could not detect any hatred in the hearts of their hosts.

On January 20, 2004, a group of Americans went to observe Israelis building a fence behind a row of Palestinian homes, cutting those Palestinians off from their land on the other side of the fence, land that Israeli settlers were confiscating for the Harsina settlement, near Hebron. We decided to walk down the new road on the settler side of the fence and talk with a group of about 30 Israeli high school boys who were building the fence, accompanied by armed security guards. They were quite friendly as we approached them. Apparently they took us for Jews. After all, we were on the Jewish side of the fence. One of our group was Jewish. We introduced ourselves, began chatting, and taking pictures of each other. They asked about who we were. It wasn't long before the settler guards realized who we were and ordered us to go to the Palestinian side of the fence and leave the area. About eight soldiers arrived to enforce the settler order. The students seemed stunned. Suddenly, the people who they thought to be their friends were now identified as their enemies. Suddenly we became Palestinians. Now we were to be shunned and feared. We were no longer to be seen as sharing a common humanity. Now we had to be separated by a fence. We could no longer be friends or even talk with each other. We wondered what impressions that left with those teenagers. Were they able to make the quick perceptual transition? After connecting with us in such a positive way, were they able to suddenly see us as enemies? Did this experience have any effect on their perceptions of the fence dividing us?

There is something inhuman and unnatural about fences and walls that separate people. On December 25, 2003, the Israeli military put up a high fence on the street outside our team apartment in Hebron, to separate the settlers and the Palestinians, one small part of the larger Apartheid Separation Wall the Israeli government is building. Six weeks later, on February 4, 2004, I heard a noise in the street and discovered a settler man and about five boys on the Israeli side of the fence and one of the local chicken merchants on the Palestinian side, haggling over two pigeons the settler wanted to buy. I noticed them passing the pigeons through a hole in the fence. The wall was breeched that day. It could not keep the Jewish settlers and the Muslim merchant apart. A week later, the chicken merchant stopped me on the street and told me one of his chickens had gotten through the fence and was on the other side of the Jewish only street. He wanted me to crawl through a hole under the fence and retrieve his chicken. That sounded scary to me, but I decided I needed to do that for him. With some difficulty, I caught the chicken, was not seen by settlers, and crawled back under the fence. The wall was breeched again.

On November 28, 2005, Tom Fox, Jim Loney, Norman Kember, and Harmeet Sooden, four people associated with the CPT team in Iraq, were kidnapped by armed men on a street in Baghdad, raising deep concern around the world for their safety and demands for their release. Out of this horrible act came an incredible story of solidarity and support. When something bad happens, we can accept that as an opportunity to confront evil on its own turf. That is what happened in this case.

It wasn't long before our Palestinian Muslim friends in Hebron began contacting Palestinian religious and political groups for their assistance in describing the work of CPT in Palestine for the Arab media and urging the Iraqi captors to release the four CPTers. Soon a statement, signed by groups as diverse as Hamas, Fatah, and the Democratic Front for the Liberation of Palestine, calling for the release of the captives, was read at a press conference at a mosque in Hebron.

Muslim leaders and Islamic groups around the world, including al Qaida, issued statements calling for the release of the four Christians. Many imams in mosques in Iraq called for the release of the four. Practically every important Muslim leader in the world joined this call.

On December 2, I joined Muslims in the small village of At-Tuwani for a demonstration and march through the village calling for the release of the CPTers. Several Israeli Jews joined the demonstration. The next week, over a hundred of those villagers joined a demonstration in Hebron, about ten miles away. That the Muslim world would respond in this way in support of four Christians was truly humbling.

As a response to the outpouring of Muslim support for the four Christian peacemakers taken hostage in Iraq, the United Church of Canada issued a proclamation calling the Christian community to speak out on behalf of human rights for Iraqis. Their statement read: "For far too long, thousands of Iraqis have been illegally detained, abused, and tortured. . . .This grave situation is the result of the illegal foreign occupation of Iraq. . . . We believe the occupation is the underlying source for this disregard of human rights. The occupation must end." In response to this call, Christians in the United States called on American Christians to also stand up in support of Muslims who are being mistreated by Western powers. Sadly, the Christian world has not adequately united in support of Muslim detainees, many who had been tortured.

On March 9, 2006, Tom Fox's body was found in Baghdad. Two weeks later, Jim, Norman, and Harmeet were released. An elderly Muslim woman in At-Tuwani planted an olive tree in memory of Tom, who had spent some time in At-Tuwani.

My wife tells the story of a meeting of the Muslim Peacemaker Team in Karbala, Iraq, in 2005. These Shia Muslims were wrestling with whether to take an action of visiting the Sunni city of Fallujah, which had been almost completely destroyed by U.S. bombing a few months earlier. The idea was to express condolences and help with cleanup in the city. The MPT members expressed a lot of fear. "We are Shia and they are Sunni. What if they reject us? What if they kill us?" After some discussion, one of the Shia said, "But that is what peacemaking is about. We want to use our suffering, not for revenge, but for healing." The Karbala Shias took the risk and visited Sunni Fallujah and were warmly received. There were a total of seven visits in 2005.

One day in Hebron I had a long talk with an Israeli soldier who was considering becoming a refusenik and refusing to continue working in the Israeli military. I promised to pray for him. I then went to the noon prayer in the local mosque and prayed for the Israeli soldier there in the mosque. A Christian prayed for a Jew in a mosque. He now is an Israeli peace activist, with whom I have maintained contact.

Media Benjamin, of Code Pink and Global Exchange, tells the story of being in Lebanon in August 2006, while Israel was dropping bombs on the Lebanese people. She says it was difficult being an American Jew there as Israelis dropped those U.S.-made bombs around her. She identified herself to the Lebanese people as a Jew. The Lebanese people warmly welcomed this American Jew, in spite of the horror Americans and Jews were raining on them, because she went to the Lebanese people with love and compassion.

On April 15, 2007, I attended a Holocaust memorial vigil in Athens, Ohio. The Athens Jewish community organized the vigil and included Muslims, mainline Christians, Jehovah's Witnesses, and others. The program commemorated all 11 million victims of the Holocaust, not just Jewish victims, and also contemporary victims of genocide. That inclusiveness indicated spiritual maturity on the part of the Athens Jewish community.

During the Gulf war in 1991, before I ever considered any participation in Islam, a Muslim friend one day thanked me for all the time and effort I was putting into the peace movement. He concluded his words of gratitude by saying, "You must have a deep love for humanity that you would work so hard for peace." "No," I said, "I am doing this because of my love for Allah." He seemed stunned and surprised, and then hugged me. I understood that as his recognition of the faith we had in common.

In September, 2001, about a week after the 9/11 attacks, a group of local people and people from Ohio University encircled the mosque in Athens Ohio, in response to threats against Muslims. After the vigil, all were invited into the mosque for food and conversation. This included Jews, Christians, and people from other traditions.

On May 28, 2008, Israeli settlers stole bundles of wheat that Palestinians from the village of At-Tuwani had just harvested. Israeli soldiers caught the settlers in the act of stealing the grain. The soldiers ordered the grain to be returned to the field and ordered that no one was allowed to remove the grain from the field until the Israeli courts had ruled on who the wheat belonged to, a common procedure in occupied Palestine. Israeli settlers often steal land or property from Palestinians, and the Palestinians cannot retrieve their property without suing in the Israeli courts. In this case, Israeli peace activists associated with Ta'ayush came to the village two days later, removed the wheat from the field, and took it to the owners in the village. The Palestinian family had their grain, but they could not be charged with disobeying the military order.

On February 6, 2009, Muslims, Jews, and Christians gathered on a hilltop near Hussan, a village west of Bethlehem, to land near the Green Line, just north of the Beitar Illit settlement, a brand new city for Ultra Orthodox, just south of a Palestinian village that Israelis demolished in 1948. We were there to plant olive trees, brought by Ta'ayush and Rabbis for Human Rights. The owners of the land had feared to go on their land because of the presence of Israeli settlers and soldiers. Our planting those olive trees made a statement of support for the Palestinian owners of the land. We also expressed hope for peace and reconciliation, symbolized by the olive trees themselves, and by Jews, Christians, and Muslims working together.

My heart was filled with joy as Jews, Muslims, and Christians worked together demonstrating that peace and reconciliation are possible. I was especially moved by the willingness of these Israeli Jews to come and work with people who are supposed to be their enemies, and the willingness of the Palestinian Muslims to accept these Jews after all the oppression they had experienced from other Jews. These Israeli Jews had come to these Palestinian Muslims to express solidarity, but also as an act of repentance for what their people, their culture had become. This was religious liturgy at its best as we celebrated our common faith planting olive trees.

Three Israeli soldiers with their guns walked by us. One of the local Muslim leaders said to them, "I hope you will put your guns away and come to us in peace." One of the soldiers responded, "I don't hope." What a contrast in spirits: hope and rejection of hope.

In the last chapter I mentioned the Al Ghawi family in the Sheikh Jarrah neighborhood in East Jerusalem living in a tent on the sidewalk in front of their home from which Israeli police had evicted them. The family now lives in that tent. Every day, Jews, Christians, and people of other religions come to that tent to show solidarity with this Muslim family. Every day the Jewish settlers who live in the house must walk by the people they dispossessed.

There are dangers in interfaith solidarity. It is important that dialogue and inter-faith relationships not be used to cover up injustice and oppressive relationships, making things look rosy and fine when they are not rosy and fine. Those in power can use "dialogue" to cover up and legitimize their control, soothe their consciences, and co-opt the goals of less privileged groups.[5]

It has been difficult for many Western people to treat non-Western people as equals and as partners. This problem applies also to interfaith relationships. When people from dominate groups dialogue with or stand in solidarity with people from the groups they oppress, power dynamics affect the dialogue, and unhealthy relationships are often actually perpetrated by the dialogue, making dialogue and solidarity between oppressors and the oppressed difficult, or sometimes even counter productive. It is difficult to give up our arrogance, our ideas of superiority, and hegemonic dreams of ultimately imposing our worldview and values on others.

This has also been a struggle for Western peace activists as we live and work with Palestinians in the West Bank, since it is so easy to fall into the roles of domination/oppression we have absorbed from our own cultures, and act out of our privilege, which gives us huge amounts of unrecognized and unaccountable power. In our arrogance, it is easy for us to think we know better than people from the rest of the world. To counter this dynamic, during my work in At-Tuwani (2004–2009), our team tried hard to take our directions from the people of the village.

Israeli peace activists have the same struggle, since much of Israeli culture is rooted in Western worldviews. Palestinians in At-Tuwani repeatedly have told us that they want us all to work as partners. Although the Palestinians deeply appreciate the support of their Israeli activist friends, they also resent Israelis coming into their village to engage in actions without first consulting with the villagers. While in the village many Israeli activists display a common Western arrogance and leave the people who could be their partners standing on the sidelines.

Although we have done a good job of taking directions from the people of the village, we still have much to learn about being partners.

---

5. For an in-depth evaluation of dialogue encounters between Israeli and Palestinian students, see Abu-Nimer, *Dialogue*, 149–67.

Maybe our reluctance to engage as partners is a legitimate recognition of our Western tendencies to dominate and control and for a time it may be necessary for us to simply take directions from the villagers, with the hope that sometime we Westerners may become mature enough to become partners with the Palestinians. Our first task is to learn to be servants.

⇒ SEVEN ⇐

Religion and Violence

THERE ARE NO RELIGIOUS wars anywhere in the world. Wars are fought for social and economic reasons; for power, control, and greed. I know of no religious issue or theological proposition that is the core of any modern war. Even in conflicts between or within religious groups, usually the real conflict is not actually about religion or theology, but comes out of a historical context of suspicion, bigotry, and hatred rooted in colonialism, class conflict and power struggles, or some other oppression.

Rather than "a clash of civilizations," the major conflicts in the world are power struggles between nation states. It is nation-states that have been the cause and perpetrators of most of the violence in the world, much of which has come from the Western world. Within nations, the deeper social conflict is between those seeking to dominate and control, and those with a humane outlook.

All sides in wars use religion to justify, enflame, and psychologically support the ensuing carnage. In every war, God is declared to be "on our side." Religion is used to mobilize people in conflicts. By rejecting allegiance to nation-states, and finding our identities in the roots of our faith, in our relationship with God, religious movements can transcend political conflicts and stand together against the idolatrous power of nation-states.

Wars are rooted in greed, in the desire to steal from others. The Book of James in the Bible puts it well:

> What causes wars, and what causes fightings among you? Is it not
> your passions that are at war in your members? You desire and do

not have; so you kill. And you covet and cannot obtain; so you fight and wage war.[1]

There is one basic religion in the world today: the belief in the redemptive power of violence. The basic religion of the world is the belief that violence is redemptive, that only violence can hold back the threatening forces of chaos and evil, that only violence can save us. Since the cosmos is chaotic and violent, our only hope for salvation is through the use of violence to hold back the forces of chaos that threaten us. We cannot reason with our enemies. They are evil. They only understand force. The only answer is to crush our evil enemies. Almost every nation is committed to this belief.

This belief is rooted in the ancient Babylonian creation myth in which there is a war in heaven, the goddess Tiamat is killed, her body cut in pieces, and flung throughout space, thus creating the universe. In this myth, the cosmos is understood as chaotic and violent. Since people are created out of drops of Tiamat's blood, violence runs through our veins.

This myth is played out and repeated every day in our culture. In every film that involves violence, violence is portrayed as the only possible answer to any threat, preferably ending in the death of the one or ones who embody the threat of chaos. In every film, after a few minutes of violence, magically, the threat of chaos is gone and peace returns. Many people believe this myth, but in the real world, reality is much different. In the real world, violence does not magically bring peace, but rather leaves a trail of suffering and usually actually makes the situation worse.

Every day our political leaders repeat this lie, telling us that evil threatens us, that we cannot negotiate or reason with our enemies who understand only force. The only answer is to crush our enemies. George Bush promised that he would root out evil from the world. He said he would move heaven and earth to do it. This, of course, was blasphemy. How would he move heaven and earth? He was not God. Instead of crushing evil, Bush increased the evil in the world.

How different this myth is from the creation stories of the Bible and the Qur'an in which a good God creates a good earth with evil entering our world only later. Violence and evil are not part of creation. Violence is a perversion of a good creation, an act of rebellion against God. In the biblical, Qur'anic view, creation is good, God is generous, and redemption is

1. Jas 4:1–2.

possible without violence. If the Jewish, Christian, and Muslim Scriptures are true, then the religion of redemptive violence is a lie. It is a perversion of Scripture to use religion to support violence. People who claim they can create peace through violence are deceived both spiritually and politically.

The argument that peace is not possible, that nonviolence is naïve and unrealistic, is also rooted in the Christian heresy of original sin perpetrated by Augustine, the idea that we were created with an evil nature, that we are all condemned to a life of sin, and that redemption is finally possible only in the next world. Acceptance of violence affects even people's perception of God. So pervasive is the acceptance of violence, that even God is perceived as violent.[2]

War is rooted in fear. We are taught to fear each other, to fear our neighbor, to fear the stranger. We fear the cosmos. We cannot even trust ourselves. We produce scapegoats on which we project our fears, and then seek to destroy the scapegoats. Yet repeatedly in the Bible we find the words, "Do not be afraid."

My wife has traveled all over Iraq with no armed protection, going to places American soldiers warned her not to go because the people there were "terrorists," and would kill her. But the Iraqi people always warmly welcomed her in those places. American soldiers were shocked to see her in dangerous places. They said to her, "Don't you know how dangerous it is here! And you do not even have a gun or armed protection." Peggy would respond to them saying, "I am safer than you are, and I can go places you cannot go."

Too often people have used worldly power in the name of religion. Religious bodies have been transformed from servant communities into corrupt, imperial, hierarchal institutions based on worldly power. All too often we fail in our religious communities. All too often people are abused, condemned, labeled, rejected, isolated, and removed. It has been a deep disappointment for me how both devoted religious people and peace activists can act in oppressive ways.

If God is the Sovereign Lord of history, there is no need for us to seize power to insure that things will turn out right. All three religions teach that ultimately God is in control of history, but all three also recognize that God has given people a role in managing the events of history. We have forgotten, however, our subordinate role in history, usurped

2. For an introduction to recent questioning of the violence of God, see Weaver and Mast, *Work of Jesus Christ*. Also see Weaver, *Nonviolent Atonement*.

God's role, and made ourselves gods. Too often people are convinced they are doing something so good and so important that they feel justified in manipulating others to get done the good they think they need to do.

There is especially no need to ignore God's command to love your neighbor in order for us to insure that God's will be accomplished. There is an alternative to the vision of some Christians and Muslims who see their religion ruling and dominating the world (Christendom or Dar al Islam). There are people in all three religions who do not accept using political power to establish God's rule on earth, who have caught a vision of nonviolent social change.

There is a deep basis for a nonviolent vision in all three religions. Judaism emerged out of the violence of intertribal warfare to develop a prophetic nonviolent vision of beating swords into plowshares. Both Christianity and Islam began with a nonviolent vision that gave way to the perceived need to dominate and control. Sadly, with horrendous results, many Muslims, Christians, and Jews have traded in their historic faith for belief in redemptive violence and domination

Although most people in the three Abrahamic religions see their own religion as being a religion of peace, many see the other two religions as being inherently violent. They bolster their views by quoting Scriptures from the other religions, and by using examples from history and current events to prove how violent those other religions are. Each religion has used their holy books to instill hatred and justify genocide. Each religion has been twisted and used for narrow ideological, class, or nationalistic interests.

I remember discussing this with a Christian who expressed concern about violent tendencies in the other religions. When I said that this tendency also exists in Christianity, she seemed puzzled and questioned me. When I said that many Christians support dropping bombs on Muslims, she replied, "Oh, you mean that." She apparently had not thought before that Christians also support violence, or considered the violence of her own country to actually be violence. It is difficult to recognize our own sin.

The caller on a radio talk show (July, 2006) decried the violence in the Qur'an and claimed the Bible to be superior to the Qur'an because "the Bible teaches forgiveness." "Because Muslims are violent and a threat to Christians," he said, "America should immediately bomb the Islamic world into submission." How blind he was to his own violence. Was he not aware of biblical passages that talk of dashing baby's heads against the rocks? Was he not aware of Jerry Falwell, who referred to the war on terror, and said, "Blow them all away in the name of the Lord?" Jesus said for us to take the log out of our own eye before we attempt to take the speck out of our neighbor's eye.

I am continually impressed with the emphasis on peace I encounter as I worship with the three religions. Muslims stress that Islam means peace, that Allah calls us to peace. Jews repeat the word "Shalom" over and over in the readings and prayers I hear in the synagogue, readings that stress peace and justice. Christians call Jesus "the Prince of Peace," and proclaim that anyone believing in Jesus will know peace. Yet adherents of all three religions perpetrate horrible violence. Over and over again, Jews, Christians, and Muslims forsake their faith in God and give in to their fears. We know the results: air force bombings, suicide bombings, occupation, and threats of more wars to come. People of all three religions have nuclear weapons.

The story of the Bible parallels the existence of many of the great empires of human history: the Assyrian, Egyptian, Babylonian, Persian, Greek, and Roman empires. A striking fact about the Bible story is that never in the Bible are the people of God expected to identify themselves with any of these kingdoms. In fact, they are harshly condemned when they look to Assyria or Egypt for help. Instead, the people of God saw those empires as oppressive occupiers. The people of God were called to a different identity. They had a different understanding of reality, a different vision for the future.

It is striking how many Christians in America today identify themselves with the American empire and support military conquest. They not only have American flag decals on their cars, they even prominently display the American flag in their places of worship, putting the American flag in the place of honor, to the left of the pulpit, and the Christian flag to the right of the pulpit, in an inferior, subordinate position. They are first of all, Americans. They pledge their allegiance to the American flag. They have exchanged the biblical ideas of exiles, sojourners, and aliens, for American citizenship. To illustrate this, consider these quotes from popular American religious leaders. "The American empire is the embodiment of God's will for the earth." "America is the last best hope for the world." "We have been divinely chosen to order the world." In the total scheme of God's redeeming work in history, the American empire is but a sad footnote. It is God's work that is significant.

The cost of this transfer of loyalties has been high. With the acceptance of empire comes the acceptance of violence, war, domination, and control. There is also the horrific cost of what this does to our souls personally, and to our religions.

Truth and justice are always sacrificed as soon as war begins. In times of war, leaders in all three religions not only support the wars of their own countries, but often try to silence their own people from opposing their wars. Labels like unpatriotic, self-hating, treasonous, and even racist are thrown at people who simply are repulsed at the mass killing of children. Consider the uncritical support for Israel from many Jews, the Christian Right's uncritical support for American military adventures, and Muslim support for corrupt governments. When faith is reduced to cheerleading for political strategies, faith is degraded and impoverished.

We turn now to a short history of the three religions and their relation to violence.

JUDAISM AND VIOLENCE

The roots of Judaism go back to the biblical stories of a monotheistic religion developing in a context of intertribal warfare, a horrible, bloody story told in the books of Joshua and Judges. The remarkable aspect of these bloody stories is not the blood and gore, which is expected in warfare, but rather the prophetic warnings to not trust in chariots and horses, to not think victories are won by the strength of military might, and the command to trust exclusively in God for security. "Not by might shall a man prevail" (I Samuel 2:9). Even the bloody books of Joshua and Judges point away from militarism and toward nonviolence. The Hebrew Scriptures prohibit having a standing army.

According to the Hebrew Scriptures, God created a good earth. Sin entered creation and disrupted community. God's work since then has been to seek redemption and reconciliation. The Hebrew Scriptures are full of stories of reconciliation. Isaac and Ishmael together bury their father. Jacob and Esau are reconciled after twenty years of separation. The longest story in the Hebrew Scriptures ends with Joseph forgiving and being reconciled with his brothers who had sold him into slavery in Egypt. David turned down two opportunities to kill Saul and the two were later reconciled.[3] Because King David had much blood on his hands, including exterminating seven ethnic groups, David was not allowed to build the temple. There is a grand Passover celebration involving both sides after a war between Israel and Judah.[4]

When Simeon and Levi massacred the people of Shechum (Nablus) because of the rape of their sister, Dinah, their father Jacob was disturbed that they had acted out of anger and deceit and had engaged in collective punishment.[5] Jacob rejected his sons' argument that the massacre was justified because of its deterrent value. In Deuteronomy 24:16 and Ezekiel 18:20, the idea of collective punishment is clearly rejected. Only those who are guilty may be punished, and not people related to the guilty party, a lesson still needing to be learned in our modern world.

The story of the Hebrews winning an important battle as long as Moses held his arms above his head points to the need to trust in God alone.[6] Moses, like all of us, could not keep his arms lifted for a long time, so his comrades held his arms high until the battle was won. Try to imagine a modern military strategy based on this Scripture: "Not by power, not by might, but by my Spirit says the Lord of hosts."[7] In Joshua 6 the Hebrews won the battle of Jericho, not by military might, but by marching around the city seven times and blowing trumpets.

The story of Gideon in Judges 6–7 is instructive. Because "the Israelites did evil in the eyes of the Lord," the Midianites oppressed the Israelites for seven years. In response to being oppressed, Gideon called for volunteers to drive out the Midianites. Twelve thousand people responded. God told Gideon that he could not fight with that many troops, because if they would win they would think they had won the battle by the strength of their own hands. Instead, God asked Gideon to tell anyone who was afraid, to go home. Two thousand left. The force was then further reduced to 300, who went into the huge Midian camp in the night,

3. 1 Samuel 26.

4. 2 Chronicles 30.

5. Genesis 34; 49:5–7.

6. Exod 17:8–13.

7. Zech 4:6.

armed only with trumpets and torches. They scared the Midianites so deeply they fled.

In addition to not trusting in weapons, another significant moral advance, even in Joshua and Judges, was the prohibition of taking any booty in war. In other words, no blood for oil. Why fight wars if there is no profit?

Seeking revenge also was prohibited. "You shall not take vengeance or bear any grudge, . . . but you shall love your neighbor as yourself: I am the Lord."[8] An important Biblical law against vengeance is the naming of cities of refuge, places where a murderer could flee from people seeking revenge and be assured safety. "Do not rejoice when your enemy falls, and let not your heart not be glad when he stumbles."[9] The Biblical idea of an eye for an eye and a tooth for a tooth is a severe limitation on the use of violence and vengeance. I cannot do more to you than you have done to me. Imagine the world advancing even to this level of morality. In response to the killing of almost 3,000 people on September 11, 2001, the U.S. government has killed hundreds of thousands of Muslims.

One of the central themes of the Hebrew prophets is the longing for shalom. This hope is rooted in the peace of the Garden of Eden and the vision of lions lying down with lambs. The Jewish hope for the coming of the Messiah is a hope for peace, which stands in fundamental opposition to militarism and imperialism. Many of the messianic texts talk of beating swords into plowshares and a new age of peace.

Shalom is one of the ten names of God in the Torah. A prayer in Talmud Berachot 55b states, "Great and mighty one, who dwells on high, You are Peace and Your name is Peace. May it be Your will that You place upon us Peace."[10] Gideon, who we just referred to, said, "The Lord is Peace."[11] Rabbi Marc Gopin claims that "The Zohar, the classic text of Jewish mysticism, makes the claim that one who fights against peace fights against the name of God."[12] The biblical command is to "Seek peace and pursue it."[13]

8. Lev 19:18.

9. Prov 24:17.

10. Gopin, "Is There a Jewish God of Peace?," 34; in Polner and Goodman, *The Challenge of Shalom.*

11. Judg 6:24.

12. Gopin, "Is There Jewish God of Peace?," 35; in Polner and Goodman, *The Challenge of Shalom.*

13. Ps 34:15.

Although zealotry, with horrible consequences, has also been part of Jewish history, Jews traditionally have generally understood the folly of securing peace through war.

The Hebrew idea of shalom is more than the absence of war. It implies wholeness, integrity, justice, healing, salvation, having relationships in order. Shalom is a major theme not only of the Jewish Scriptures, but also of the Jewish prayer books and rabbinical writings. Many rabbis have even gone so far as to say that seeking peace is to seek the presence of God. Peace is a way of identifying God's presence in our hearts and in society. Those who prepare for war have turned their hearts away from God.

It is simply wrong to see "the God of the Old Testament" as violent and harsh, and the God of the "New Testament" to be merciful and loving. None of this anti-Jewish bigotry is supported by the Bible or by history. All of Jesus' statements of love of neighbor and rejection of violence are rooted in the Jewish tradition. They were not new with Jesus. Jesus' command to "Love your neighbor as yourself" comes from Lev 19:18. The Jewish Scriptures are full of references to mercy, forgiveness, and peace. Martin Buber believed Jesus embodied the essence of Judaism. As the Hasidic rabbi of Rizhyn put it, "Just as it is man's way and compulsion to sin and sin again and again, so it is God's way and his divine compulsion to forgive and pardon again and again."[14] The Hasidim emphasized that to love God is to love one's neighbor and one's enemy. Martin Buber quotes a Hasidic teaching: "Pray for enemies that things go well with them, and if you think, that is no service of God: know that more than any other prayer, this is service of God."[15]

The pacifism of the first-century Jewish/Christian communities was rooted in Judaism and continued in Rabbinic Judaism, but was for the most part abandoned in the Christian communities as they became less Jewish. As John Howard Yoder put it, "For over a millennium the Jews of the Diaspora were the closest thing to the ethic of Jesus existing anywhere on any significant scale anywhere in Christendom."[16]

The rabbis used the biblical story of Moses and the burning bush as symbolic of peaceful coexistence between opposites, in that the fire did not consume the bush. That means we need to learn to live in peace with

---

14. Friedman, "Hasidism and the Love of Enemies," 42; in Polner and Goodman, *The Challenge of Shalom*.

15. Buber, *Two Types of Faith*, 77.

16. Yoder, *Jewish-Christian Schism*, 81–82.

those who are different from us. For Judaism, turning to God does not mean turning away from my family and neighbors, or the denial of self and passions, but the fulfillment of self as we give ourselves wholeheartedly to loving and serving our neighbor.

The first story of nonviolent resistance in the Bible, and possibly the first recorded act of civil disobedience in history, is the story of the Hebrew midwives, Shiphrah and Puah, defying Pharoah's order to kill all male Hebrew babies.[17] According to the biblical text, the reason they disobeyed was because they "feared God." Although a political act, they resisted not for political reasons, but because of their respect for God, the Creator. They did not compromise their integrity. They listened to their consciences.

Possibly the first recorded act of civil disobedience by soldiers refusing to obey orders is found in 1 Sam 22:6–17. King Saul ordered his soldiers to kill the priests of the Lord and their families. His soldiers refused to obey his orders.

In Daniel 6, there is the story of the Babylonian king ordering that for thirty days no one was allowed to pray to God, with the penalty of being thrown into the lions' den. Instead of obeying the order, or quietly praying alone, Daniel opened his windows and defiantly and publicly prayed toward Jerusalem, and was thrown into the lions' den. When Babylonian King Nebuchadnezzar set up a golden idol, Shadrach, Meshach, and Abednego refused to bow down and worship the idol. They were thrown into a fiery furnace, but were not consumed.[18]

There are many stories in the four books of Maccabees of refusal to break Torah regulations during the forced Hellenization of Judah. "We are ready to die rather than transgress the laws of our fathers," they said.[19]

Jeremiah advocated surrender rather than to fight against the advancing Babylonians, or ally with the Egyptian empire. For that, he was arrested, accused of treason, beaten, and thrown into a dungeon. Isaiah also rejected resisting the Babylonian assault on Jerusalem. In another

17. Exod 1:15–20.

18. Daniel 3.

19. 2 Macc 7:2.

case, Isaiah walked the streets of Jerusalem naked for three years to protest the shame of his people's sins.

The central event in the Jewish Scriptures is the Exodus, God's liberating the Hebrew slaves from oppression, the rejection of people having power over other people. Throughout the Hebrew Scriptures there is the theme that there is a higher authority than the state. This includes belief in the sanctity of human life, that we are created in the likeness and image of God, "a little lower than the angels."

At first, the Israelites operated with a decentralized system of rule under judges and charismatic leaders. But in time, the Israelites wanted to be like the other nations, and have a king and centralized rule. The prophet Samuel warned that having a king would lead to military conscription, high taxes, and ultimately, slavery (1 Samuel 8). Samuel warned that to have a king would be to reject the kingship of God. Against Samuel's advice, they chose a king and proved Samuel right. The Israelites, for the most part, did not fare well under their kings, and ultimately were conquered by surrounding empires. Consider this quote attributed to the Hassidic Rabbi of Apt:

> When God promised to make of Abraham "a great nation," the
> Evil Urge whispered to him: "'A great nation'—that means power,
> that means possessions." But Abraham only laughed at him. "I un-
> derstand better than you," he said. "'A great nation' means a people
> that sanctifies the name of God."[20]

While there was the idea of holy war in Joshua and Judges, many Jews at the time of Jesus had rejected the whole idea of kings and their wars. For them, the point of the holy war tradition of Joshua and Judges and the prophetic tradition (i.e., Amos, Isaiah, and Jeremiah) was to trust only God, not in chariots and horses or military alliances with neighboring empires.

For most first-century Jews, the Maccabean rebellion (168–35 BCE) only reinforced the idea that violence was not a viable option for Jews.

---

20. Milgrom, "Nonviolence and Judaism," 122; in Smith-Christopher, ed., *Subverting Hatred.*

The Jewish revolt in 70 CE, against overwhelming Roman power, resulted in the destruction of Jerusalem and the Jewish temple, and the scattering of Jews throughout the world (Diaspora). After this, Judaism mostly rejected military force as a means of overcoming evil and developing security. The final act of Jewish violent resistance was the Bar Kochba revolt in 120 CE. For 1700 years, the failure of these revolts pretty much ended revolutionary hopes for a violent reestablishment of Jewish sovereignty.

Rabbinic Judaism understood the experiment with civil kingship and the Maccabean and Zealot adventures into violence as failures. In the era of Rabbinic Judaism, Jews accepted that they could not topple the great military powers, and chose to live in secluded communities on the edge of the Gentile world. For the past 1900 years, Judaism has been essentially pacifist. Rabbinic Judaism did not have a vision of militarism and domination of other peoples. Such ideas would have been considered anathema, totally contradictory to the Jewish way of living a life of trusting in God. An essence of Jewish identity has been its not being like other nations with their oppressive structures. As John Howard Yoder put it, "Jewry represents the longest and strongest experience of religious-cultural-moral continuity in known history, defended without the sword."[21]

Here are three stories that articulate the essence of Jewish nonviolence.

There is a story from Muslim Spain where Sh'muel Ha-Nagid was an official in the government of the Caliph of Granada. A visiting Muslim verbally abused the Jew in front of the caliph, whereupon the caliph ordered the Jew to cut out the tongue of the rude Muslim. Later the caliph saw the Jew and the Muslim having a friendly conversation. The caliph asked the Jew why he had not cut out the man's tongue. Sh'muel answered, "I removed an enemy's tongue and replaced it with a friend's tongue."[22]

Abraham Joshua Heschel tells the story of how in the spring of 1921, the Grand Mufti of Jerusalem, Haj Muhammed Amin el-Husseini, instigated attacks against Jews. Shots rang out when a group of Arabs was ready to attack Jewish homes between Tel-Aviv and Jaffa. Rabbi Ben Zion Uziel put on his rabbinical robes and went out on the battlefield between the warring parties and convinced both sides to stop shooting. The Rabbi

21. Yoder, *Jewish-Christian Schism*, 125.

22. Bentley, "Hasidism and the Love of Enemies," 29; in Polner and Goodman, eds., *The Challenge of Shalom*.

appealed for peace and to share the land as brothers.[23] Sadly, this expression of trust was soon betrayed.

Joseph Abileah, a well know Israeli pacifist, tells the story of being surrounded by a group of Palestinians in 1936, a time of deep tensions and violence between Jews and Arabs. When the Palestinians threatened to kill him, he responded, "If it is your duty, go ahead. I am in your hands." It was soon clear that they didn't have the heart to kill him. When one proposed they throw him in a nearby well, he walked to the well and stood on its edge. No one had the heart to do what they knew to be wrong. Abileah later reflected that there was something of God in their hearts that prevented them from killing him. If he had used a violent defense, it would have been much easier for them to kill him.[24]

There were problems with the passive Rabbinic vision. Judaism became ingrown, lost its vision of being a servant and a light to the world, and failed to maintain vital relationships with their neighbors. Along with Rabbinic Judaism came pogroms and expulsions, and finally the Holocaust.

The most recent innovation for Judaism has been the founding of the state of Israel, and accepting the Gentile model of military power. The state of Israel has decided that survival cannot be trusted to God, that only militaristic nationalism can lead to salvation. Some Jews see the establishment of the state of Israel as the fulfillment of messianic promises and the beginning of the messianic age. A new vision, from Theodore Hertzl to Benyamin Netanyahu, has rejected Rabbinic Judaism in favor of a new accommodation to the ways of the Gentiles. Some militant Israelis now honor people like Bar Kochba and their violence.

Relying on an earthly kingdom based on violence, Zionism now has taken a path similar to that of Constantinian Christendom. Israel now relies on massive military force, including nuclear weapons, for her security. With the collapse of the Rabbinic vision, and the establishment of the state of Israel, many Jews adopted the vision of a militaristic state

23. Heschel, "A True Story," 26; in Polner and Goodman, eds., *The Challenge of Shalom.*

24. Abileah, "Meeting at Our Roots," 108–9; in Polner and Goodman, eds., *The Challenge of Shalom.*

prepared to crush and dominate any foe. The frightening results of that vision can be seen not only in Israel's distorted relationships with her neighbors, but also in the spiritual and psychological toll it has exerted on Judaism itself. Many Israelis have told me that the only answer for Israel is to have more guns and bombs than the Arabs. Only with armed might and keeping the Arabs suppressed can there be peace, they say.

It has been a deep pain for me to see how Judaism has been used to justify and support the domination and subjugation of the Palestinian people. My experiences with Israeli settlers and soldiers in the West Bank are quite different from the Judaism I experience in the synagogue in Athens, where I experience compassion, sensitivity, love, grace, and a commitment to social justice for all. Those are two radically different Judaisms.

The Jewish settlers and Israeli soldiers in Hebron maintain their control over the Palestinians with guns, violating the rule of the prophets, "Not by power nor by might, but by my Spirit says the Lord of Hosts."[25] It is by the power of the gun that they rule over the Palestinians, a relationship built not on trust in God, not on mercy and kindness. God is absent from the equation, except that the name of God is used to justify oppression. As Avraham Burg, former speaker of the Israeli Knesset, put it, "Jews and Israelis have become thugs."[26] Quoting the Midrash, Burg compares Jews mistreating Palestinians with Jews eating pork.[27]

When secular Zionists began to migrate to Palestine, the local Palestinian Orthodox religious Jews were horrified by both the philosophy and the antics of these Zionist zealots, which they saw as a threat both to their Jewish faith and their good relations with their Muslim and Christian neighbors. The Ultra-Orthodox Neturei Karta refused to support the establishment of the state of Israel, seeing it as usurping God's role in redeeming Israel and making the new state of Israel an authority independent of Torah. The following is a quote from a leaflet distributed by Neturei Karta in Montreal on Israeli Independence Day, 2001.

> Worse than the toll of suffering, exploitation, death, and desecration of the Torah, has been the inner rot that Zionism has injected into the Jewish soul. It has dug deep into the essence of being a

25. Zech 4:6.

26. Burg, *Holocaust Is Over*, 51.

27. Ibid., 89.

Jew. It has offered a secular formulation of Jewish identity as a replacement for the unanimous belief of our people in Torah from Heaven. It has caused Jews to view golus [exile] as a result of military weakness. . . . It has wreaked havoc among Jews both in Israel and America, by casting us in the role of Goliath-like oppressors. It has made cruelty and corruption the norm for its followers.[28]

Yisrael David Weiss, an Orthodox anti-Zionist, wrote,

Only blind dogmatism could present Israel as something positive for the Jewish people. Established as a so-called refuge, it has unfailingly over the past five decades, been the most dangerous place on the face of the earth for a Jew. It has been the cause of tens of thousands of Jewish deaths, of families torn apart; it has left in its wake a trail of mourning widows, orphans and friends. . . . And let us not forget that to this account of the physical suffering of the Jews, must be added those of the Palestinian people, a nation condemned to indigence, persecution, to life without shelter, to overwhelming despair, and all too often to premature death.[29]

Moshe Saber, an Israeli rabbi, rejects the violence of Israelis toward the Palestinians.

The notion that we can do whatever we please, succumb to any kind of temptation, or engage in any form of foolish self-aggrandizement without fear of penalty because we have an inside track to the Almighty is the plain opposite of religious faith. It is in fact an affront to the Divine, whose authority to determine the course of history we are usurping. . . . Such blind faith is not really a faith in God at all, but rather faith in ourselves. It makes a tool out of the Almighty. . . . It is an idolatrous concept that masks what is actually an irrational belief in our own invincibility.[30]

Whatever one thinks about these quotes, there is no question that the formation of the state of Israel has had a huge impact on Judaism, creating a new Judaism. This includes political empowerment and rejection of the prophetic and rabbinic traditions. Many Israelis believe Jews are superior to Arabs. Jewish identity is now rooted in ethnicity rather than in obedience to God. Avraham Burg says that for some, Judaism

28. Quoted by Rabkin, *Threat Within*, 1.

29. Ibid., 199.

30. Ibid., 77.

has been reduced to "a race theory."[31] This means a major shift from seeing redemption coming from God to redemption rooted in military and political action.

Justification of Israel takes three forms: believing in the innocence of Israel, seeing Jews as perpetual victims, and support for political and military superiority with no need for any moral justification. Loyalty to Israel trumps loyalty to Judaism. Marc Ellis puts it this way: "If it is true that powerlessness is, after the Holocaust, unethical for Jews, it can also be said that power without ethics is a kind of moral suicide."[32] The Wailing Wall symbolizes Jewish suffering, while the Apartheid Wall symbolizes Israel's infliction of suffering on others.

Israel is an important arena for the struggle for the soul of Judaism. People like Martin Buber, Judah Magnes, and Aron Cohen advocated a bi-national state of Israel with equal rights for Palestinians. Many Israelis continue to believe that a Jewish nation must recognize and defend the rights of minorities in Israel. Already in 1891, Asher Ginzberg, an important Jewish philosopher, could see where Zionism was heading.

> Palestine is not an uninhabited land and can offer a home only to a very small portion of the Jews scattered throughout the world. Those who settle in Palestine must above all seek to win the friendship of the Palestinians, by approaching them courteously and with respect. But what do our brothers do? Precisely the opposite. They were slaves in the land of their exile, and suddenly they find themselves with unlimited freedom. This sudden change has aroused in them a tendency to despotism, which is what always happens when slaves come to power. They treat the Arabs with hostility and cruelty, rob them of their rights in a dishonest way, hurt them without reason and then pride themselves on such actions.[33]

Helen Fein said it well.

> Ruling over another people who claim not merely minority rights but the right to self-determination as a people should be as abhorrent to Jews as was our powerlessness. Governing without consent demands the use of repression. No more than the Americans, or the British, or the French do Jews have the capacity to rule over another people without becoming captive to their rule, without

---

31. Burg, *Holocaust Is Over*, 181.

32. Ellis, *Reading Torah Out Loud*, 89.

33. Quoted by Wagner, *Dying in Land of Promise*, 89.

playing the role of oppressor. This endangers the moral integrity of the Jewish state from within and makes it prone to crime, disorder, and terrorism.[34]

The high points of Jewish morality and spirituality were during times when Jews had no political power. Sadly, like Christians and Muslims, when Jews have had political power, they also have acted in brutal ways. As Roberta Strauss Feuerlicht put it, "Judaism survived centuries of persecution without a state; it must now learn how to survive despite a state."[35]

Any discussion of nonviolence and Judaism must wrestle with the Holocaust. There was some armed Jewish resistance to the Holocaust, as for example, the Warsaw Ghetto uprising, but it was not effective. Most people are not aware of the amount of successful nonviolent resistance, as it has not been as well documented or publicized as armed resistance, partly because it was more secret and hidden.

In February-March, 1943, Hitler arrested about 1,000 Jews who were married to non-Jewish spouses. The non-Jewish spouses organized demonstrations in front of Hitler's headquarters in Berlin, with 6,000 people demanding the release of their family members. Hitler backed down and released the Jewish spouses. (Although this story is widely told, there are some who dispute its historicity.)

Jewish nonviolent resistance took many forms, including escape, refusal to register or report, hiding, getting false papers, volunteering to die in the place of other Jews, forming support groups inside and outside the concentration camps, finding homes where Jews could hide, arranging transportation to safe areas, or working with non-Jewish groups.

Along with refusal to cooperate with Nazi edicts, non-Jewish protection of Jews was extremely important. It is significant that in eight out of the twenty-one countries allied with or occupied by Germany, over half of the Jews survived. It is not true that Jews stood alone.[36] Mordecai

34. Fein, "Reading the Second Text," 80; in Polner and Goodman, eds., *The Challenge of Shalom.*

35. Feuerlicht, *Fate of Jews,* 287.

36. See Wilcock, "Impossible Pacifism," 59–69; in Polner and Goodman, eds., *The Challenge of Shalom.*

Paldiel, Director of Vad Vashem's "Department for the Righteous Among the Nations," estimates that as many as 250,000 Gentiles helped save as many as 250,000 Jewish lives.[37] It is true that out of 6,000,000 Jews killed, the number saved was quite small. In the countries where the majority of Jews survived, non-Jewish support was essential in the survival of those Jews. In almost every case where Jews survived, they were aided by non-Jews, sometimes called "Righteous Gentiles (hasidei ummot ha-olam)." Interdependence is essential for survival. Going it alone for any group will lead to disaster. This is especially true of minority groups.[38]

The idea that Jews stood alone is used by militant Zionists to argue that Jews today must stand alone, that no non-Jew can be trusted. Right wing Zionists use this perspective to argue that Jews are eternal victims, stand alone and isolated (a self-fulfilling prophecy), and to argue against any negotiated settlement with Palestinians. These ideas blind Israelis from seeing the reasons why Israelis are hated and feared, and result in Israelis advocating denial of Palestinian rights, separation of Jews and Palestinians, and even mass expulsion of all Palestinians from Israel. Some Zionists even advocate genocide against the Palestinians. This not only undermines support for Israel, but makes Israelis less secure by increasing the threat and undermining the legitimacy of Israel.

The vision of Israel against the world is a denial of the call in the Torah for Israel to be "a light to the nations," to serve the world. As Israelis lose their spiritual foundation, they are left with nothing but nationalism, militarism, and materialism, a massive defeat for Judaism.

Some Jews are now saying the task for Judaism is to find a third way beyond passive withdrawal and military supremacy. There are voices in the Jewish community saying that recovery of the essence of Judaism will need to include a recovery of Jewish nonviolence. Groups like the Jewish Peace Fellowship are calling for active nonviolence. (Other progressive Jewish

37. Gushee, *Righteous Gentiles*, 9.

38. See Niewk, *The Holocaust: Problems and Perspectives of Interpretation,* for a collection of various perspectives on the Holocaust. Especially instructive is Yahuda Bauer's article, "Forms of Jewish Resistance," in detailing examples of both nonviolent and violent resistance to the Holocaust, 129–45. For a discussion of Polish help in saving Jews, see Richard C. Lukas' article, "The Poles Were Fellow Victims," 176–90.

groups include Jewish Voices for Peace, Progressive Jewish Alliance, Shomer Shalom Institute for Jewish Nonviolence, The Shalom Center, J Street and Tikkun.) As Rabbi Steven S. Schwarzchild put it, "I believe on the basis of intense, life-long and professional studies, that pacifism is the best, the most authentic, interpretation of classical Judaism." [39] Many Jews are saying that the profound ethical tradition of Judaism needs to be recovered. Marc Ellis maintains that like Christians who cannot retreat to pre-Auschwitz days, so also Jews cannot retreat to pre-Israel days, but rather will find healing and redemption only in relationship to Palestinians.[40]

In spite of all the attempts at separation and Apartheid, the policies of the Israeli government, like scattering settlements throughout the Palestinian territories, Israelis and Palestinians have become irrevocably part of each other's lives. Marc Ellis goes so far as to suggest that Israeli actions have served to include the Palestinian people as part of the Jewish covenant. The effect of Israeli actions has been the opposite of the goal of an exclusive Jewish state.[41] Maybe the creation of the state of Israel will one day lead to healing the feud between Isaac and Ishmael.

I am always impressed with the Scriptures, readings, and sermons shared during the Jewish Holy Days. If Israelis would live by the clear commands in their Scriptures, the problems with the Palestinians would soon be resolved. If the worldwide Jewish community could stand up to the atrocities of the Israeli government and once again put morality above narrow nationalistic interests, the Jewish people could rediscover what it could mean for Jews to be a Chosen People and recover their call to be "a light unto the nations." One suggested reason for the weakness of the Israeli peace movement is the lack of support from progressive Jews in the rest of the world. Because of international Jewish support for Israel's commitment to military supremacy, Israeli doves are left stranded with no support from their natural allies around the world. The crisis of morality in Israel is an opportunity for Judaism to find spiritual renewal.

39. Schwarzchild, "Shalom," 19; in eds. Polner and Goodman, *The Challenge of Shalom*.
40. Ellis, *Reading Torah Out Loud*, 124.
41. Ellis, *O Jerusalem*, 54.

CHRISTIANITY AND VIOLENCE

The history of Christianity is a bloody history. No religion has ever blessed as much killing as have Christians. Think of the crusades, the Thirty Years' War that wiped out half the population of Europe, two world wars, Vietnam, Iraq, and Afghanistan, plus all the smaller wars in which Christians have been killing each other and people of other religions.

It did not start out this way. Jesus transformed the expectation of the Messiah being a political ruler who would violently restore the kingdom of David and bring political power and dignity to the Jewish people to an understanding of a nonviolent kingdom rooted in spiritual power based in nonviolent, suffering love.

Not one verse in the New Testament supports the idea of violent self-defense or killing one's enemies. On the night before his crucifixion, Jesus washed the feet of the one (Judas) who would betray him. Then while in unimaginable agony on the cross, Jesus called on God to forgive the ones who had carried out his torture. Jesus commanded his followers to not repay evil for evil. It is difficult to imagine Jesus killing his enemies. Jesus rejected self-defense, laid down his life, and sought to include and redeem his enemies. The early Christians agreed with their Jewish brothers and sisters that war was to be rejected. As John Howard Yoder points out, it was in the process of rejecting its Jewish identity that Christianity rejected its pacifist beginning.[42]

Up until 170 CE, there is no evidence of Christians being soldiers in the military. All the early Church fathers were clear that a Christian may not be a soldier. After the year 170, there are a few accounts of Christians in the military, but participation in the military was controversial. Writing between 170 and 180, Celsus, the pagan critic of Christianity, berated the Christians for refusing to participate in war. Tertullian wrote about people withdrawing from military duty when they became Christians. He said that "Christ in disarming Peter ungirt every soldier." Justin Martyr wrote,

> We who were filled with war and mutual slaughter and every wickedness have each of us in all the world changed our weapons of war. . . . swords into plows and spears into agricultural implements. . . .We who formerly murdered one another now not only

---

42. Yoder, *Jewish-Christian Schism*, 72.

do not make war upon our enemies, but that we many not lie or deceive our judges, we gladly die confessing Christ.[43]

Arnobius wrote sometime around 304–10 CE:

For since we in such numbers have learned from the precepts and laws of Christ not to repay evil for evil, to endure injury rather than to inflict it, to shed our own blood rather than to stain our hands and conscience with the blood of another, the ungrateful world now long owes to Christ this blessing that savage ferocity has been softened and hostile hands have refrained from the blood of a kindred creature.[44]

A primary basis for rejection of war was the Christian commitment to love. Tertullian asked, "If we are enjoined to love our enemies, whom have we to hate? If injured we are forbidden to retaliate, who then can suffer injury at our hands?"[45]

Gradually, Christians did begin to become soldiers, but this was widely condemned by all Christian leaders. Up until the time of Constantine, the Christian church was essentially pacifist.

The "conversion" of the Roman emperor Constantine to Christianity in 312 marked a drastic change in Christianity. Constantine was pro-claimed to be "God's Anointed." Whereas it had been illegal to be a Christian, soon it would be illegal not to be a Christian. Earlier, Christians were prohibited from being soldiers. Now only Christians would be al-lowed in the Roman army. The baptizing of the Roman Empire brought little change to the Roman Empire. The church, however, underwent drastic change as it sold its soul to the empire and became like the empire.

Such a major shift in power and allegiances required a correspond-ing theological shift to fit the needs of the empire. Christian pacifism and the teachings of Jesus were now to apply only to private and interpersonal relationships, and to religious orders. Monks and priests were not to par-ticipate in war. They were to continue to follow the way of Jesus. However, religious military orders soon developed and priests and bishops par-ticipated in battle. Roland Bainton records that between 886 and 908, ten German bishops died in battle. They sometimes did try to preserve the letter of the law. Rather than use a sword, the archbishop of Mainz in

43. Bainton, *Christian Attitudes*, 72.
44. Ibid., 73.
45. Ibid., 77.

1182 used a club to kill nine people in battle because he did not want to shed blood.[46]

Up until the time of Pope Gregory VII (1073–85), soldiers needed to do penance for killing in war. Gregory, however, preached that killing in war was meritorious rather than sinful as had been taught by the church up to that time. This ruling gave church support for massacres during the crusades.

Ambrose, and then Augustine, developed the just war doctrine to accommodate Christianity to the needs of the empire. Borrowing from Stoicism, Plato, Cicero, and the Hebrew Scriptures, Augustine developed a set of rules of conduct to govern warfare. Augustine did this partly to justify Rome protecting itself from the threat of a Barbarian invasion. In spite of Augustine's support for killing Barbarians, the Barbarians conquered Rome and the church thrived. Augustine was wrong both politically and theologically. The main threat to our faith comes from compromising our faith.

There have been various lists of criteria to be used in discerning whether or not a particular war is just or unjust. Sometimes the list includes seven criteria, sometimes as many as fourteen. John Howard Yoder put together a list of traditional criteria for war to be considered justifiable. These criteria represent the official position of most churches.

The authority waging the war must be legitimate.

The cause being fought for must be just.

The ultimate goal ("intention") must be peace.

The subjective motivation ("intention") must not be hatred or vengefulness.

War must be the last resort.

Success must be probable.

The means used must be indispensable to achieve the end.

The means used must be discriminating, both quantitatively, in order not to do more harm than the harm they prevent ("proportionality"), and qualitatively, to avoid use against the innocent ("immunity").

The means used must respect the provisions of international law.[47]

---

46. Ibid., 104.

47. Yoder, *When War Is Unjust*, 18.

Any honest person who studies this list must say that it is an impressive list. How could any decent person disagree with these criteria? Three responses to this list come to mind.

First, the doctrine of the just war assumes that ethical judgments can be made about the use of violence. It means that the violence of the state is not a law unto itself, and not only can be, but must be questioned. Governments are not the final authority over what is moral or immoral. Sadly, many religious people do not believe that the violence of the state may be questioned. "My country right or wrong."

Second, if these criteria are to be taken seriously, practically all wars would need to be declared unjust, for I know of no war that fits all of these criteria. In all modern wars, for example, most of the victims are innocent civilians. The U.S. war on Iraq met hardly any of the criteria.

Third, instead of being a set of criteria for discerning whether or not any particular war is justifiable (a noble quest), the just war tradition has been used only to justify wars, not to declare wars unjust. I am not aware of any war in history that ever was declared unjust by any major church. The only example I know of a church declaring a war unjust was John Michael Botean, Bishop of the Romanian Catholic Diocese of Canton, Ohio. In a pastoral letter delivered on March 7, 2003, on the eve of the U.S. war on Iraq, Bishop Botean declared the war unjust, and any participation in or support for that war to be murder and a mortal sin.

Even when Christians were fighting on opposite sides, Christians on both sides were convinced that their war was a just war. The just war tradition has been a total farce. It has been a fig leaf used by the church to justify every war that has come along. How can any argument for war be used to justify people of the same religion fighting on both sides of any war? All the popular preachers who have said, "Right or wrong, we support our nation's war efforts," have abandoned the just war theory and any ethical discernment concerning war, and given ultimate allegiance (worship) to the state.

Even Pope John Paul II, who vigorously opposed George Bush's unnecessary, illegal, and immoral war against Iraq, did not declare that war to be unjust, which would have made it a mortal sin for Catholics to participate in the war. Even in that grossly unjust war, the Pope did not implement the just war tradition, but allowed the just war theory to be used to support the unjust war.

Some people have taken these concerns seriously and have supported or opposed particular wars based on these or other moral criteria. They have sometimes been referred to as selective conscientious objectors. They are to be respected.

Actually, most people do not think ethically about war. They support their country, right or wrong. For them, national self-interest is the primary criteria, a philosophy spelled out by Machiavelli. Their thinking is totally outside the Abrahamic tradition. For them, ethical questions are not considered relevant. National sovereignty replaces any other concerns. The only argument about the war in Iraq they would listen to, for example, was whether or not the war was in America's best interest.

A popular basis for ethics is pragmatism, doing what we can to make situations come out right, with the best possible results, with the greatest good for the greatest number of people. Christian ethics, however, are based on following Jesus, becoming servants. Instead of grasping power "to do good," we give up control, take up the cross, accept suffering, and make ourselves vulnerable. This is the very opposite of worldly do-goodism which has created so much oppression and suffering in its attempt to make history "come out right."

The church never took the just war tradition seriously. But even the just war theory collapsed in the Middle Ages as Christians faced first the Barbarians and then the Muslims in the crusades. The ideas of holy war and crusade replaced philosophical ideas about just war. Our nation's enemies are seen as the enemies of God, forgetting that all of us have been enemies of God. Today, the two main options for most Americans in looking at warfare are national interest and holy war. A high percentage of American Christians support the idea of a new crusade against Muslims. One even hears self-professed Christians calling for nuclear annihilation of the Muslim world.

For too many Christians, Jesus has no authority in discerning right from wrong. They confuse national ambitions with the will of God. White, American, evangelical Christians overwhelmingly supported George Bush's unnecessary and illegal war against Iraq, even arguing that that war would open the way for the conversion of the Muslim world to Christianity. Instead, the war weakened the Iraqi Christian church and made a mockery of Christianity for much of the world.

Although rooted in the biblical holy war tradition, the Medieval crusades differed from Hebrew holy war in that the Israelites trusted in God to win the battle, while the crusaders were fighting for God, which justified anything they did. In a holy war, since one is fighting for God rather than some political interest, neither human rules, nor religious rules for that matter, apply. The worst evils are committed for lofty reasons: wars to end wars, wars to spread democracy, wars to rid the world of terrorism, etc.

In holy war, war need not be the last resort. Negotiations are considered naïve, dishonorable, and treasonous. Having a good chance of winning is not important. To die as a martyr is victory. In holy war, the enemy has no rights. The enemy may represent Satan, or even be considered less than human. Often racist perspectives come to the fore. "The only good enemy is a dead enemy." American wars have had some of the qualities of holy war. Islamic and Jewish militants also fit in this category.

The Christian pacifist tradition of the early Christians continued to be expressed in every century. The religious orders in the Roman Catholic tradition were one means of continuing the tradition. There was opposition to the militarized church throughout the Middle Ages. There were the Cathari, Waldensians, Franciscans, Peter Chelciky, and many others. The Reformation for the most part continued the views of the Medieval church, officially supporting the just war theory, but in practice sanctioning mass killings of their opponents. Both Luther and Calvin, like Augustine, recommended the killing of people with whom they disagreed.

There was radical opposition to the mainline Reformers. The Anabaptists rejected not only war, but also infant baptism, merger of church and state, and religious coercion. They called people to follow Jesus, to live simply, and to live in community. In his trial before his execution in 1527, the Swiss Anabaptist, Michael Sattler, stated:

> If the Turk (Muslim) comes, he should not be resisted, for it stands written: Thou shalt not kill. We should not defend ourselves against the Turks or our other persecutors, but with reverent prayer should implore God that He might be our defense and our resistance. . . . If waging war were proper I would rather take the field against the so-called Christians who persecute, take captive, and kill true Christians, than against the Turks.[48]

48. Krabill et al., *Anabaptists Meeting Muslims*, 101.

Coming out of the radical wing of the Protestant Reformation, the Mennonites (and associated bodies such as the Amish and Hutterites), the Quakers, and the Church of the Brethren constitute what have been called the Historic Peace Churches. These churches have always taught that followers of Jesus are called to love their enemies and are prohibited from killing them. Therefore those churches have always taught their members to refrain from participation in war or preparation for war, and for most of their histories have made this commitment a condition of church membership.

The Historic Peace Churches have not only opposed wars, but have actively worked to relieve hunger and human need, have reached across boundaries of nation, race, class, and religion to promote understanding in the world.

Christian pacifism was never limited to the Historic Peace Churches, however, but has been a minority presence in all of the mainline Christian churches. In the early years, Pentecostals were pacifists. In recent years, atrocities like saturation bombing of cities in World War II, the advent of nuclear weapons, and the war in Vietnam raised issues of war/peace that many mainline Christians could no longer ignore, which has caused many Christians to rethink their stance toward war. The witness of Mahatma Ghandi and Martin Luther King, Jr. has made the philosophy of nonviolence a real option for many people. There now is renewed interest in the pacifism of the Historic Peace Churches.

Christians involved in nonviolent action look to the Jesus who drove the money changers from the temple, and to the Book of Revelation where the government is described as a "beast" to be resisted.

ISLAM AND VIOLENCE

Like Judaism, Islam emerged out of a tribal society marked by cycles of violence and oppressive social relations. Islam was a message of peace. Loyalty to the Ummah, the larger Muslim community, became more important than loyalty to one's tribe. Muslims were forbidden from fighting against other Muslims. Mohammad's egalitarian message of peace was welcomed as liberation by the common people, but was seen as a threat to the power structures of his time. A major reason for the early growth and spread of Islam was Mohammad's ability to bring reconciliation to the warring tribes of Arabia, based on the proclamation of the oneness of God. Tribal warfare and blood revenge were largely banished.

It is unfair and inaccurate to describe Islam as a religion of violence. We do not use the violent conquest of Canaan to define the essence of Judaism, or the crusades or Inquisition to define Christianity. Neither should we use Muslim extremists to define Islam.

For the first thirteen years, Islam was a totally nonviolent religion. Even though he was humiliated, persecuted, and even tortured, Mohammad counseled against retaliation and emphasized nonviolent resistance. Mohammad even opposed cursing one's enemies. Mohammad responded to persecution by saying, "Forgive them, Lord, for they know not what they do."[49] There are many verses in the Qur'an that support nonviolence. Consider these verses.

> If anyone slew a person—unless it be for murder or for spreading mischief in the land—it would be as if he slew the whole people. And if anyone saved a life it would be as if he saved the life of the whole people.[50] (This is actually a quote from Jewish sources.)
>
> O ye who believe! Stand out firmly for Allah, as witnesses to fair dealing, and let not the hatred of others to you make you swerve to wrong and depart from justice. Be just; that is next to piety, and fear Allah. For Allah is well-acquainted with all that ye do.[51]
>
> O you who believe! Stand out firmly for justice as witnesses to Allah even as against yourselves or your parents or your kin and whether rich or poor: for Allah can best protect both. Follow not the lusts [of your hearts] lest you swerve, and if you distort or decline to do justice, indeed Allah is well-acquainted with all that you do.[52]

Muslims consider Islam to be a religion of peace. The word "peace" (salaam) is used constantly in Muslim conversation and writings. Muslims greet each other with Salaam alykum (peace be unto you). The word *Islam* itself means both submission to God and peace. A Muslim is one who lives in submission to God and is at peace with God's creation. In the Qur'anic story of Cain and Abel, Abel says to Cain, "If thou doest stretch thy hand against me to slay me, it is not for me to stretch my hand against

49. Quoted by Abu-Nimer, *Nonviolence and Peace*, 67.
50. Qur'an 5:32.
51. Ibid., 5:8.
52. Ibid., 4:135.

thee to slay thee, for I do fear Allah, the Cherisher of the Worlds."[53] In decrying Muslim support for violence, Jawdat Sai'd wrote,

> I don't see anyone in this world who has clearly explained when it is incumbent upon a Muslim to behave like (Abel) the son of Adam! Nor does anyone teach the Muslims that the Messenger of God said to his companion Sa'd Ibn Abi Waqqas, "Kun ka-ibni Adam (Be as the son of Adam)!" at the time when Muslims turn to fight one another. The Prophet said to his companion Abu Dharr al-Ghifari in a similar situation, when Abu Dharr asked him, "But what if some-one entered into my home (to kill me)?" The Prophet replied: "If you fear to look upon the gleam of the sword raised to strike you, then cover your face with your robe. Thus will he bear the sin of killing you as well as his own sin." And in the same situation, the Prophet told his companion Abu Musa al-Asha'ri: "Break your bows, sever your strings, beat stones on your swords (to break the blades); and when infringed upon by one of the perpetrators, be as the best of Adam's two sons."[54]

I have often heard Muslims say that we may never kill anyone. They quote a saying (hadith) from Mohammad that it would be better to destroy the Kab'ah in Mecca (the most holy shrine in Islam) than to kill one person. It is better to let people kill us than for us to kill anyone. It is against Islam to kill for any political purpose. We can only trust the future to God. This, of course, is only one strain of Islam, but any Muslim would recognize these ideas.

It is significant that the Muslims captured Mecca in 630 CE without bloodshed, after which Mohammad granted amnesty to all residents of Mecca, including people who had persecuted and killed Muslims. When offering forgiveness to the people of Mecca, Mohammad referred to Joseph forgiving his brothers. It is important to note that both Joseph and Mohammad offered forgiveness and reconciliation from a position of power. A whole chapter of the Qur'an is dedicated to the story of Joseph and ends with an affirmation of Jewish and Christian Scriptures.

Mohammad is quoted as saying,

> Shall I inform you of the best morals of this world and the hereafter? To forgive he who oppresses you, to make a bond with he who

53. Ibid., 5:28.
54. Quoted by Abu-Nimer, *Nonviolence and Peace*, 44.

severs from you, to be kind to he who insults you, and to give to he who deprives you.[55]

There is a clear vision of democracy and freedom in Islam, based on the concepts of consultation (shura) and consensus decision-making (ijma) in the Qur'an and the practice in Medina. Mohammad rejected the trappings of worldly power and insisted in trusting only God. He saw the temptation of domination and warned against it. "You people will be keen to have the authority of ruling, which will be a thing of regret for you on the Day of Resurrection. What an excellent wet nurse it is, and how bad for weaning!"[56] Even Mohammad's later reluctant acceptance of limited warfare indicates that peace, not war, is the goal of Islam. War, though permissible, is not desirable.

Muslims have not been perfect. They, like Christians and Jews, in spite of God's revelations, have been influenced by the violence of their time. Muslim violence, including massacres and ethnic cleansing, should be seen as aberrations, as regression to ancient Arabic tribal values that at times took precedence over the vision of the Qur'an. There is no need to see early Muslim military conquest and Muslim intrigue and murder between Muslim groups as normative. At times, tribal vengeance rather than submission to God, was the guiding force for Muslims. Three of the first four caliphs were murdered. Muslims have often killed Muslims in obscene power struggles.

Islam began as a beloved community centered on the Prophet and his companions. It was not long, however, before Muslims began wars of conquest for the purpose of territorial expansion of the Muslim state. Often this included plunder and the enrichment of Muslim leaders. This soon developed into Arab empires, ruled by the Umayyad and Abbasid dynasties, based on Persian, Roman, and Byzantine hierarchal models of pomp, power, and control. Empires became the center of Islam with resulting civil wars and rebellions. Class distinctions developed between the powerful and wealthy, and the poor. After 40 years of an amazing system of openness and democratic decision-making, Muslims reverted to a centralized, hereditary monarchy. Obedience to the caliph, rather than obedience to God, became the primary obligation of Muslims. Those, like

55. Quoted by Shirazi, *War, Peace and Nonviolence*, 103.

56. Bukhari 9:262, quoted in Harris, "Nonviolence in Islam," 109. Smith-Christopher, ed., *Subverting Hatred*.

the Christian Anabaptists, who believed in piety, social equality, and the unity of the Muslim community were seen as a threat to those in power, and often were killed.

It is troubling how quickly after Mohammad's death the early Muslim community abandoned its nonviolence and began a century of conquest. Within fifty years of Mohammad's death, the Muslim empire stretched from the Atlantic coast of North Africa to Central Asia. The simplicity of faith and lifestyle of Mohammad soon was transformed into political rulers amassing great amounts of power and wealth.

Actually the main tools for spreading Islam were through traveling merchants and traders, and through treaties in which all were promised protection and peace. Those treaties sounded attractive to people who had experienced much warfare and felt unsafe. The actual battles were few and short, and were won with the help and support of the local people who welcomed the Muslims as liberators. Coptic Christians, for example, welcomed the Muslim conquest of Egypt in 641 as liberation from Byzantine oppression.

Muslim rules of war were similar to the Christian just war doctrine. Prerequisites for war included a just cause, right authority, right intention, proportionality, and last resort. Severe limitations were placed on the conduct of war. Women, children, and the elderly were not to be harmed, trees and crops could not be destroyed. Many Muslim scholars argued that war could be fought only in self-defense. "Nor take life—which Allah has made sacred—except for just cause."[57] "Fight in the cause of Allah those who fight you, but do not transgress limits, for Allah loveth not transgressors."[58] The Qur'an states that hostilities must cease immediately when the enemy offers peace.[59]

There are harsh condemnations of Judaism and Christianity in the Qur'an, based partly on Christian and Jewish violent resistance to Islam. Verses in the Qur'an in which permission is given to kill the enemy are not different from Jewish and Christian writings that justify killing one's enemy. These harsh verses should be seen as exceptions to the norm of tolerance, not the norm.

57. Qur'an 17:33.
58. Ibid., 2:190.
59. Ibid., 2:192–93; 8:61.

It took almost 300 years for Christianity to embrace empire and seek to rule the world. The transformation of Islam parallels that of Christianity, only Islam changed more rapidly. On the other hand, it is a tribute to both Christianity and Islam that in spite of all the seductions of empire, the radical vision of the early faith survived in both Islam and Christianity, and continues to this day to be a transforming force.

Like in Christianity, violent power struggles came to the fore and the doctrines of Islam were compromised to meet the needs of the expanding Muslim empire. A major argument in support of war was the idea of necessity. "Necessity makes permissible the prohibited" (*al-darurat tubih al-mahzurat*). With this doctrine, anything can be justified. There is no longer any standard of morality. Even the clear teachings of the Qur'an can be ignored because someone considers it "necessary" to do so.

Like Christians, most Medieval Muslim commentators wrote only to justify war, not to wrestle with the deeper issues of the relationship between ethics and war. Seldom did Muslim leaders ask if a war was just before engaging in the war. As in Christianity, there is a long history of Muslim justification for war. In fact, many Medieval Muslim scholars blindly accepted the universality of war, a given that was seldom questioned. Some argue that later Muslim use of violence made obsolete (abrogated) earlier teachings of Mohammad which point to nonviolence.

Some Muslims continue an uncritical attitude toward war, suicide bombings, and killing one's enemies. The senseless killing of Muslims by Muslims in the Muslim world brings shame to the whole Muslim ummah. Sadly, some Muslims have interpreted jihad to mean something quite similar to Christian and Jewish concepts of holy war. Even though they are a minority, it is these Muslims who receive most of the attention of the news media. To be fair, we should view them in the same way we view pro-war Christians and right-wing Zionists.

One interesting experience during my 2008 trip to Indonesia was going to the jail at a police station in Jakarta to visit Habib Riza Syihab, the leader of Islamic Defenders Front (FDI), who was in jail accused of fomenting violence. The FDI tries to enforce morality and sometimes uses violence, like destroying liquor stores and attacking "heretics." I was told they were not associated with al Qaida.

We went in to the jail and into a large room where Habib was sitting talking with maybe 25 of his supporters who were visiting him. Women and his children were also there.

Habib, an impressive man dressed in white, stood up to greet me. He hugged and kissed me. I then sat down beside him and began a short conversation in Arabic. I gave him a copy of my book. We then switched to Indonesian with a friend translating. I started out by saying I had heard of him and respected him for taking action on his convictions. I told him a little about CPT. He said he had heard of me.

Then began an intense conversation about nonviolence. His basic argument was that nonviolence is unpractical and utopian, and gave the usual shallow arguments like I have to protect my family if an intruder comes into my house. I said I am safer without a gun and that nonviolent responses are more likely to protect my family. I said the overthrow of the Shah of Iran demonstrates nonviolence is also practical on a political level.

In order to reach him, I gave the example of my writing a letter to the editor protesting a sexy billboard advertising beer in Athens, Ohio, and asking people to call the beer distributor. In a few days the billboard was gone. I suggested the best way to protest immorality and stand up for what is right is to take nonviolent action against the perpetrators of evil. He said that was impractical, because in Indonesia the police will beat the protestors. I referred to Gandhi's salt march in which wave after wave of protestors got beaten. I suggested that if every day 20 protestors were beaten in front of a liquor store, that would soon have a deep effect in the society there. The police would look bad and support would build for the protestors. I said that soldiers are prepared to die. Is our commitment to *jihad* less than that? For jihad to be faithful to Muslim teachings, jihad needs to be nonviolent.

I took it one step further. I suggested that in jihad, it is important to take action, but to trust only in Allah for results. To use violence is to say we cannot fully trust Allah, but feel the need to take things into our own control. He heard me.

Sadly, our time ran out and I had to leave. We hugged and kissed each other. I left feeling an incredible high, praising God for this wonderful opportunity to dialogue with that man. I felt a deep connection with him. I don't think he knew I also am a Muslim. I did not bring up the subject. I do wish I could have prayed with him and his followers.

Later people told me more about his violent activities and the support he gets from right wing military groups. It did not sound good. Was I naïve? I don't think so. Knowing what I know now, I still would have done the same thing.

The next day we went to visit some Ahmadiyah people. The main religious violence in Indonesia at the time was being directed against the Ahmadiyahs. The Ahmadiyahs said that Habib was behind the violence and were not impressed with my story of visiting him. They recounted the persecution they faced. There are a half million of this Muslim sect in Indonesia. We talked about persecution strengthening religious groups. We talked about what nonviolent actions might be helpful.

Many modern Muslims have criticized classical interpretations of jihad as being too influenced by the imperial needs of the caliphs, thus compromising the original vision of Islam and violating essential Islamic principles. The actions of modern violent Muslim extremists have raised these questions in a way that cannot be ignored and have stimulated a rethinking of these issues. In July, 2005, the Fiqh Council of North America, issued a *fatwa* (religious edict) against terrorism and religious extremism, which included these words:

> Islam strictly condemns religious extremism and the use of violence against innocent lives. There is no justification in Islam for extremism or terrorism. Targeting civilians' life and property through suicide bombings or any other method of attack is haram—or forbidden—and those who commit these barbaric acts are criminals, not "martyrs."

Islam teaches us to act in a caring manner to all of God's creation. The Prophet Muhammad, who is described in the Qur'an as "a mercy to the worlds" said: "All creation is the family of God, and the person most beloved by God [is the one] who is kind and caring toward His family."

In the light of the teachings of the Qur'an and Sunnah we clearly and strongly state:

All acts of terrorism targeting civilians are *haram* (forbidden) in Islam.

It is haram for a Muslim to cooperate with any individual or group that is involved in any act of terrorism or violence.

It is the civic and religious duty of Muslims to cooperate with law enforcement authorities to protect the lives of all civilians.

We issue this fatwa following the guidance of our scripture, the Qur'an, and the teachings of our Prophet Muhammad—peace be upon him. We urge all people to resolve all conflicts in just and peaceful manners.

We pray for the defeat of extremism and terrorism. We pray for the safety and security of our country, the United States, and its people. We pray for the safety and security of all inhabitants of our planet. We pray that interfaith harmony and cooperation prevail both in the United States and all around the globe.

Like Jewish and Christian violence, Muslim violence is a sad story. Muslims probably have suffered much more from Muslim violence than have any other people. Can Muslims rethink Muslim history and come up with a new Islamic understanding of violence and war? There is no theological basis in Islam for rejecting nonviolence.

The first step is to ask ourselves whether or not we can trust God for our security. To look to any other source than to God for our protection is not only a rejection of God, but also idolatry. We need no protection except for the protection of Allah.

An important Muslim basis for peace is the strong sense of justice, social responsibility, equality, and honesty in Islam. Surrender to or acceptance of injustice is sin. Active nonviolence is a way of resisting injustice. It is those who work for justice who are on the right path.[60] "Allah commands justice, the doing of good."[61] The goal is to win over one's opponents. "Nor can goodness and evil be equal. Repel (evil) with that which is better; then will he between whom and thee was hatred become as it were thy friend and intimate.[62]" Bawa Muhairjadeen, a Sri Lankan

60. Ibid., 6:82–83.

61. Ibid., 16:90.

62. Ibid., 41:34.

Sufi, makes the same point. "It is compassion that conquers. It is unity that conquers. It is Allah's good qualities, behavior, and actions that conquer others. It is this state that is called Islam. The sword doesn't conquer; love is sharper than the sword. Love is an exalted, gentle sword."[63] Since struggling against injustice is a primary justification for warfare (which in itself would rule out participation in most wars), and since nonviolent struggle is the best means for achieving justice, there is a strong basis in Islam for nonviolence.

According to the Qur'an, Allah's primary characteristic is mercy. Mohammad is quoted as saying that when God created the cosmos, he inscribed on His throne, "My mercy overpowers my wrath." God has mercy on those who are merciful to others.[64] Because I am in need of God's mercy, I must be merciful to others. If I am not merciful, I cannot expect mercy. I will be judged by the standards with which I judge others.

Another Muslim basis for nonviolence is the concept of *sabr* (patience). "Nay, seek (Allah's) help with patient perseverance and prayer: it is indeed hard, except to those who are humble."[65] Patience is a product of trusting in the goodness of God. I have repeatedly been with Palestinian shepherds grazing their sheep on their own land when Israeli soldiers come and order all the shepherds to leave the area. I always become angry and bent out of shape. The shepherds, however, walk toward home with their heads held high. I stand there humbled as I see the hope and faith in the faces of those shepherds. I have so little faith. Those simple Muslim shepherds actually believe that the future is in God's hands. Why should they despair?

Through the discipline of regular fasting, praying five times a day, and trusting in the goodness of God, Muslims have the basis for the personal discipline and self-sacrifice needed for commitment to nonviolent struggle.

Jihad means not holy war, but struggle. Mohammad distinguished between the greater and the lesser jihad. The greater jihad is the inner struggle against sin and temptation, while the lesser jihad is the struggle against injustice and oppression. Everyone is called to engage in this spiritual struggle. Some Muslims consider *al-da'wah* (evangelism) to be

63. Muhaiyaddeen, *Islam and World Peace*, 34.
64. Qur'an 7:151.
65. Ibid., 2:45.

the primary meaning of the lesser jihad, with the promise of God's protection for those sharing the good news of Islam. Farid Esack describes the struggle against apartheid in South Africa as jihad.[66]

During a deep conversation with a Muslim leader in Hebron, I quoted Eph 6:12 to him, which states that our struggle is not against particular people, but rather our real struggle is a spiritual struggle against the principalities and powers of evil. He readily agreed and said that he believed the same thing. Jihad is the struggle described in Eph 6:12.

There is a conflict between good and evil. What has gone wrong is that we have understood this as a conflict between "us " and "them," with we being good and they being evil. The answer is in seeing the conflict between good and evil as something with roots in our own lives. This view should lead to a deep humility instead of an imperial view of us conquering evil people out there. The important spiritual warfare is the struggle within our own souls.

Physical weapons are useless in that struggle. The way to engage in jihad and not violate either God's commands or other people is through nonviolence. Murder is one of the four major sins in Islam. Only through nonviolence can we follow both the command to not murder and the command to practice jihad. In the struggle against social evils, tools like education, creating peaceful relationships, and nonviolent resistance to injustice and oppression are important.

Although the Qur'an is not as clear as the Christian scriptures in rejecting violence, there are only a few verses in the Qur'an that justify violence, but there are many verses about mercy and peace. In the law of qisas (law of equality and mercy), Muslims are permitted to seek revenge, but seeking revenge is not required. In fact, the Qur'an states that it is better to forgive because God forgives us.[67] Forgiveness is better because good and evil are not equal. Evil is to be replaced with something better.[68] When enemies of Islam, people who had killed Muslims, converted to Islam, Mohammad forgave them and held nothing against them.

There is a ritual among the Awlad Ali tribes of North Africa used in cases of murder. The offender lies beside a sheep on the ground. Someone from the victim's family is given the choice of killing the offender or the

---

66. Esack, *Liberation and Pluralism*, 106–10.

67. Qur'an 16:126–28; 42:40–42.

68. Ibid., 41:34ff.

sheep. The sheep is killed, but the fact that the victim's family had the opportunity for revenge restores the honor of the victim's family. The cycle of violence is broken and community is restored.

The Qur'an does not demand nonviolence. There is a concession to the use of violence. However, in a world of technological warfare in which most victims are innocent civilians, some Muslims now say that in order to be faithful to Islam, Muslims need to reject violence and develop Islamic concepts of nonviolence.[69]

There have been many nonviolent Muslim campaigns throughout history. One of the most famous is that of Abdul Ghaffar Khan (Badsha Khan), an associate of Gandhi, who led a nonviolent army of a hundred thousand Pashtuns in a twenty-year struggle against the British occupation of India. The movement was solidly rooted in Muslim faith and practice, using Mohammad as their example.[70] The Muslim Peace Fellowship is a modern American Muslim pacifist movement associated with the Fellowship of Reconciliation, the oldest and largest religious pacifist organization in the United States.

The first Palestinian *Intifada* (1987–93) was essentially nonviolent, using boycotts, strikes, marches, civil disobedience, and community organizing, which were brutally repressed by the Israeli military. Although in many ways unsuccessful, it did mobilize international sympathy for the Palestinians and portrayed Israel as the aggressor. The main failure of the Intifada was the failure of the international community to adequately support the Palestinians.

Muslims must ask, is their loyalty to the ummah (the world Muslim community), or to their nation-states? Muslims have traditionally rejected separation of church and state because they do not want to separate the spiritual and secular. Muslims believe that submission to God must involve our whole lives. Submission to Allah, however, is not the same as submission to corrupt nation states. Often submission to God will mean opposing nation-states.

Some Islamists argue that if Muslims are in a situation where they are weak, they should use nonviolence, but if they are in a stronger position, the use of violence is preferred, if not obligatory. Ironically, this perspective seems to unconsciously recognize that nonviolence is stronger

69. An excellent introduction to Islamic nonviolence is Abu-Nimer, *Nonviolence and Peace Building.*

70. See Easwaran, *Badshah Khan.*

than violence. The weakness of the contemporary Muslim world is an opportunity for Muslims to move from identifying with the history of conquest to identifying with the beginnings of Islam as a small, persecuted minority who put faithfulness to God's revelations above any practical rationalizations.

A CALL TO NONVIOLENCE

Maybe someday we will learn that it is a lie that war will bring peace and security. Every time we kill an enemy, we have created more enemies. Killing for peace makes as much sense as fornicating for virginity. Seeking to destroy evil through violence is the height of naiveté. Trying to destroy evil only escalates evil in the same way the blood of the martyrs strengthens the causes for which they die. When we return evil for evil we legitimize the rationale that was used to do evil to us.

Wars are the result of a lack of creativity and imagination, and usually are the prelude to the next war. Instead of reverting to primitive animal instincts, we can creatively analyze each situation and come up with real solutions to problems. Working through conflicts is the best way to build trust. We have choices. It is a lie that wars are necessary and inevitable. We can break the cycle of violence.

Faith-based nonviolence is more than a strategy or a political philosophy. It is a way of life. Nonviolence is an attempt to bring together the practical and the ideal. It is a rejection of the lie that the life of someone else is worth less than my life. We can say we would rather die than kill. We can love our enemies. Vengeance belongs to God, not to us. For us to take vengeance against another person is to usurp God's place, to play God.

It has been argued that the Abrahamic religions are inadequate for dealing with reconciliation because of their long history of violence and oppression. On the other hand, within the three religions there also is the vision and challenge of reconciliation, unity, and the universality of God's justice and salvation, which for too long have been neglected. Those roots of social justice, nonviolence, and shalom/salaam, can be recovered, revitalized and implemented.

Momentous possibilities for peace could spring up around the world if the three religions, which include over half the world's population, could put submission to and trust in God ahead of their own narrow religious, ethnic, and national interests. We, like Abraham, who was willing to sacrifice his son and his future, can lay down our selfish interests. We can embrace each other, demand an end to all hostilities, and cooperatively create structures of communication, cooperation, and mutual support. The very fact that all three Abrahamic religions are international, transcending national boundaries, would lead one to expect that allegiance to one's religion would bind one more deeply with adherents of one's religion in other countries than to one's own government, thus weakening loyalty to one's nation-state. Maybe today love of enemies is the primary test of faithfulness to God.

All three religions can move to a post-Constantinian faith, a faith not rooted in nationalistic, racial identity, coupled with idolatrous commitment to a nation-state. The answer for all three religions is cooperation, mutual respect, and standing together. Only in this way will we find security and be faithful to God's commandments. Let Jews, Muslims, Christians, and all other believers in God, promise each other that we will not kill each other, no matter what propaganda and lies may be used to convince us to do so. We can turn to the roots of our faith, deepen our relationship with God, and pray for those toward whom we are tempted to harden our hearts.

In every part of every society, there are those who out of their fear want to dominate and control. They can be resisted. Living in submission to God is not compatible with a lifestyle built on the oppression of others. There is no good reason why we cannot be free. No one has been given authority by God to control others.

Peace is not the highest good. More important than peace is obedience to God, resistance to evil, and love of enemy. These are so important that they may never be sacrificed on the altar of violence. Being faithful may result in conflict, but faithfulness to God cannot lead us to kill our enemy who God also created and also loves.

We have been taught that peace and security are obtained only through violence and through oppressing others. There is another power, the power of love, the power of graciousness and humility, the power of creativity, solidarity, and community, a power that is the gift of God rather than the result of oppressing others. The power of love is not passive. Love is active, takes risks, crosses boundaries, breaks down walls, and builds bridges. Love reaches out to enemies, overcomes stereotypes, and builds community. Love reconciles enemies, overcomes fear, and creates a new world.

≫ EIGHT ≪

Faith and Ethics

WHAT DO THE SIMILARITIES between the three religions mean for ethics? What can we learn from each other? In this chapter I will offer my own synthesis on some ethical issues as examples of some results of my struggles within the three religions. I have already dealt with the issue of violence and war in the previous chapter.

Ethics for the Abrahamic communities is discernment of how to live faithfully in the midst of a corrupt society, in cultures that are living far from God's intention for the world.

An important contribution of the Abrahamic religions is their social ethic, something missing in most other religious traditions. Much of modern Hindu and Buddhist social ethics is a response to Abrahamic social ethics. God's covenant with and promise of the land to Abraham and his descendants was conditional on the practice of social justice. All three religions call us to struggle for social justice, to a new social order lived in obedience to God. An important part of obedience to God is to love one's neighbor as one's self. That includes not only the neighbor down the road, but also the neighbor who will live down the road fifty years from now, and the neighbor who lives on the other side of the globe.

True faith is not to reject God's creation (asceticism) or to believe unintelligible dogmas, or discover secret mysteries that can lead to salvation. True faith involves wrestling with how our faith impinges on the critical issues we face. Muslims are right in seeing Islam as a way of life and in rejecting all attempts to relegate religion to one's private concerns. Sadly, too many people have been happy to turn all social-political ethical

176

questions over to governments. All actions of individuals and governments are subject to moral critique.

There is both great value and great danger in doing all the correct rituals of one's religion. Discipline, commitment, and steadfastness are essential. We can, however, become more concerned about the outward form than the inner content. We can become self-righteous, rigid, or focus on unimportant details of our religion. Submission to God cannot be reduced to formal rituals devoid of spiritual depth, while serving the false gods of wealth, power, and privilege. Submission to God involves joining the struggle for liberation and resisting idolatry

Taqwa, awareness of God's presence, is connected to human relationships. It is to be aware of the suffering of the oppressed. Do I selfishly focus on my own salvation, or look for God's transforming power at work in the events around me? It is easy to fall into a selective morality. We can oppose sexual immorality but support militarism, imperialism, and racism. We can become sanctimonious about social injustice, but say nothing about personal morality. People seem to have an extraordinary ability to inflict pain and injustice upon each other. Even activists for peace and justice also seem to have a great ability to inflict suffering on others. God have mercy on us.

True faith is deeper than outward practices of piety. Most important is what is happening in our hearts, the nature of our relationship both with God, our neighbors, and the rest of God's creation. Love, generosity, and humility are more important than prayer and fasting. Although Muslims place great emphasis on outward actions and lifestyles, these outer actions are to be expressions of an inner equilibrium, an awareness of the compassion and mercy of God. The outer practices are empty unless they express an inner reality. Muslims expect there to be a unity between the inner and the outer. This sounds like my Anabaptist background.

Attempts in all three religions to rigidly apply their Scriptures have resulted in disaster. Rigidly applying revelation objectifies revelation and leaves God out of the equation. Our task is not to be morally pure (none of us are pure), but to act out of gratitude, love, and a deep desire to please God—and to love our neighbor.

Let's look at some Jewish/Christian/Muslim themes and consider some of their meanings for today. We will look at idolatry, the goodness of creation, modesty, kosher/*halal*, Sabbath, and Jubilee.

IDOLATRY

According to the Bible and the Qur'an, idolatry is the worst sin. Idolatry is making ultimate what is not ultimate, to make absolute what is not absolute. It is to put anything in place of or alongside of God, to share God's sovereignty with something else. It is to blur the distinction between the Creator and the creation.

Islam makes a big point of not naming anything as a partner with God. The Torah commands us to have no other gods alongside God. Jesus said we cannot serve two masters. He didn't say it is wrong to serve two masters: he said it is impossible. To serve more than one master is to be divided, unfocused. Modern life confronts us with competing loyalties, contradictory values, and opposing commitments. Do we serve only God, or do we submit to or trust in other competing powers?

Worship is about seeking salvation. In what or whom do we trust for our security? Do we trust in God, or in guns and bombs, in investment portfolios, in our power to manipulate and control? To what or whom do we pledge allegiance and loyalty? From what do we derive our identity?

The Bible tells the story of Adam and Eve not wanting to be creatures, but to be like God. Practically nobody would be so crass as to say, "I am God," but saying "I can do anything I want to do" is close to claiming I am God. Many political leaders act as if they were God. False religion justifies human pride and egoism. True faith moves us to love, sharing, and cooperation.

Too often we replace ethics with a tribal code. Too often American Christians say, "We are Christians, but we are Americans first." Being willing to kill a person of another race, religion, class, or nationality for the sake of my race, religion, class, or nation is idolatry, in that this is putting my race, religion, class or nationality above God. I have had repeated conversations with Israeli soldiers in which I challenged them to treat Jews and Palestinians alike. When they justify treating Palestinians and Jews by different standards, I suggest that they are putting the Jewish people above God's demand for justice. I name their attitude to be idolatry. There are people in every country who make the same idolatrous commitment to their country. If nothing is more important than my nation, my people, I am guilty of idolatry. Idols are those things for which we are willing to kill. All human endeavors are human, less than God. Even religion can be made into a idol, subjecting God to the dictates of my religion.

Commitment to institutional preservation is often in conflict with faithfulness to God. Our ultimate loyalty is to God, not to any nation state. All three religions have experienced the seductiveness of political power. The history of oppression and corruption resulting from more than a thousand-year merger of church and state is a tragedy. We know the results in Christendom when popes became repressive, corrupt worldly leaders instead of spiritual leaders. There have been similar developments in the Muslim world. Muslims do not want to separate the sacred and secular, but there is a problem when mosques are dominated and controlled by corrupt political leaders. One of the most serious threats to the three religions is their captivity to nationalistic, economic, and ideological powers.

The strong opposition to God's prophets, even to the point of killing them, was not opposition to some abstract belief in one God as Creator, but to their call for people to pledge their loyalty only to God, and not to human persons, institutions, or ideologies. Pledging our allegiance to God is a threat to human power. Those rulers who seek to reduce people to instruments of their control are seeking to usurp God. This can be done by raw power, or through claims of special knowledge or special access to God.

Oppressions are the result of idolatry. The domination of some people over other people is the result of the refusal to serve only God. If God is not worshiped, other gods are created for us to serve. One problem is that the idols we create end up controlling us and limiting our freedom. Much of humanity is enslaved to the service of false gods. We create and then devote our lives to what we have created. Our things become our masters. Our possessions possess us. There is no hope for salvation and liberation without renouncing the worship of all false gods.

Believers in God can surrender all desire to control, dominate, or exercise authority over other people. No one is obligated to obey people who seek to dominate others. The Qur'an says, "The authority rests with none but Allah. He commands you not to surrender to any one save Him."[1] Jesus said, "You know that the rulers of the Gentiles lord it over them. . . . It shall not be so among you; but whoever would be great among you must be your servant."[2] The teachings of the Bible and the Qur'an are

1. Qur'an 12:40.
2. Matt 20:25–28.

a reproach to those hungry for power, to those who would put themselves in the place of God. The claims of all imperialists and oppressors have been relativized.

I am always troubled by the bumper stickers on so many cars in the United States that proclaim: "God bless America." This slogan is almost always put beside the American flag. Calling on God to bless MY country, MY political views, sounds not only parochial, but arrogant and idolatrous. Is God the water boy for the current United States government, for its policies? The real purpose of these bumper stickers seems to be using God as support for American wars. Who are we to use God for our purposes? God is not on our side. That is blasphemy. Both John McCain and Sarah Palin in their 2008 presidential campaign in the United States stated, "America is the greatest source of good in the world." That pretty much leaves out God. That is idolatry.

A bumper sticker that counters this view carries the message, "God bless the whole world: no exceptions." This slogan recognizes the greatness and oneness of God. This slogan calls us away from idolatry to worship of the one true God.

It is false religion that holds on to traditions out of fear of weakening the social fabric of society. Truth is truth, and may never be compromised, even if the truth is seen as a threat to my country, my society, my religion. All idols must go. I cannot make my faith compatible with the worship of other gods. Nationalism, racism, bigotry, violence and materialism are idols that stand against the claims of the one true God. All idols must be rejected. Too many people believe, "My country right or wrong." To make one's obligation to the state more important than obeying God is idolatry.

Do we realize how serious a sin it is to put God in a box, to seek to control or limit God, to make God my servant, to demand that God conform to my ideas, values, and goals? Idolatry results in devastating destruction, both spiritually and socially.

Sin is turning away from God, denying who we are in relationship with God. The smallest sin can be the beginning of my destruction. Even one illicit glance can destroy me. To sin, I must deny that God sees me in my sin. To continue to sin is to develop unbelief, to separate myself from God.

THE GOODNESS OF CREATION

As I have worked with Muslims in Palestine, I have experienced that every time something bad happens, be it the demolition of their homes, imprisonment, death, or any other hardship, the Muslims always say, "*Allah karim.*" "God is generous," they say. I have come to understand that they express a profound truth when they affirm the goodness of God and God's creation.

The three Abrahamic religions reject the idea of the physical world being evil or controlled by spirits, and affirm the sovereignty of God over the natural world. There is no need to placate the spirits. Islam does not deny the existence of the spirits (*jinn*), but sees them as being restricted to the unseen and not in control of the cosmos or of humanity. Salvation is found not in renouncing the material world, but in finding a proper relationship to it. Doing God's will is experienced in relation to God's creation, not in escape from it.

Sadly, this profound understanding of reality has been twisted to see nature as a machine, subject neither to the spirits nor to God, but as valueless matter to be dominated and exploited. The objectification of creation is at the core of our ecological crisis. We need to recover a sense of the goodness and sacredness of creation.

From the perspective of the Abrahamic traditions, creation is sacred and good because God created it. The cosmos is an expression of God's will and purpose. It came into being by God's command. It all fits together. Everything is connected in the natural world between people and the rest of creation, between all humanity. There is a connection between how we treat creation and how we treat each other. Harm to one is a harm to all. This is based in the oneness of God (tawhid).

Most people believe that the cosmos is evil, violent, chaotic. They believe they cannot trust God. The only source of salvation is domination and violence.

MODESTY

Whenever I see Muslim or Amish women, I see not a sex object, but a person who loves God. The modest dress of those women reminds me of God who has created all things good. I rejoice when I see these women and turn my heart toward God. I have a different reaction when I see scantily dressed women. My heart is not turned to God. I think of myself and my selfish desires.

Western culture is saturated with sex. Every day in America we are assaulted with sexual images. Even in most churches, conservative and liberal, people are dressed in provocative ways, calling attention to their sexual attributes. It is difficult to worship in many American churches without struggling with lust because of the provocative ways in which people are dressed. For many Christians, not even in worship is there any concern for modesty. As one American Christian friend said to me, "I would never invite Muslims to visit my church, because I know how offended they would be by the immodesty." As a sign of respect, Muslims cover themselves when bowing before God.

It is especially troubling to see parents dressing little girls in sexy outfits, teaching them early to accept their role of being little more than playthings for boys. Our culture starts early in socializing women to be sex objects. The sexualization of children has horrific results.

Our bodies are not our own. We belong to our Creator. We do have the freedom to use our bodies in any way we wish, either in degrading, destructive ways, or in ways that are life affirming and liberating. The objectification of women leads to horrible oppression, both emotional and physical. The rates of emotional, physical, and sexual abuse of women in Western society are alarming. Muslim culture also has deep problems in how women are treated. Western culture promotes freedom for women while degrading and exploiting women, turning them into objects.

Like with early Christianity, the coming of Islam meant liberation for women. Although not comparable to modern Western freedom for women, the rights given to women were revolutionary. It was not until the nineteenth century that women in Christian Europe had anything close to the rights women enjoyed under Islam. Karen Armstrong says, "In the Middle Ages the Muslims were horrified to see the way the Western Christians treated their women in the Crusader states. And Christian scholars denounced Islam for giving too much power to menials like slaves and women."[3]

I am a male homo sapien who gets excited seeing cleavage and thighs. This is certainly partly due to the indoctrination of my culture,

---

3. Armstrong, *Muhammad*, 199. For more details about early Islam and women, see pp. 190–92, 197–99. For an excellent introduction to Islamic feminism, see Barlas, "Believing Women."

but it probably also is rooted in my genes. I know that I, like many men I know, have a problem with lust when seeing provocatively dressed women. Women tell me they experience similar urges when seeing provocatively dressed men.

It has been liberating for me to live in Muslim cultures where everyone dresses modestly. There I do not have the same struggles with lust or seeing women as objects. Orthodox Jews and some Christian groups also have maintained a concern for modesty. Many people may not realize that just fifty years ago most Christians and Jews were committed to dressing modestly. Recently, it is Muslim culture that has most clearly maintained a witness for modesty.

An important objection to dressing modestly is to argue that the problem of lust is in the mind of the beholder, not with the object of the lust. It is we men who need to take responsibility for our attitudes and actions, and not force women to hide themselves so that men will not need to be self-disciplined. Men are not beasts who cannot be expected to have any self-control. We men need to take this seriously and accept responsibility for our thoughts and actions.

The answer is neither in hiding women, nor in women ignoring the effects of how they relate to others. All of us, men and women, can be responsible moral people who take responsibility for how our actions affect other people. We can move beyond individualistic thinking to an attitude of social responsibility. We can resist all forms of oppression and exploitation. We can all be responsible for how our dress or lack thereof affects other people. There is no good reason to sexually stimulate another person outside a committed relationship.

I want to ask whether any of my actions may cause someone to stumble. When King David stood on his roof and looked down and saw Bathsheba bathing, he was so overcome with lust that he not only arranged to rape her, but also had her husband killed so that he could keep her.[4] The tragic consequences of that sin were horrific for David's family for years to come. The responsibility for that sin was all David's, but think of all the pain that could have been avoided if Bathsheba had been a bit more discrete in her bathing.

In a sexist society where women are programmed to dress in ways that invite men to see them as objects, and where men think, talk, and

---

4. 2 Samuel 11.

act in degrading ways toward women, it seems reasonable to ask how we might resist that programming. Some suggest that we dress in ways that call attention to our faces rather than the rest of our bodies. Muslim headscarves do that.

It is not for me to tell others how to dress. I need to start with myself. In order to express my concerns for modesty, I dress more modestly than may be necessary. I do not want to publicly expose more of my body than I believe is appropriate for women to expose. I do this partly to protest immodesty, and partly to protest male privilege. I question doing things that women are not free to do. It is deeply troubling for me to see a Muslim man wearing shorts on a hot day while his wife is fully covered.

I dress modestly as an act of resistance to a society that disrespects our humanity, cheapens the value of human life, turns people into commodities, and ridicules the sacredness of sexuality. I reject the slave mentality of Western society. I reject the images of bondage so many have embraced.

Everything we do is an expression of something deeper. To cover our bodies with clothes can be an expression of a spiritual covering of our egos with humility and repentance. Both our inner selves and our bodies need covering. Prostration in prayer is an expression of an inner surrender and submission to God. The important thing is to have a modest heart. Whatever we do, without that inner modesty, our actions will be immodest even if we are covered from head to toe.

For me, modesty means showing deep respect for the goodness of the human body, the sacredness of sexuality, and a search for humility. I do not want to call attention to self or give others a cause to stumble.

KOSHER/HALAL

There is a strong emphasis in Judaism and Islam on some things being acceptable (kosher or halal) and some things being forbidden (*trefe* or *haram*). There is almost no similar concept in Christianity, except for awareness of the concept from the Jewish Scriptures. Most Western Christians dismiss the concept as belonging to Jewish ceremonial law and not applicable to Christians.

The issue of kosher or halal foods can be a problem in interfaith relationships. Often Jews and Muslims are uncomfortable eating with Christians unless Muslims or Jews prepared the food. A simple way to avoid this problem is for Christians not to serve meat at gatherings with Jews and Muslims. Most Jewish and Muslim food regulations involve meat.

The whole concept is rooted in a desire to obey God in our daily lives, even when we do not understand. It comes out of sensing the sacredness of all creation, and our own need to live lives of holiness. If we truly believe in God, we cannot fit into a normal Western lifestyle. There are things that we should simply say are forbidden.

There is a close similarity between Jewish and Muslim understandings of this idea, with Muslim restrictions being somewhat less strict than Jewish restrictions. Kosher/halal rules are closely related to tradition, identity, and community. Not eating pork, for example, sets Jews and Muslims apart from other people. Jews and Muslims often have a much clearer sense of identity than do Christians. There is no agreed upon answer to the question of what is a Christian lifestyle. That is much clearer in Islam and Judaism.

Many of the rules relate to food and the preparation of food. What is more common than eating? To be conscious of God's will for us every time we eat is a profound reminder of who and whose we are. Both Jews and Muslims have clear regulations and rituals concerning the slaughter of animals. Slaughter must be humane. But the concern goes far beyond religious ritual. Both Jewish and Muslim traditions forbid cruelty to animals. The *Shulkhan Arukh* states, "It is forbidden, according to the law of the Torah, to inflict pain upon any living creature." How we treat animals is a test of our character. Showing disrespect for animals is to show disrespect for God's creation and demonstrates hardness of heart on our part. According to the Bible and Qur'an, justice must be established for all, including animals and all the rest of God's creation. The Bible and the Qur'an both state that even in war, trees may not be destroyed.

Everything has a purpose. Consider a pin, a hammer, a piece of paper. These things have purposes. Animals and the rest of creation are not machines, not objects, but have value in God's sight beyond any utilitarian use they might have for us. People of faith see creation from a moral, spiritual perspective. Creation is not to be subjected to our desires with no thought to God's purposes for that creation. The purpose of creation is greater than to serve my desires. I have shut God out of an important part of my life if I do not recognize the rest of creation as fellow creatures. We are moral, not just economic beings.

Even if slaughtered in a ritually correct way, can we call meat kosher or halal if the animals were mistreated, if they were fed nasty byproducts from other animals, including animal manure, injected with growth hormones, and antibiotics to keep them alive in spite of their unhealthy diet and unsanitary living conditions? Is the meat kosher or halal if the animal spent its whole life in a cage unable even to turn around?

Much of the meat certified kosher or halal in the U.S. is raised in the same way, and comes from the same feedlots and animal factories as non-kosher and non-halal meat. The only difference is in the ritual involved in killing the animals. We do serious violence to our faith traditions if we reduce obedience to God to performing correct rituals. If ritual is all that matters, then the focus of obedience shifts to performing the rituals correctly. To eat meat from an abused animal that has been slaughtered in a ritually correct way is to miss the point. There is no kosher/halal way to slaughter a pig.

We can take this one step farther. If the product we buy or consume is a product of injustice, then that product is not kosher or halal. If the workers who produced the product are exploited, if the production of the product pollutes God's creation, or if the corporation that sells the product is corrupt, that product is not kosher or halal. What about chemical pesticides, workers enduring dangerous working conditions, or slave wages? What about issues of sustainability and global climate change? Can we see these issues as related to the biblical and Qur'anic idea of kosher/halal? Not eating pork can be a basis for not eating foods rooted in oppression.

Sadly, many of my Jewish and Muslim friends shop at Walmart while trying to keep kosher or halal. Because of the unjust practices of Walmart, I would ask if anything Walmart sells is kosher or halal. When I participate in actions that support oppression, I increase the oppression in the world. When I refuse to participate in oppression, I hope, to some small extent, to increase liberated space for others and myself. The book of James says it well,

> Look! The wages you failed to pay the workmen who mowed your fields are crying out against you. The cries of the harvesters have reached the ears of the Lord Almighty. You have lived on earth in luxury and self-indulgence. You have fattened yourselves in the day of slaughter. You have condemned and murdered innocent men, who were not opposing you.[5]

5. Jas 5:4–6.

The issue is not purity. Actually the word kosher does not mean pure. It means prepared for ritual. Mixing purity with religion causes a lot of problems, including racism. If you are not pure, then I cannot associate with you, because associating with you would make me impure. Since I am pure and you are not pure, I am better than you. The truth is, none of us is pure. Purity or holiness can be approached only with the greatest of humility, recognizing we are all in need of God's grace. Jesus was harshly critical of purity connected with self-righteousness.

On Saturday, January 12, 2008, Israeli settlers attacked a Palestinian home near the Kiryat Arba settlement near Hebron, injured a number of Palestinians, knocked one of my teammates to the ground, and destroyed Palestinian property. Although the settlers were violating the rule of no physical exertion on Shabbat, they strongly objected to being photographed on Shabbat. Something is wrong with this picture.

Ritual worship is not the only way to obey God. Resisting oppression, serving those in distress, pointing people to God is the real meaning of kosher/halal. Social justice is a kosher/halal religious obligation.

SABBATH, THE CLIMAX OF GOD'S CREATION

Sabbath is one of Judaism's great gifts to humanity. Modern people are obsessed with controlling and possessing the space around us. To have, to own, to control, are our goals. We want power. Things are what matter. We fill every moment with business. The gift of Sabbath is mercy, providing us with the grace of being still, a time for reflection, reevaluation, and restoration. Sabbath is a reminder that enough is enough.

The material world is not the only reality. Sabbath is a focus on time, on being instead of having. Time is about relationships, meaning, unity. In Judaism, pagan agricultural festivals were transformed into remembering historical events. Historical events were remembered as acts of God in time. In a similar way, Muslims stopping their work and praying five times a day brings the reality of time into each day. The word "holy" appears first in the Bible in Genesis in relation to the Sabbath. "And God blessed the seventh day and made it holy"[6] (Gen 2:3). Abraham Joshua Heschel notes,

6. Gen 2:3.

> The meaning of the Sabbath is to celebrate time rather than space. Six days a week we live under the tyranny of things of space; on the Sabbath we try to become attuned to holiness in time. It is a day on which we are called to share in what is eternal in time, to turn from the results of creation to the mystery of creation; from the world of creation to the creation of the world.[7]

Observant Jews not only do not work on Sabbath, but also do not travel, use electrical appliances, smoke, write, or fix things. Practically everything modern or industrial is put aside. One day each week they stop work to remember and honor the Creator. It is a time to stop, to pause, to reflect, to get a new perspective.

According to the Torah, God did not finish creation on the sixth day. It says "On the seventh day God finished his work."[8] On the seventh day God created Sabbath. It was Sabbath that completed creation. A time of peace, rest, happiness, harmony, and contemplation completed and gave meaning to creation. All three Abrahamic religions root Sabbath in creation. Sabbath is the epitome of creation. Sabbath points to our own re-creation through prayer and rest.

For Jews, the Sabbath also remembers freedom and deliverance from slavery in Egypt. Sabbath is about liberation. Sabbath is a day to be human, unencumbered with work and responsibility. It is a time to enjoy family and community.

Sabbath is the most often mentioned of the 613 laws in the Torah. It is the fourth of the Ten Commandments and the longest.[9] There are two commands regarding Sabbath. One is to observe the Sabbath and the other is to remember the Sabbath. Even if we do not always completely observe the Sabbath, we can still remember the Sabbath. In fact, we can remember the Sabbath all week long and allow the truth and beauty of Sabbath to inform our daily lives. We can remember that in whatever we do, we have another commitment, another loyalty, that transcends our normal activities. On Sabbath, we pause to remember, to reflect, to renew our relationship to the One who transcends all that we do and are.

In reality, if all days are holy, none are holy. Making one day holy encourages us to see all days as holy. The more deeply we realize the holiness of one day, the more we can carry with us that holiness into other

---

7. Heschel, *The Sabbath*, 10.

8. Gen 2:2.

9. Exod 20:8–11; Deut 5:12–15.

days. Sabbath is a time to step back and see the big picture. The Sabbath changes our perceptions for the coming week. Practicing Sabbath moves our faith away from the abstract to the concrete.

Another less important meaning of Sabbath is rest. God rested on the seventh day. "Whoever enters into God's rest, rests from his own work as God did from his."[10] Muslims point out that God does not need to rest, which is true in a human sense. Muslims tend to reject any attempts to see God in human terms, yet in the Qur'an God has human characteristics. God hears, sees, sits, loves, gets angry, etc.[11] Although not to be taken literally, according to the Qur'an, God has hands, eyes, a face. But God is not like humans. God's hands are not like our hands. God should not be equated with anything else. However the Qur'an suggests that God did change pace after creation.[12]

We all need rest, breaks from our work. For me, Sabbath, a day of rest, is grace, a gift. Athletes, like marathon runners, rest the day before a strenuous event. For the secular world, Sabbath has been reduced to "weekend." This can be seen as a gift, a blessing religion has bestowed on the world. With a forty-hour week and two days free each week, there is now more time for family life, personal pursuits, and leisure. No working people are proposing repealing weekends. In fact, there is a movement toward a two and one-half day weekend, beginning Friday noon. That would accommodate all three religions.

A friend of mine who died of cancer decided she would discuss her health issues with other people only during the week. On weekends, she took a break from such discussions. On the weekends, she focused her energies in other directions.

For religious people, Sabbath is something deeper than rest or a free weekend. Abraham Heschel says, "The Sabbath is not for the sake of the weekdays; the weekdays are for the sake of the Sabbath." Heschel goes on to note,

> To the Biblical mind, however, labor is the means toward an end, and the Sabbath as a day of abstaining from toil, is not for the purpose of recovering one's lost strength and becoming fit for the forthcoming labor. The Sabbath is a day for the sake of life. Man

10. Heb 4:9–10.

11. Qur'an 42:11.

12. Ibid., 7:54; 10:3; 32:4.

is not a beast of burden, and the Sabbath is not for the purpose of enhancing the efficiency of his work.[13]

For Muslims, *Yom Juma* (I am using the word *Shabbat* to refer to the Jewish Sabbath, Yom Juma to refer to the Muslim Sabbath, and the Lord's Day to refer to the Christian Sabbath) is more a day of prayer than rest. It is the day when Muslims are required to join together in prayer in mosques. My experiences of Yom Juma are some of my most pleasant experiences in Muslim cultures. It is always special to go to Friday prayers and them visit with families. Yom Juma is a family day.

These experiences remind me of my childhood. My parents took the Lord's Day seriously. Only necessary work was done. We gathered with other members of our church for worship. We visited relatives and friends. And the food on Sundays was always special. In fact, we had a feast every Sunday. I didn't need to be told that the Lord's Day was holy. I experienced it as holy.

Most Christians and Muslims have not taken Sabbath as seriously as have Jews. Christians changed the Sabbath from Saturday to Sunday (the day to worship the sun god) in order to distance themselves from Judaism. Muslims moved their Sabbath to Friday to distance themselves from both Judaism and Christianity. Although not identical, all three religions have a concept of Sabbath. To recover a deeper understanding, it will be helpful if both Christians and Muslims look to the Jewish understanding of Sabbath.

For Jews, Shabbat is a day of joy and feasting, not a day to be somber. The Sabbath is a day of joy. Sabbath is a combination of denial and luxury, solemnity and pleasure. The Rabbis encouraged couples to engage in sex on Shabbat. It is a day of grace, not a day of earning God's favor. Jews look upon *Shabbat* as a special guest. As part of the Friday evening Shabbat service, all rise, face the door, and sing a song to welcome Shabbat. The Jewish Shabbat avoids both making Sabbath a stern legalism on the one hand, and spiritualizing our faith to the extent it is not a way of life. Observing Sabbath is an offering of gratitude to God.

Sabbath is about trusting God. It is a recognition that we are not in control. Sabbath protects us from ourselves, our pride, our arrogance, our greed. Observing Sabbath is letting go, giving up control, recognizing our dependence on God. One of the important rules developed by the Jewish

13. Heschel. *The Sabath*, 14.

community is not to fix anything on Shabbat. This is to remember that it is God who heals, repairs, who makes things right. The world is already created and we did not do it. The world will survive without my help.

Sabbath raises the question of whether we can trust God. Can we let go one day a week and trust God? Can we give up control? Sabbath confronts us right in our guts with this all-important question. To make the point clear to the Israelites, God ordered them to not gather more manna than they needed for one day.[14] Only on Friday could they gather double, enough for Friday and Shabbat. The Torah tells us that when the Israelites gathered extra manna, a sign they did not trust God, God provided maggots to pollute their stash. Our stash also has become polluted.

Sabbath not only has deep spiritual meaning; it has radical social implications. Sabbath is about community. In all three religions, members are expected to assemble together on their Sabbath day. What a wonderful counter to the individualism of Western society. What a release from bondage to self!

Sabbath is counter-cultural in that it points to a set of values, a lifestyle, a belief system at odds with economic interests. To observe the Sabbath requires one to be intentional. It is not easy to stop our business, to put aside worldly concerns, and rest from our labors. To observe Sabbath pits us against the demands of the exploitative, cumulative, capitalist system that commands more and more, not less. Sabbath calls us away from Mammon and to God. Sabbath calls us to remember, to meditate, to pray. Mammon resists all limitations. Mammon does not recognize God. Under Mammon, greed, domination, and control are virtues.

Large chain stores are open seven days a week, twenty-four hours a day, 365 days a year. They never close for holidays. For them, nothing is sacred except money. Locally owned businesses, that have some respect for community values, are not open 24–7–365. Part of my reasons for boycotting chain stores whenever possible comes out of my respect for Sabbath. We do not need to be at the mercy of the big corporations.

Sabbath is about social justice and equality. The Prophet Isaiah decries celebration of holy days that are ritually pure but divorced from social justice.[15] In the Torah, all are given the day off on Sabbath, including women, slaves, strangers, and animals. All are to share in God's grace. All

14. Exodus 16.

15. Isaiah 58. For a detailed Biblical study of Sabbath and social justice, see Lowery, *Sabbath and Jubilee.*

deserve a day of rest. Sabbath for all, including slaves, is a basis for treating all people justly. Sabbath laws forbidding work on Sabbath liberated menial workers. With the modern overturning of blue laws, however, many workers now again are separated from their families and have to work weekends so that more wealthy people, who have the weekends off, can "enjoy" their weekends. The Sabbath reminds us that no one is to be considered a cog in the machine.

Just because we can do something does not mean we should do it. Sabbath is about setting limits. Sabbath is a day in which we do not impose our will on God's creation. We will never recover ecological sanity without recovering some sense of Sabbath. In the biblical Sabbath, animals and the earth are also given rest. There is to be one day a week, plus the Sabbatical Year, without dominating and controlling nature. During the Sabbatical Year the land was to lie fallow. Even the land has its right to rest. If we could get that straight, maybe we could extend the idea of not dominating and controlling to the whole week, to the whole year. Sabbath leads us to a different relationship with God's creation, a relationship of respect in which we consider creation to be holy.

On Sabbath we declare peace with all of God's creation. Sabbath is about developing an intentional relationship with creation. The Torah teaches us that unless we grant the earth its rightful Sabbath, the earth will find its rest through drought or other natural rebellion against human oppression. Ecological disaster threatens unless we rediscover Sabbath.

Even if Sabbath may not be the key to world peace, it is not unreasonable to suggest that Sabbath can help bring the three religions together. Rethinking Sabbath can help us rethink the relationship between the three religions, help us see our common heritage, and offer opportunities for people of different religions to meet together on holy days.[16]

I am uncomfortable with legislation that would mandate Sabbath observance, but I would support legislation to protect the right to observe Sabbath. For example, no corporation should be able to force anyone to work on their Sabbath day. The responsibility for observing Sabbath, however, must be on the believers. In a pluralistic society, Sabbath is chosen voluntarily, as it always should be.

I continue to stop all work on Sundays. I know a Christian pastor who works hard on Sundays, but has incorporated Sabbath into her busy

16. An interesting book in which the author experiences and examines Sabbath in all three religions is Ringwald, *A Day Apart*.

life by starting Sabbath each Lord's Day with a short ceremony after her pastoral responsibilities end on Sunday and ends her Sabbath on Monday. I doubt God cares about the exact time or day of Sabbath, but it is important that we not observe Sabbath at our convenience. Sabbath requires more discipline and transcendence than that. I like the way the Prophet Isaiah put it:

> If you turn back your foot from the Sabbath
> from doing your pleasure on my holy day,
> and call the Sabbath a delight
> and the holy day of the Lord honorable;
> if you honor it, not going your own ways,
> or seeking your own pleasure, or talking idly;
> then you shall take delight in the Lord.[17]

JUBILEE

Judaism has given us not only the gift of Sabbath, but also the concept of Jubilee, an extension of the concept of Sabbath. Every seventh day is Sabbath. Every seventh year is a Sabbath year, an ecological year of Sabbath for the land. For that year the land is to lie fallow. Nothing is to be planted. People are to trust God to provide. All debts were to be canceled and all slaves freed.

Every fiftieth year, the year after a cycle of seven Sabbatical years, a trumpet was to be sounded in the land on the Day of Atonement (*Yom Kippur*), announcing the Year of Jubilee. According to Leviticus 25, the Year of Jubilee was to be a year of massive social, economic revolution. All debts were to be forgiven and all slaves freed, and the land redistributed. People could return to their ancestral lands that had been sold, lost, or confiscated. Jubilee was sharing and passing on of resources to the next generation.

The Jubilee was a recognition that the land belongs to God, not people. Under this system, one could not actually buy a piece of land. Instead, one would pay for the number of harvests one could expect before the next Jubilee when the land would again be redistributed. Creation does not belong to us. The earth does not belong to us. The land and resources of the earth do not belong to us. When we act as if the earth belongs to us,

17. Isa 58:13–14.

we deny God, we engage in idolatry, with the resulting consequences of alienation, oppression, poverty, ecological devastation, violence, and war.

There are many reasons why people might lose their land: personal tragedies, natural disasters, mismanagement, or injustice. There are also many ways in which people accumulate possessions: clever management, deceit, or injustice. There seems to be a natural tendency to accumulate power and wealth, with fewer and fewer people controlling the land and resources. The result is poverty, alienation, crime, and war.

The Jubilee recognizes that more is needed than handouts for the poor to keep society healthy. Land, wealth, capital, and the means of production and distribution need to regularly be redistributed to restore peace and equilibrium.

Some Biblical scholars suggest that the Year of Jubilee may not have ever actually been carried out in practice. That would explain why the Hebrew prophets regularly cried out against accumulated wealth, the devouring of widows and orphans, and the putting of people under bondage. Moses had reminded the Israelites that there would be no poor among them if they obeyed God's commands.[18] The prophets understood the fall of Israel and Judah into bondage as God's judgment for injustice.

There is an important truth here for modern society. Growing inequalities of wealth and power destabilize societies. There is something about inequalities of wealth and power that creates fear in people's hearts, particularly in the hearts of the rich. Inequalities not only have to be defended by violence, but those inequalities also produce violence. Inequalities and injustice are the enemies of shalom/salaam/peace. It is unconscionable that true Christians, Muslims, and Jews would live in luxury while others starve, for to do so negates the concept of community and that everything belongs to God.

Do we want a two-level society with those on top living in luxury while the rest struggle to survive and do the dirty work for those living in luxury? This inequality produces resentment against those on top, leaving those on top feeling insecure and searching for new ways to defend themselves and cut themselves off from those below them. This system of inequality requires police, prisons, and repression to maintain stability and order, ignoring the reality that stability and order are the products

18. Deut 15:4–5.

of justice, equality, and a sense of belonging. Some people are not more important than other people. We all share a common humanity.

All three Abrahamic religions call for social justice for all, including economic justice. Economic systems need to be based in the idea that everything belongs to God. Economics must conform to standards of social justice, lead to an equitable distribution of the world's resources, and enhance the dignity and freedom of all people.

All three religions call for redistribution of wealth, either through *zakat*, tithes and offerings, or Jubilee. Love leads us to share with others. In love there are no distinctions of ethnicity, religion, social class, race, or gender.[19]

God's intentions for sharing are carried out in many ways. Many people do not realize that the biggest economy in the world is the economy of sharing. What happens in families, between friends and neighbors, in charitable institutions, is a huge amount of sharing, cooperation, and serving the needs of others. Usually this is unpaid, and often unrecognized. All this happens without enforcement of governments or bosses. God calls us to give all we have and take only what we need.

Living in solidarity with the poor is more important than charity. In both the Bible and the Qur'an, Moses was born in slavery, but became part of Pharoah's household. Moses' leadership involved renouncing his privilege, identifying with the slaves, and demanding liberation rather than improved conditions under slavery. We also can choose to live in solidarity with the oppressed, the marginalized.[20] A theology of liberation will bring us to an awareness and understanding of injustice and oppression, including its structural foundation, and a vision for undoing bondage and exploitation based on class, gender, race, religion, etc.

When Jesus began his ministry and announced his Nazareth Manifesto, he quoted from the Prophet Isaiah: "The Spirit of the Lord is upon me, because he has anointed me to preach good news to the poor. He has sent me to proclaim release to the captives and recovering of sight to the blind, to set at liberty those who are oppressed, to proclaim the acceptable year of the Lord." [21] There is general agreement among biblical

---

19. Gal 3:28. For a clear statement on the Qur'an and social justice, see Esack, *Liberation and Pluralism*, 103–6.

20. See Esack, *Liberation and Pluralism*, 98–103, for a call to identify with the poor.

21. Luke 4:18–19.

scholars that "the acceptable year of the Lord" is the Jubilee. Jesus came proclaiming the Year of Jubilee.

There was one difference in Jesus' proclamation, however. For Jesus, the Jubilee was not to be practiced every fifty years, but rather every day. Jesus' followers were to forgive sins and debts, heal the sick, liberate the oppressed, and work for reconciliation. The early Church was clear that tithes and offerings were not to be used for church buildings, but for Jubilee redistribution to the poor. The early Christians implemented the Jubilee by selling their possessions, giving everything to a common treasury, and having all things in common. They rejected private property. Jesus and the early Christians were communists, but not Marxists.

Instead of following God's way of Jubilee, during the last two decades of the twentieth century the world saw the most extensive redistribution of wealth in history, a redistribution from the bottom up to a small global elite. In a world of violence and war, great concentrations of wealth, and massive poverty, it is clear to me that God's people are called to live the Jubilee, to renounce private property, to share all we have, and trust our future to God. But can we trust God?

All three religions have found ways to live out the Jubilee. The Jewish Kibbutz movement comes to mind. Jews moving to Israel tried to reinvent a Jewish lifestyle rooted in a vision of social justice. In the Kibbutzim there was no private property, all were to be considered equal, and decisions made democratically.

The early Church established the Christian vision of Jubilee, carried on by religious orders and sectarian movements that renounced private property. The Hutterites in North Western United States and Canada have been living communally for almost 500 years. There are many newer intentional communities scattered all over the world.[22]

Muslims have a vision of economic systems distinct from capitalism and communism. The Qur'an clearly rejects stockpiling personal wealth. Wealth is to be shared.[23] The Prophet lived very simply and condemned luxury. Instead, he identified with the poor. Mohammad said, "He is not a true Muslim who eats his fill when his next-door neighbor is hungry."[24]

---

22. See Gish. *Living in Christian Community*.

23. Qur'an 63:9–10; 102:1.

24. Quoted from Bukhari by Chapra, *Objectives of the Islamic Economic Order*, 186.

A major problem for the poorer nations is their oppressive load of debt to the rich nations. Debt payments are huge and keep those nations in poverty. Based on the concept of Jubilee, many activists around the world have been calling for a Jubilee and cancellation of the debts of poor nations.

All three religions warn those who would hoard gold and silver and not expend wealth in the cause of good. The Qur'an talks about being obsessed by greed for more and more.[25] Psalm 10 describes the greedy, the arrogant, and the oppressors as people who have rejected God. One response is to live simply so that others can simply live. We can be liberated from our slavery to consumption.

25. Qur'an 102:1–2.

⇒ NINE ⇐

Where Do We Go from Here?

I AM NO LONGER much interested in arguing about differences of belief with people of other religions. Much more exciting is when we can talk together about our faith and how our faiths affect our lives. I think of all the deep conversations I have had in Muslim homes in Palestine and Iraq, talking about our struggles with faith, forgiveness, and love. Praying together, eating together, crying together, and laughing together: these are aspects of real dialogue.

On February 19, 2004, I visited one of the top *Shia* leaders in Baghdad. In the course of our intense conversation, I asked him what for him was the essence of his *Shia* faith. Without a moment's hesitation, he said, "Forgiveness. We need to forgive each other." What person of faith could disagree?

I remember a conversation Peggy and I had with a Palestinian Muslim family in January 2005. The family had been regularly praying for Peggy while she was working in Iraq. They expressed to Peggy their fears for her, which led to a time of deep sharing about fear and trusting in God. Peggy shared with them her struggles with fear, and told them that the only way she can raise above her fears is to daily ask God for love. The family shared their daily struggles with fear of attacks from both nearby Israeli settlers and from Israeli soldiers. This sharing of fear and faith took interfaith dialogue to a deeper level. Our hearts were joined together by our faith.

God is bringing together the three religions as God's witness to the world of God's love and mercy, of the good life God wants to give to us.

In all three religions there are people who are deeply committed to their faith, are open to dialogue both with other religions and modern philosophy, and have taken courageous stands against the rigid, oppressive, conservative movements in their countries, cultures, and religions.[1]

Don't ask how we can bring God into any situation. Know that God is at work everywhere and in the hearts of all people. We do not take God anywhere. Wherever we go, we look for signs of God's presence. We expect to find signs of God's presence. How often have I been humbled by the clear evidence of the work of God in the life of the Muslim, the Jew, the Hindu, and yes, in the life of the atheist. We rejoice and affirm that Presence when we sense that Presence in another person. We bear witness to Light wherever we find it.

We can celebrate together the oneness and unity of God (*tawhid*). The unity of humanity is a reflection of the oneness of God. Everything is interconnected. We reject the division between us and them, slave and free, male and female, rich and poor, secular and spiritual. All these divisions are an affront to the oneness of God.

The majority of Christians in the world are non-Western. It is these Christians who are most involved on a daily basis with Muslims. How can a secularized West that has lost its moral and spiritual core dialogue with the Muslim world? Western secularists seem poorly equipped to dialogue with Muslims. Maybe the impetus for international understanding must come from people in the three religions. As I write these words, many Americans are fanning the flames of war with Iran. At the same time Mennonites are engaging in dialogue both with Iranian religious leaders and with Achmad Achmadinajad, the President of Iran. This dialogue includes having Mennonites studying at a theological center in Qom, the spiritual capital of Iran, the most conservative city in Iran.

I have helped in bringing Israeli Jews into Palestinian Muslim homes in the Hebron area. I once had a small role in helping develop a friendship between a Jewish man and a member of Islamic Jihad in Hebron. Israeli Jews sometimes visit and sleep in the homes of Palestinians killed by Israelis. This is usually a stretch for everyone. It is scary for people to go into the homes of people who are supposed to be their enemies. It is scary for an Israeli Jew to go into a Muslim home. It is also a big step for the Palestinian Muslim family to welcome "the oppressor" into their home. But they do it.

1. Küng, *Islam*, 539–50.

When I work side by side with people of other religions, the important questions for me are not whether we have disagreements about fine points of doctrine, or whether we pray in the same ways, but rather, what unity do we have in our working together? Are we working for the same goals? Do we agree on the methods we are using to reach those goals? In what spirit do we come together?

The important issues of faith, however, will affect how we work together. Do we love God and neighbor? Do we believe in forgiveness and grace? Do we act in faith and love? Where are our loyalties and commitments? Do we engage in idolatry by making things ultimate that are not ultimate? Are we open to God's Spirit working among us?

When people cross boundaries, exciting things happen. Each time in Israel/Palestine that I experience Jews, Muslims, and Christians eating, working, laughing, and crying together I sense a foretaste of the coming kingdom of God, a demonstration of how things could be, and one day will be. Those are my most exciting experiences.

In the fall of 2008, I had a small crisis of faith after participating in Rosh Hoshanna services at the synagogue in Athens, something similar to feelings after participating in worship with Christians. The Scriptures and readings were profound and inspiring. I was reminded again of the profound wisdom revealed in the Abrahamic Scriptures. I was deeply moved. But then I wondered, who, if anyone, believed that stuff. I admit I was being judgmental. But if people actually lived by the lofty precepts of the Jewish Scriptures, this would be a beautiful world. There would be social justice for all. Wars and oppression would cease. We would live in harmony. Life would be full of joy.

I have become weary with listening to empty preaching. Often the radical perspectives of Scripture are de-politicized and spiritualized. I recently heard a sermon on the book of Ruth. The sermon was about kindness, and never mentioned the anti-racist, inclusive message of the book. There was no mention of Moabites. Too many sermons repeat profound truths from Scripture, but never seem to get to the profound, radical, implications of what too often sound like empty clichés. Most of the time I have no idea what preachers mean when they repeat their abstract concepts. I want the word to be made flesh, to be made concrete. How could it be possible to hear those words without our lives being radically changed? Is religion a vaccination against the transforming power of God's Truth? Too often the Word of God is reduced to ritual.

Today the world still needs the call to turn from the false gods of money, sex, power, war, and self, to the One who created us all, the One in whom we can understand our destiny, the One who can liberate, transform, and empower the creation of a new humanity, a new community of love, respect, and sharing. The world needs people who with God's help will rise above their fears. We need to be reminded that salvation comes from God, not from governments, corporations, or armies, not from our good works, however important they may be, or even from our religion. Our call is to give up power, privilege, and independence. That call is to live on the edge of the empire, to identify with the victims and outcasts of society, and to trust God.

There is something more compelling about the call of God than all the glitter and lies of Western society. Direct, personal experience of that Creative Mystery and Power that sustains, shakes, and renews us makes everything else as appealing as dirt.

Most every movement of God's Spirit results in the transformation of people in community. Powerful examples are the formation of the Jewish community, the early Christian Community, the new community in Arabia that resulted from the proclamation of the Qur'an. The *ummah*, the Body of Christ, the Jewish community, form a nation, a community built not on race, military might, wealth, or any human manipulation, but on faith in God and love for our neighbors. It is that community that can transcend race, class, gender, and religion, and live out the call given by God to the prophets. It is that community that can make visible God's reign on earth. Can Christians, Muslims, and Jews renounce their marriage to capitalism, militarism, and imperialism, and turn to God?

Before returning home to Ohio after spending three months in Hebron, I spent the night of February 26, 2005 in Jerusalem. I decided to go to the Al Aksa Mosque, the third most holy place on earth for Muslims, for sunset prayers. I walked very slowly across the large plaza of what Jews call the Temple Mount, thinking about the Jewish temples which once stood there, thinking about Jesus in the temple there, thinking about Jews and their pain, thinking about the history of that place and its importance for Jews, Christians, and Muslims.

I was deeply moved in the Muslim prayers as I knelt in prayer, praying for the coming of God's kingdom, praying for the Muslim world, praying for the peace of Jerusalem. I sensed that it was not I who was praying, but God's Spirit praying for me and through me. I walked out of the Aksa Mosque and heard the ringing of church bells. My heart leapt with joy. After doing Muslim prayers, I was reminded of my Christian roots. I was called back to Jesus. Those Christian bells spoke to my heart, recalled for me who I am. I am a Christian.

I walked back through the narrow streets of the Old City and saw a sign pointing to the Western Wall. Something inside me immediately told me I had to go pray with the Jews. Soon I was standing at the Wailing Wall surrounded by Jews, all of us praying to the God of Abraham and Moses. I prayed the Lord's Prayer. I prayed Muslim prayers. I repeated Hebrew words of praise, I sang "*Shalom Haverim*." I was reminded of my Jewish roots.

I am a Jew. I am a Muslim. I am a Christian. I can do no other. There is one God. Who are we to restrict God?

As I stood there in the courtyard, I had a vision that in addition to the Al Aksa Mosque on the Temple Mount, there could also be a Jewish temple and a Christian sanctuary. There would be no separation between them, with people freely going from one place of worship to another. Why not? It may be politically impossible at this time, but people of faith could demand it. The Bible calls us to pray for the peace of Jerusalem. Could that include people of all three faiths praying on the Temple Mount, the *Haram al Sharif*? We can pray. We can dream. We can take action for peace.

The Apostle Paul points out in Ephesians 2–3 that God's purpose throughout history has been to create one humanity by bringing Jews and Gentiles together. Mohammad's dream of a larger community of faith that would connect the three Abrahamic religions has not been realized, but it points to the truth that faith in God can bring us together.

We face momentous problems in the world. Those problems impinge on people of all religions. How much better it would be for people of all religions to stand together in facing those problems. We can learn from each other as we apply our faith to those problems.

From the beginning in the Garden of Eden, people have been given the choice of two paths. One of those paths is seeking power and control, self-centeredness, doing things because I can and because I want to, all of which lead to murder and death. The other path is submission to God, seeking God's will in everything we do. The call of God comes from beyond where and who we are. It is an awesome and costly call. The call is to give up our lives, to surrender everything we have and everything we are.

From my Anabaptist heritage I learned the German word, "*gelassenheit*," which means submission, yieldedness, surrender, serenity, peace. *Gelassenheit* is what one has after giving up everything to trust in God alone. It is yielding to God's will, living a new way of life under the reign of God, and resisting all domination. Jesus used the image of a seed dying to become a new plant.[2] In contrast to burial signifying the end of life, surrender to God means the beginning of life. In the giving up of everything we find life, we find God.

As boy, I heard the call to follow Jesus with my whole life. My Anabaptist heritage taught me that following Jesus had something to do with how I lived my life, that the gospel relates to every aspect of life. When I heard the call of Islam, I heard that same call to submit all of my life to God's will, the same message as the Jewish call to love God with our heart, soul, mind and strength.

After much teenage struggle with whether I would accept this call, and continued struggle since then, I daily try to open my heart to God's Spirit, and follow those leadings, no matter how risky they may seem.

God is Good. God is faithful. God has never let me down. God has never called me to do anything that the strength for doing it was not also given. I want to give all I have.

I do not mean this in any flippant sense. To say yes to God is awesome, scary, breath-taking. When the Hebrew prophet Isaiah met God, he cried out, "I am a person of unclean lips."[3] When Moses heard the call of God, he argued with God, saying that he was not up to that kind of commitment. Neither am I. God help us.

2. John 12:24–26.

3. Isa 6:5.

Afterword

WHILE I WAS READING this manuscript, I received the news that Art Gish had died in a tragic farm accident. Though I did not know Art personally, I felt as if I had been given a glimpse of the depth of his heart and soul through his words, and I mourned his death. I was convinced that the legacy left by Art Gish needed to be passed on through this book for it speaks of hope, but also suggests a direction and vision for creating peace in our troubled world.

That same summer that Art died, a small move toward peace was made at the peace and security sessions of the World Religions Summit 2010 taking place in Winnipeg, Canada. At that meeting, a proposal was made that a ninth millennium goal be added to the eight development goals set by the United Nations to be achieved by 2015. Adding to such goals as "eradicate extreme hunger and poverty" and "achieve universal primary education" Robert J. Suderman, a Christian leader, suggested that "our houses of faith stop teaching—and justifying—the use of lethal violence between and among our own people."[1] In the statement that was passed by all the religions represented at the summit was the following paragraph:

> We are aware that there are those who use religion to justify violent acts against others, and thereby offend the true spirit of their faith and the long-standing values of their faith communities. We condemn religiously motivated terrorism and extremism and

1. "Suderman proposes a ninth Millennium Goal," *Canadian Mennonite*, July 12, 2010, 16.

commit to stop the teaching and justification of the use of violence between and among our faith communities. Our faith traditions are steeped in the promotion of love for one another and deep respect for all humankind; peace and justice walk hand in hand. Our most inspiring teachings are stories of reconciliation and compassion. We will collaborate to create paths of peaceful and sustainable coexistence.[2]

In this book, Art Gish has begun the process of fulfilling this statement. It is full of inspiring stories of reconciliation and compassion that move toward countering religiously motivated violence. But more than that, Art points us in a direction that is even more radical, one that will require deep collaboration by the peoples of the Abrahamic religions. He calls us to worship the one God through our words and actions.

By radical, I do not mean a political radicalism of the left but rather a move to the roots or the source of our faith. Probably the most radical move that Gish makes is the move to ground the conversation between religions in worship rather than in religious convictions alone. Each religion, including the Christian religion, has grown a variety of vines from its own root that need pruning in order that peaceful interactions may ensue. And Gish wants more than mere "coexistence." He wants radical engagement between the faith groups, something that he has demonstrated in his own life.

Clearly, this book will not answer all the theological questions that arise when people of faith engage each other in conversation. My own experience in Mennonite/Shi'i dialogue has shown me that both differences and similarities need to be addressed in honesty and transparency so that respect can be developed and space be created for new understandings to blossom.[3] However, a dialogue with words is not enough; there needs to also be a dialogue of life, a getting to know each other as fellow humans on a journey of faith. This becomes risky when persons are divided from each other by both the physical and mental force of political differences.

---

2. Interfaith Leaders in the G8 Nations, *A Time for Inspired Leadership and Action, Final Draft*, 3–4.

3. For an overview of these dialogues, see the summaries by the editors of the book, *On Spirituality: Essays from the Third Shi'i Muslim Mennonite Christian Dialogue*, M. Darrol Bryant, Susan Kennel Harrison and A. James Reimer, 7–10; 211–28. Note also my own letter of invitation to one of these dialogues where the focus is on the dialogue of life rather than only a scholarly dialogue (247–48).

But Gish's book points us in a direction that is practical and that is rooted in the one God.

That direction includes getting to know each other's history, getting to know each other's Scriptures and getting to know the God who can bring us together into a bond of peace. For me as a Christian it also means a truthful encounter with the history of violence and injustice in my own faith tradition, something that is easy to whitewash or to cover up when I am tempted to compete instead of converse with persons of a different faith.

This is why I was most intrigued with the stories that Gish gives us of his own experience of worship in all three religions. Some of my most in-depth encounters with another religion came when I too discovered I could say "amen" to the prayers of my Muslim friends. It is worship that connects us with the God who can bring about spiritual transformation, whether we are Jew, Muslim, or Christian. The stories in this book witness to that fact. Thank you, Art Gish, for giving us hope and inspiring us to action.

Lydia Neufeld Harder
Adjunct Professor of Theology (retired)
Conrad Grebel University College and Toronto School of Theology

Bibliography

Abunimah, Ali. *One Country: A Bold Proposal to End the Israeli-Palestinian Impasse*. New York: Metropolitan Books, 2006.

Abu-Nimer, Mohammed. *Dialogue, Conflict Resolution, and Change: Arab-Jewish Encounters in Israel*. Albany: State University of New York Press, 1999.

———. *Nonviolence and Peace Building in Islam: Theory and Practice*. Gainesville: University Press of Florida, 2003.

Abu-Nimer, Mohammed, and Muhammad Shafiq. *Interfaith Dialogue: A Guide for Muslims*. Washington, D.C.: The International Institute of Islamic Thought, 2007.

Ahmad, Khurshid, editor. *Islam: Its Meaning and Message*. London: The Islamic Foundation, 1980.

Alpert, Michael. *Crypto-Judaism and the Spanish Inquisition*. New York: Palgrove, 2001.

Armstrong, Karen. *A Short History of God: The 4000-year Quest of Judaism, Christianity and Islam*. New York: Knopf, 1993.

———. *Islam: A Short History*. New York: Random House, 2000.

———. *Muhammad: A Biography of the Prophet*. New York: Harper, 1992.

Ayoub, Mahmoud M. "Toward an Islamic Christology II, The Death of Jesus: Reality or Delusion?" In *The Muslim World* 70 (1980) 91–121.

Bainton, Roland H. *Christian Attitudes Toward War and Peace*. Nashville: Abington, 1960.

Barlas, Asma. "Believing Women." In *Islam: Unreading Patriarchal Interpretations of the Qur'an*. Austin: University of Texas Press, 2002.

Bhutto, Benezir. *Reconciliation: Islam, Democracy, and the West*. New York: Harper Collins, 2008.

Bodian, Miriam. *Dying in the Law of Moses: Crypto-Jewish Martyrdom in the Iberian World*. Bloomington: Indiana University Press, 2007.

Brown, Brian Arthur. *Noah's Other Son: Bridging the Gap between the Bible and the Qur'an*. New York: Continuum, 2007.

Buber, Martin. *Two Types of Faith: A Study of the Interpenetration of Judaism and Christianity*. Trans. Norman B. Goldhawk. New York: Harper Torchbooks, 1961.

Burg, Avraham. *The Holocaust Is Over: We Must Rise From Its Ashes*. New York: Palgrave Macmillan, 2008.

Byrant, M. Darrol, Susan Kennel Harrison, and A. James Reimer, editors. *On Spirituality: Essays from the Third Shi'i Muslim Mennonite Christian Dialogue*. Kitchener, Ontario: Pandora, 2010.

Carey, Roane and Jonathan Shainin. *The Other Israel: Voices of Refusal and Dissent*. New York: New Press, 2002.

Chapra, Mohammad Umar. *Objectives of the Islamic Economic Order*. Leicester, England: Islamic Council of Europe, 1996.

Courbage, Youssef and Philippe Fargues. *Christians and Jews under Islam*. London: I. B. Tauris Publishers, 1997.

Cragg, Kenneth. *The Christ and the Faiths*. Philadelphia: Westminster, 1986.

D'Costa, Gavin, ed. *Christian Uniqueness Reconsidered: The Myth of a Pluralistic Theology of Religion*. Maryknoll, NY: Orbis, 1990.

Diouf, Sylviane. *Servants of Allah: African Muslims Enslaved in the Americas*. New York: New York University Press, 1998.

Ellis, Marc H. *O Jerusalem! The Contested Future of the Jewish Covenant*. Minneapolis: Fortress, 1999.

————. *Reading the Torah Out Loud: A Journey of Lament and Hope*. Minneapolis: Fortress, 2007.

Esack, Farid. *Qur'an, Liberation and Pluralism: An Islamic Perspective of Interreligious Solidarity against Oppression*. Oxford: Oneworld, 1997.

Feuerlicht, Roberta Strauss. *The Fate of the Jews: A People Torn Between Israeli Power and Jewish Ethics*. New York: Times Books, 1983.

Fletcher, Richard. *The Cross and the Crescent: Christianity and Islam from Muhammad to the Reformation*. New York: Viking, 2003.

Gish, Arthur. *At-Tuwani: Hope and Nonviolent Action in a Palestinian Village*. Scottdale, PA: Herald, 2008.

————. *Hebron Journal: Stories of Nonviolent Peacemaking*. Scottdale, PA: Herald, 2001.

Gish, Peggy Faw. *Iraq: A Journey of Hope and Peace*. Scottdale, PA: Herald, 2004.

Gushee, David P. *The Righteous Gentiles of the Holocaust: A Christian Interpretation*. Minneapolis: Fortress, 1994.

Haddad, Yvonne Yazbeck, and Wadi Zaidan Haddad, editors. *Christian-Muslim Encounters*. Gainsville: University Press of Florida, 1995.

Halevi, Yossi Klein. *At the Entrance to the Garden of Eden: A Jew's Search for God with Christians and Muslims in the Holy Land*. New York: William Morrow, 2001.

Hay, Malcolm. *Europe and the Jews: The Pressure of Christendom on the People of Israel for 1900 Years*. Boston: Beacon Press, 1960.

Heschel, Abraham Joshua. *The Sabbath: Its Meaning for Modern Man*. New York: Farrar, Straus and Giroux, 1951.

Hick, John, and Paul F. Knitter, editors. *The Myth of Christian Uniqueness: Toward a Pluralistic Theology of Religions*. Maryknoll, NY: Orbis, 1987.

Hick, John, and Edmund S. Meltzer, eds. *Three Faiths—One God: A Jewish, Christian, and Muslim Encounter*. Albany: State University of New York Press, 1989.

Husein, Fatimah. *Muslim-Christian Relations in the New Order Indonesia: The Exclusivist and Inclusivist Muslims' Perspectives*. Bandung: Mizan Pustaka, 2005.

Interfaith Leaders in the G8 Nations. *A Time for Inspired Leadership and Action, Final Draft*, 3–4, June 23, 2010. Online: http://www.peacenext.org/profiles/blogs/world-religions-summit-in.

Kaltner, John. *Ishmael Instructs Isaac: An Introduction to the Qur'an for Bible Readers.* Collegeville, MN: Liturgical, 1999.

Krabill, James R., David W. Shenk, and Linford Stutzman, eds. *Anabaptists Meeting Muslims: A Calling for Presence in the Way of Christ.* Scottdale, PA: Herald, 2005.

Kramer, Martin, ed. *The Jewish Discovery of Islam.* Tel Aviv: The Moshe Dayan Center for Middle Eastern and African Studies, 1999.

Kung, Hans. *Islam: Past, Present, and Future.* Trans. John Bowden. Oxford: Oneworld, 2007.

Laqueur, Walter. *The Changing Face of Antisemitism from Ancient Times to the Present Day.* New York: Oxford University Press, 2006.

Lewis, Bernard. *The Jews of Islam.* Princeton: Princeton University Press, 1984.

Lowery, Richard H. *Sabbath and Jubilee.* St. Louis: Chalice, 2000.

Madjid, Nurcholish. *The True Face of Islam: Essays on Islam and Modernity.* Edited by Rudy Harisyah Alam and Ihsan Ali-Fauzi. Ciputat, Indonesia: Voice Center Indonesia, 2003.

Mohammed, Ovey N. *Muslim-Christian Relations: Past, Present, Future.* Maryknoll, NY: Orbis, 1999.

Mortenson, Greg, and David Oliver Relin. *Three Cups of Tea: One Man's Mission to Fight Terrorism and Build Nations . . . One School at a Time.* New York: Viking, 2006.

Muhaiyaddeen, M. R. Bawa. *Islam and World Peace: Explanations of a Sufi.* 2nd ed. Philadelphia: Fellowship, 2007.

Niewyk, Donald L. *The Holocaust: Problems and Perspectives of Interpretation.* Lexington, MA: Heath and Company, 1992.

Novak, David. *Jewish-Christian Dialogue: A Jewish Justification.* New York: Oxford University Press, 1989.

Polner, Murray, and Naomi Goodman, eds. *The Challenge of Shalom: The Jewish Tradition of Peace and Justice.* Philadelphia: New Society Publishers, 1994.

Perez, Joseph. *History of a Tragedy: The Expulsion of the Jews From Spain.* Chicago: University of Illinois Press, 2007.

Qa'im, Mahdi Muntazir. *Jesus through the Qur'an and Shi'ite Narrations.* Translated by Muhammad Legenhausen. Elmhurst, NY: Tahrike Tarsile Qur'an, Inc., 2005.

Rabkin, Yakov M. *A Threat from Within: A Century of Jewish Opposition to Zionism.* New York: Zed Books, 2006.

Raisanen, Heikki. "The Portrait of Jesus in the Qur'an." *The Muslim World* 70 (1980), 122–33.

Ringwald, Christopher D. *A Day Apart: How Jews, Christians, and Muslims Find Faith, Freedom and Joy on the Sabbath.* New York: Oxford University Press, 2007.

Roth, Norman. *Jews, Visigoths and Muslims in Medieval Spain: Cooperation and Conflict.* New York: Brill, 1994.

Sha'ban, Fuad. *For Zion's Sake: The Judeo-Christian Tradition in American Culture.* Ann Arbor, MI: Pluto, 2005.

Shirazi, Iman Muhammad. *War, Peace and Non-violence: An Islamic Perspective.* Elmhurst, New York: Tahrike Tarsile Qur'an, Inc., 2001.

Smith-Christopher, Daniel L. *Subverting Hatred: The Challenge of Nonviolence in Religious Traditions.* Cambridge: Boston Research Center of the 21st Century, 1998.

Torrey, Charles Cutler. *The Jewish Foundation of Islam.* New York: Jewish Institute of Religion Press, 1933.

Wagner, Donald E. *Dying in the Land of Promise: Palestine and Palestinian Christianity from Pentecost to 2000.* London: Melisende, 2003

Watt, William Montgomery. *Muslim-Christian Encounters: Perceptions and Misperceptions.* New York: Routledge, 1991.

Weaver, Alain Epp, and Gerald J. Mast, editors. *The Work of Jesus Christ in Anabaptist Perspective: Essays in Honor of J. Denny Weaver.* Telford, PA.: Cascadia, 2008.

Weaver, J. Denny. *The Nonviolent Atonement.* Grand Rapids: Eerdmans, 2001.

Yoder, John Howard. *The Jewish/Christian Schism Revisited (Theology in a Postcritical Key).* Edited by Michael Cartwright and Peter Ochs. London: SCM, 2003.

———. *Preface to Theology: Christology and Theological Method.* Grand Rapids: Brazos, 2002.

———. *When War Is Unjust: Being Honest in Just-War Thinking.* Minneapolis: Augsburg, 1984.